Compassionate Confinement

CRITICAL ISSUES IN CRIME AND SOCIETY
Raymond J. Michalowski, Series Editor

Critical Issues in Crime and Society is oriented toward critical analysis of contemporary problems in crime and justice. The series is open to a broad range of topics, including specific types of crime, wrongful behavior by economically or politically powerful actors, controversies over justice system practices, and issues related to the intersection of identity, crime, and justice. It is committed to offering thoughtful works that will be accessible to scholars and professional criminologists, general readers, and students.

For a list of titles in the series, see the last page of the book.

Compassionate Confinement

A Year in the Life of Unit C

Laura S. Abrams
Ben Anderson-Nathe

Rutgers University Press
New Brunswick, New Jersey, and London

Library of Congress Cataloging-in-Publication Data

Abrams, Laura S.
  Compassionate confinement : a year in the life of Unit C / Laura S. Abrams,
Ben Anderson-Nathe.
      p. cm. — (Critical issues in crime and society)
  Includes bibliographical references and index.
  ISBN 978-0-8135-5413-6 (hbk. : alk. paper) — ISBN 978-0-8135-5412-9
(pbk. : alk. paper) — ISBN 978-0-8135-5414-3 (e-book)
  1. Juvenile corrections—United States.   2. Juvenile detention homes—
United States—Case studies.   3. Juvenile delinquents—Rehabilitation—
United States.   I. Anderson-Nathe, Ben.   II. Title.
  HV9104.A27   2012
  365′.420973—dc23
                                                              2012005100

A British Cataloging-in-Publication record for this book is available
from the British Library.

Copyright © 2012 by Laura S. Abrams and Ben Anderson-Nathe

Visit our website: http://rutgerspress.rutgers.edu

Manufactured in the United States of America

This book is dedicated to the youth and the staff of Unit C, in appreciation of their willingness to welcome us into their worlds and the insights and experiences they shared with us that made this work possible.

Contents

FOREWORD

UNLESS WE LIVE IN the end-time of ultimate enlightenment, the coveted truths we now hold most self-evident, the products of our best science, will not only seem outdated and wrong in a few decades, but laughable. Of the candidates for ridicule by a future Stephen Jay Gould, I would nominate early twenty-first century notions of youth violence and juvenile crime founded in developmental-stage and brain-maturity science that hasn't advanced much in a century.

I suspect that today's generic notion that crime prone youth engage in adolescent risk taking due to impulse-wired teen brains spurred by always-negative peer pressures will seem as ludicrous as nineteenth-century crime theories resting in racial hierarchies, cranial metrics, and tortured phrenologies that criminal behavior could be read in atavistic countenance. Stereotypes of the typical teenager will become as offensive as yesterday's delineations of the typical Jew, darkie, and Injun.

For all the claims to scientific validation, popular, persistent theories inevitably flatter their adherents as the wisest ontogeny of the superior phylogeny, with statistics and evidence bent to upholding and perpetuating them long after debunking by reasoned analysis. Typically, the sin is data selectivity.

Biodevelopmental theorists generalized youth proclivities from certain facts (such as that youths in a single Oakland, California, zip code suffered dozens of homicides over the last two decades) while ignoring challenging facts (that youths in a similarly populated Marin zip code an hour's drive away, likewise manifesting adolescence, experienced none). Crime and political authorities endlessly deplored the early 1990s spike in homicide and violence among poorer urban young people (in fact, many seem reluctant to let it go) but utterly ignored the even larger, longer-term surges in drug abuse and crime among middle-agers (merely the parents). Credentialed alarmists hyped the increase in arrests for one offense, assault, among girls in the early 1990s as proof of some new crime nexus (often linked to modern young females' worldliness) but failed to notice the larger, broader leap in arrests, especially for assault, among their midlife mothers and fathers. Experts avoided level-playing-field comparisons of adult and youth behavior;

for example, under similar economic conditions, middle-agers display risk outcomes similar to those of teens. It's 1910 all over again.

However, there are good antidotes to the dubious doctrine of adolescent risk taking. The statistically grounded ethnography that locates the individual in the group and the group in the individual is, in my view, the philosopher-king of social science literature. Ethnographies complicate and humanize statistics and quantitative research by illuminating the individuality of youths within the worlds they (unlike most researchers and theorists) have to negotiate.

Laura Abrams and Ben Anderson-Nathe have authored an incisive contribution to complicating juvenile crime, incarceration, and rehabilitation discussion. They locate several teenagers, none of them typical, within their environments inside and outside the juvenile facilities where they are confined, showing how youths adapt one setting to the other with a hybrid of promising and troubling results. It's unsettling how smoothly skills learned in the gang, street, and difficult-family worlds prove useful in juvenile prison heirarchies and vice versa—a reinforcement pattern the correctional system is supposed to interrupt. Judge for yourselves the detailed, highly personal accounts of young men and staff in Unit C that Abrams and Anderson-Nathe present in critically refining the dilemmas of crime prevention and management.

Mike A. Males
Oklahoma City, Oklahoma
January 1, 2012

ACKNOWLEDGMENTS

WE ARE GRATEFUL TO many extraordinary individuals who offered their insights into this project in many stages. We thank our former colleagues from the University of Minnesota, Jane Gilgun and Kyoungho Kim, for their support in the project's initial formation and implementation. At UCLA, Jorja Leap, Stuart Kirk, and Zeke Hasenfeld offered us wonderful advice for constructing a book proposal. At Portland State, we thank Harold Briggs and Vikki Vandiver for the wisdom they offered in the early formation of the prospectus. We are extremely grateful for the keen intellect of our colleague and friend Laura Curran, who offered a lovingly critical review of the full manuscript and helped us to clarify and sharpen our ideas. Our research assistants, Susanna Curry (UCLA) and Stephanie Brockett (PSU), offered invaluable help with research, careful proofreading, and formatting of the final manuscript. At Rutgers University Press, we are indebted to Peter Mickulas for his sensitive stewardship of this book from prospectus to publication, to Raymond J. Michalowski, editor of the series on Critical Issues in Crime and Society, and to our external reviewers who gave us positive direction for the project. To Mike Males, we offer our thanks for holding us to a higher standard and endorsing this project from the very beginning.

There are also many friends and family members who supported us from beginning to end. From Laura: many, many thanks to my husband, Owen Fighter, and my sons, Eli and Noah, for continued inspiration and joy as well as time to complete this book. To my parents Richard and Jane Abrams and my sister Beth Abrams, I appreciate all of your love and support. Thanks to my wonderful colleagues at UCLA for intellectual community and friendship; to my graduate students and qualitative research seminar participants at UCLA for encouraging me to pursue this book; and my many caring and loyal friends who have supported me throughout my career and life transitions.

From Ben: So much love and gratitude goes to my family, most specifically to my partner, Michael, and our powerful and dynamic daughter, Sophie. To my PSU friends and colleagues—Stephanie Wahab, Jana

Meinhold, Melissa Penners, Del Quest, and Joseph DeFilippis—you've tolerated a lot from me over the past many months, and I'm grateful for it. And finally, to the students who got less from me during this process because my attention was unevenly divided, thanks for being patient.

Last, we wish to acknowledge our funders at several stages of the project: the Agricultural Experiment Station and the Faculty Senate at the University of Minnesota and the Lois and Samuel Silberman Fund.

Compassionate Confinement

Introduction

JUVENILE INCARCERATION has been legally institutionalized for over a hundred years. Yet still today, the public is mired in debate about the use of secure confinement to solve the problem of youth crime. In spite of broad consensus that the system is neither effectively helping youth nor protecting society from future harm, there is little agreement about the locus of responsibility for these failures or where to look for greater accountability. Conservative and victims' rights organizations have charged the juvenile justice system with being too soft on juvenile crime, an accusation that contributed to a major shift in the 1990s toward harsher and longer sentences for youth. In response to these trends, liberal and youth advocacy groups have argued that juvenile corrections has mistakenly abandoned its core rehabilitative mission and, due to cruel conditions and developmentally inappropriate punitive practices, ends up making youth worse.

While experts, advocates, and politicians continue to engage in public debates over the uses and misuses of juvenile incarceration, the voices and experiences of the people who live and work in these institutions have seldom been brought to bear on this discussion. In this book, we draw upon the perspectives of incarcerated youth and correctional staff to offer fresh insight into a system that frustrates everyone and satisfies no one. These are the voices perhaps best positioned to offer commentary on the system, but they are also those most routinely absent from these larger discussions. The confusion and struggle experienced by many youth moving through correctional institutions and the perspectives of the staff working with them are critical for educators, reformers, policy makers, and others to understand if the system is to be redeemed and fulfill its social charge.

To that end, we came to this project as scholars and practitioners dedicated to centering the voices of those people closest to the experience of juvenile corrections and bringing them into sharper focus in academic and public discourse. We spent more than a year immersed in "Wildwood House" (a pseudonym), a contemporary rehabilitation-oriented juvenile correctional facility for young men, observing and participating in its day-to-day functioning, meeting formally and informally with residents and staff, and reviewing the residents' records. Through hundreds of hours of engagement with the facility and the people who comprised it, we witnessed how the correctional staff managed the competing goals of punishment and rehabilitation and began to appreciate how the residents navigated their identities as young men in a system of compassionate confinement seeking to reconstruct their sense of self and reshape their futures.

THE JUVENILE CORRECTIONS SYSTEM IN CONTEXT

Founded by progressive social reformers in the early part of the twentieth century, the juvenile justice system is held publicly responsible for achieving the often competing goals of punishment and rehabilitation. For some youth, the punishment side of this equation is accomplished through mandated sentences to out-of-home placements, which are typically reserved for more severe crimes or repeat offenders, representing just 8.9 percent of court dispositions among all adjudicated minors in 2007 (Sickmund, Sladky, and Kang 2010). The system's rehabilitation goals are addressed through an array of community and home-based youth services, often focusing on first-time and lower-level offenders with the hope of diverting more significant involvement in crime. Still, rehabilitation is also accomplished through court-ordered placements; institutions as diverse as publicly funded juvenile correctional facilities, wilderness boot camps, community-based group homes, and privately funded residential treatment centers are responsible for providing programs geared toward rehabilitation. These services often include individual, group, and family therapies, as well as more specialized interventions for mental health, substance abuse, and other problems associated with offending behavior (Ruddell and Thomas 2009). Although facilities housing court-mandated youth maintain different balances of punishment and rehabilitation, most seek to accomplish both.

Nearly 160,000 youth are sentenced to correctional placements annually in the United States (Puzzanchera, Adams, and Sickmund 2011), with an average cost of $241 per youth per day—nearly four times the average for an adult due to lower staff-to-youth ratios and more intensive rehabilitation programming (Pew Center on the States 2008). Yet this extensive and expensive system of juvenile corrections tends to be viewed from all angles of the political spectrum as unsuccessful. This is because at least half of incarcerated youth—and even as many as 85 percent according to some studies—wind up reinvolved in juvenile or adult criminal justice systems within two to five years of their release (California Department of Corrections and Rehabilitation 2010; Lipsey 2009; Trulson et al. 2005). In addition to high recidivism rates, formerly incarcerated youth fare poorly in indicators of educational attainment (Bullis et al. 2002), housing stability (Hagan and McCarthy 2005), and future earnings (Hagan and Dinotziver 1999), even when compared to young people from similar economic or life circumstances without histories of criminal justice involvement (Chung, Little, and Steinberg 2005).

An abundance of evidence thus suggests that juvenile incarceration is routinely failing to improve youths' lives, or, at baseline, makes little difference in predicting future criminal behavior. However, the target of blame for these poor or null results varies according to ideological leaning. Conservative think tanks and victims' rights groups have largely attributed these failures to a system that is too lenient on youth. According to this view, young people have become more violent and more likely to commit adult-like crimes than in past years, calling for more stringent measures of longer sentences and confinement in adult or adult-like penal facilities (Stimson and Grossman 2009). During the 1990s, this view gained significant public and political traction, resulting in a major shift toward more punitive juvenile justice laws and practices (Scott and Steinberg 2008a). For example, by the turn of the twenty-first century, all US states had provisions in place to waive or transfer minors to adult court for certain classes of offenses, age thresholds, or depending upon evidence of the young person's fitness to stand trial as an adult (Sickmund 2003). Juvenile sentences in many states also become longer and more severe, and some publicly funded juvenile facilities came to resemble the locked cells and solitary conditions of adult prisons, effectively diminishing the rehabilitation side of the system's mission (Krisberg 2006). And although youth crime rates have declined dramatically since their peak in the mid-1990s, empirical studies found that these harsher practices actually contributed to greater propensity for future criminal involvement (Ryan and Ziedenberg 2007; Young and Gainsborough 2000).

Over the past decade, liberal and youth advocacy groups have responded to these trends by calling for a return to a system of juvenile justice they deem more sensible: a system that first and foremost believes in youth's immense capacity for change, and that specifically addresses young people's unique needs for education, adult guidance, and rehabilitation. From the advocacy perspective, the current system's failure can be attributed to poorly run facilities, substandard care, undertrained and potentially even abusive corrections workers, and lack of funding for high quality, evidence-based interventions. Youth advocacy and human rights organizations have also accused several state and county systems of failing to protect youth in custody from harm or to provide adequate education or mental health services (Coalition Against Institutionalized Child Abuse 2007; Human Rights Watch and American Civil Liberties Union 2006). Lawsuits against several large state and county systems on account of these breaches of care have resulted in settlements costing millions of dollars and forcing systems reform and facility closures (Hartney et al. 2010; Rabb 2011).

Amidst these debates about the uses and misuses of juvenile incarceration, there remains a limited understanding of how young people themselves experience involuntary correctional confinement, particularly in settings that are geared toward rehabilitation. Do youth view these treatment programs as a soft form of punishment, in support of the conservative view? By contrast, do they participate in rehabilitation programming and, as a result, strive to create a different future for themselves? Can both possibilities exist simultaneously, and if so, what does that mean for the system's reform?

To foreground the questions that this books seeks to address, several works have analyzed the historical, political, and legal aspects of juvenile corrections (Krisberg 2005; Krisberg and Austin 1993; Wooden 2000/1976), providing an important background to understand how we have arrived at our contemporary social and political crossroads in regard to the confinement of young people. Others have conducted ethnographic work in the juvenile justice system more akin to this project (Ayers 1997; Bortner and Williams 1997; Hume 1996; Polsky 1962; Reamer and Siegel 2008). For example, William Ayers (1997) and Edward Hume (1996) both used a journalistic approach to expose how youth and their families navigate a tireless judicial process, showcasing in a very personal way the problems and pitfalls with the juvenile justice system as a whole. Additional studies in this genre have specifically attended to juvenile correctional facilities, such as Frederic Reamer and Deborah Siegel's 2008 book, which showcased a variety of youth facilities and their shortcomings, and M. A. Bortner and Linda Williams's text (1997), which focused on the practices involved in a model correctional institution.

These ethnographic works have exposed the voices of the youth and the families who are involved in the complicated web of the juvenile justice system at many levels. Yet none of these studies has investigated how youth experience the conflicting discourses of treatment and punishment that are embedded within a juvenile correctional institution. In related work, scholars have found that involuntary confinement in mental health institutions and other mandated inpatient facilities present an array of conflicts in regard to the residents accepting their need for recovery as defined and enforced by the facility staff. Clients in these institutions often construct and assert counternarratives—meaning alternative views of the self—in order to challenge the facility's discourses of pathology or sickness (Juhila 2004; Paterniti 2000). Building on this literature, we uniquely investigate the juvenile correctional institution as a site of involuntary treatment with all of the potential complications and conflicts that are embedded in similar settings.

Moreover, existing scholarship has not adequately attended to the gendered aspects of all-boys facilities, which are the most typical configuration for juvenile corrections institutions in the United States. Young men comprise over 85 percent of all youth in correctional facilities nationwide (Sickmund et al. 2011). Still, despite the persistent and obvious gender imbalance among incarcerated young people, surprisingly little has been written about the gendered aspects of juvenile incarceration or, more specifically, the constructions and performances of masculinity (or femininity) that are embedded in an all-male milieu. In this book, we attend to the influence of institutional discourses on the formation of young men's identities with particular attention to the connections between masculinity and crime. In this sense, our approach is in line with the works of scholars such as Niobe Way (1998) and C. J. Pascoe (2007). We follow in their footsteps by centering the experiences of young people as told to us and as observed from our perspectives, situating these experiences inside larger institutional, social, and theoretical contexts to examine the identity work involved in what we view as a gendered correctional setting.

Within these nested contexts of prior work and theory, this book brings the voices of incarcerated youth and juvenile corrections workers into the current debates about what juvenile corrections can and should be able to accomplish. The ethnographic research that forms the basis for this work included more than a year of engagement with a correctional facility unit designated for young men aged fifteen and sixteen. Using multiple methods associated with participatory field research (described in detail in the appendix), we investigate how a blended system of compassionate confinement operates, how the facility is understood and experienced by the residents and correctional staff, and if and how this hybrid structure can change the course young men's lives. Ultimately, we hope that the insights offered in this work will provide a new twist to an old conversation.

OVERVIEW OF CHAPTERS

Juvenile justice scholars Elizabeth Scott and Lawrence Steinberg (2008b, 265) argue that "this is a good time to reflect on youth crime policy" due to steady decline in rates of juvenile violent crime and a softening of public opinion on youth offenders. Chapter 1 explains the historical trends that contributed to Scott and Steinberg's conclusion, covering the major pendulum swings and reforms in juvenile corrections that have unfolded since the inception of the system in the early twentieth century. Following this historical overview, the chapter then examines recent social and scientific discourses concerning youths' potential for rehabilitation, such as neuroscience and evidence-based practice, and analyzes the influence of these discourses on current policy debates. We conclude the chapter by investigating potential reasons for the persistence of punitive juvenile justice policies among a public that purports to prefer rehabilitation over punishment.

Chapter 2 situates Wildwood House within the larger playing field of juvenile corrections policies and practices. Here we also introduce the types of treatment and punitive mechanisms involved in the facility as well as the central cast of characters. This overview of the facility, its programming, and the people who lived and worked there during our field observation period sets the stage for the remainder of the book.

Chapter 3 focuses on a set of questions about treatment practices as they operate within the context of a correctional milieu, such as: How is treatment woven into an involuntary correctional context? What are some of the tensions that arise in coexisting cultures of treatment and punishment? Using narratives and case examples, we illustrate how the staff and residents of Unit C negotiated the institution's competing punitive and therapeutic frames, each entailing its own language and attributions for criminal behavior. We then articulate the challenges involved in determining residents' progress on the basis of perceived investment in a particular therapeutic discourse, particularly one that involved the identification of family problems. In this chapter and others, the views of staff and youth are considered together to present more complete and at times, more complex answers to these key questions.

As mentioned, gender is a vastly undertheorized component of juvenile incarceration. Jo Goodey (1997) and other scholars (Chu, Porche, and Tolman 2005; Majors and Billson 1992; O'Neil and Luján 2009) have suggested that the development of dominant or hegemonic masculine expressions plays a significant role in the formation and continuation of criminal identities and behaviors for young men, particularly those who are marginalized by their race and class positions. Yet with few exceptions (Reich 2010), scholarship that has addressed the relationship between masculinities, criminal identities, and prison systems has focused largely on adults (Messerschmidt 1993; Newburn and Stanko 1994; Sabo, Kupers, and London 2001). For these reasons, chapter 4 pays particular attention to discourses concerning masculinity, gender expression, and crime that contributed to the array of tangled messages in the larger milieu.

With the foundation presented in chapters 3 and 4, chapter 5 addresses a fundamental question about juvenile corrections: Can these facilities impart genuine and long-lasting change among the youth they serve? Observing and interviewing many youth who entered and exited the facility over the course of our fieldwork, we found three major patterns of response to the involuntary treatment program of Wildwood House. The patterns that we identify and explain in this chapter provide insight into why some youth respond favorably to these programs, and others would prefer to simply do their time rather than participate in any type of therapeutic intervention, even those that have a basis of evidence to support their effectiveness.

Chapter 6 focuses on community reentry. A recently released report from the Pathways to Desistance Project, a longitudinal study of over 25,000 youth offenders sponsored by the John D. and Catherine T. MacArthur Foundation, found that longer stays in juvenile facilities did not in fact promote criminal desistance, but that ongoing support upon release can reduce recidivism risk (Models for Change 2009). Responding in part to these findings, this chapter addresses an additional set of questions, such as: How do youth offenders integrate their lessons learned in correctional facilities into the contexts of their lives in the community, or as they term it, "on the outs"? What challenges arise for these youth as they attempt to reenter their communities? While much advocacy effort has been directed at promoting practices and systems that are effective for young people while incarcerated, comparatively less work has centered on understanding what youth actually do with this therapeutic programming upon their release. Chapter 6 follows some of the major players in the book, illustrating how youth adjusted to their reentry, with specific reference to the patterns of response to their involuntary treatment laid out in chapter 5. This chapter speaks to the real difficulties involved in behavior change and the internal and external struggles that even the most motivated young men faced as they transitioned out of the facility and back into community life.

In the concluding chapter, we use the information presented in this book to comment on the critical questions raised about juvenile incarceration, punishment, and rehabilitation. While we recognize that there is no panacea for a system plagued with a variety of problems and judged by diverse critical viewpoints, there are still many plausible policy and practice reforms that can improve juvenile correctional institutions from their current condition. It is our hope that the insider view we present in this book will provide concrete ideas for reform.

In the methodological appendix that ends this book, we offer a behind-the-scenes glimpse into the process of doing fieldwork in a juvenile correctional setting. We immersed ourselves for sixteen months as researchers, participants, and observers in the culture of Wildwood House, and although our interpretations and conclusions fill the pages of this book, our experiences and challenges as field researchers are less apparent in the broader narrative. In the spirit of transparency and reflexivity, and as an invitation to others who might choose to engage in the research process, we offer these reflections for the benefit of students, practitioners, and those new to interpretive research methods and ethnography.

Throughout the book, we draw upon a blend of youth voices, as interpreted through our own lenses as researchers and as practitioners, to expose the inner workings of a modern-day boys' correctional institution. By foregrounding the voices and experiences of the residents and staff of a juvenile correctional institution, we invite scholars, students, practitioners, and policy makers alike to engage with the lives of the real people impacted by this system. It is our hope that this book will offer a more nuanced perspective on longstanding debates about the fundamental malleability of youth offenders, the benefits and limitations of institutional care, and the potential for involuntary treatment programs to interrupt patterns of criminal conduct among young men.

CHAPTER 1

History and Current Tensions
in Juvenile Corrections

WILDWOOD HOUSE, the facility where we conducted our
fieldwork, did not exist in a vacuum. Nor do we believe it was unique in
composition, challenges, or successes. By all accounts, this institution, like
other juvenile correctional facilities across the United States, grappled with
the push and pull of competing demands and measures of success from several different audiences and stakeholders. The young men who spent four to
six months in the program, and the staff who supervised, challenged, and
offered treatment support to them all, lived under the shadow of society's
ambivalence about the proper uses of juvenile incarceration. In order to
appreciate the complexities of the residents' lives inside the walls of
Wildwood House, the context of the larger system must be addressed.

This chapter begins with an overview of the major movements and paradigm shifts that have shaped juvenile corrections in the United States over
the last century. Examining this history reveals several key pendulum swings
in the balance of punishment versus rehabilitation as strategies to address
the problem of youth crime. The contemporary system can be viewed as a
product of these historically rooted tensions, as current controversial topics
such as sentencing youth as adults and the humane treatment of youth within
correctional facilities are directly related to questions surrounding the
fundamental value of incarcerating young people. The bulk of this chapter is
thus devoted to the current system, its documented troubles, and conflicting
perspectives on why and how it should be reformed.

HISTORICAL BACKGROUND

Since its inception, the juvenile corrections system in the United States
has experienced a tumultuous trajectory. Following the Progressive Era's
experimental origins of the juvenile justice system, several key paradigm shifts
in thinking and practice regarding the incarceration of youth have unfolded.
A review of these shifts reveals the seemingly elusive balance between the
goals of rehabilitation and punishment as they have been embedded within
a single system. While the discussion of these trends in this section is by no

means exhaustive, we hone in on key historical turning points and events that have contributed to the current, uneasy crossroads in juvenile corrections policy and prospects for reform.

The Child Savers and the Early Juvenile Court: 1890 to 1920

The turn of the twentieth century witnessed a movement toward the institutionalization of courts and systems of confinement specifically designated for youth as separate from adults. This change coincided with the emergence of adolescence as a distinct developmental stage characterized by strife, confusion, and the loss of opportunities for meaningful social contributions on the part of young people formerly seen as capable of fulfilling adult roles. This new construction of adolescence resulted in an increased politicization of the concept of childhood and fundamental transformations in the social meanings of young adulthood (Lesko 1996; Lesko 2001). The 1904 publication of G. Stanley Hall's two-volume book *Adolescence* legitimized this category in legal and medical discourses and drew public and professional attention to this newly created developmental stage, now framed for the first time as not-yet-adults who were also no longer children. The creation of social institutions such as the juvenile courts and public secondary schools paralleled these new theoretical and cultural constructions of adolescence as a pivotal life juncture with a set of developmental concerns warranting adult guidance and intervention.

Occurring alongside these new constructions of childhood and adolescence, the Progressive Era child-saving movement emphasized civic responsibility for the well-being of children and youth. The child savers grew out of a group of mid-nineteenth-century religious and moral reformers mainly from Eastern US cities who were alarmed by the conditions of institutional care for "wayward children" (orphans and delinquents), often forced to live in almshouses or work camps alongside adult prisoners. By the late 1890s, a new wave of white, upper-middle-class and highly educated female reformers joined and subsequently moved the child-saving platform to the center of the national political stage. Noted settlement house leaders such as Jane Addams, Sophonisba Breckinridge, Grace and Edith Abbott, and Julia Lathrop launched a number of successful policy campaigns focused on the needs of poor, mostly European immigrant children and families such as child labor legislation, compulsory education, mother's pensions, and foster care (Katz 1986).

As part of this broader child-saving agenda, the first official juvenile court was established in Chicago, Illinois in 1899. By 1928, all but two states had institutionalized separate judicial systems for minors (Katz 1986; Platt 1969). Prior to the twentieth century, suspected delinquents were tried and sentenced either informally by community standards, or formally in the adult system. In response to what was deemed to be inhumane and unjust treatment, the juvenile courts suspended jury trials and established private hearings for youth, created separate facilities for detained youth, and developed probation systems that encouraged rehabilitation rather than just punishment. These sweeping reforms constituted a signature accomplishment for progressive era child savers (Katz 1986; Platt 1969; Schlossman 1977).

The early juvenile courts took on the dual responsibilities of handling cases of both delinquency (offending behavior) and dependency (when children came under the care of the state due to parental neglect or abuse), and the lines between the two were often quite blurred (Mason 1994; Schlossman 1977). Moreover, as the juvenile courts were in an experimental phase, definitions of delinquency varied widely from state to state and were often quite vague and moralistic in tenor (Schlossman 1977). For example, a 1915 California statute (as cited in Walker 1925), defined a delinquent as "any person under the age of 21 'who is in danger of leading an idle, dissolute, lewd, or immoral life.'" This type of umbrella definition, combined with experimental trial and sentencing protocols, often led to arbitrariness and subjectivity in the courts' handling of delinquency cases. For these reasons, while the juvenile court was indeed a significant child-saving accomplishment, historians have largely criticized its social control function in the lives of working-class and poor immigrant youth and their families (Katz 1986; Schlossman 1977; Schneider 1992).

While the child savers believed in the fundamental vulnerability of all youth, their views were influenced by prevailing ideas about innate biological differences between the sexes. They assumed that girls were naturally morally and emotionally vulnerable and that boys were more "redeemable," or amenable to intervention (Abrams 2000). Consequently, social responses to the conditions of wayward girls focused bolstering their moral fortitude and virtuousness, and the vast majority of correctional facilities and reform schools were crafted to meet the presumed needs of young men. These early reform houses were in many ways similar to orphanages, and took in many types of young people, including delinquents, abandoned children, and runaways. The goal of these institutions was to re-parent young men in a cottage living or family like environment, providing them with substitute care that would allow them to return to their communities as mature, law-abiding citizens. While historians have documented many problems and abuses of power in these reformatories (Brenzel 1975; Kunzel 1993; Schneider 1992), the cottage-like living model and moral intervention offered nevertheless laid the foundation for our modern system of juvenile corrections.

The Medical Model: The 1920s to 1960s

Soon after the legitimatization of the juvenile courts and reformatories, the child-saving movement was joined by a concurrent medical paradigm for understanding and intervening in juvenile delinquency. As early as 1915, Dr. William Healy of Chicago spearheaded the mental hygiene paradigm, emphasizing the need for a more scientific approach to discovering the root causes of delinquency. Although Healy studied the familial and social causes of delinquency in addition to so-called individual abnormalities, historians have often credited Healy with launching a medical frame for understanding youth crime that matured in the 1920s and 1930s and persisted for several decades to follow (Krisberg and Austin 1993). The medical model promoted the confinement of delinquent youth in out-of-home placements, intense study of individual cases, and psychological treatment by trained professionals in designated psychopathic clinics. In essence, this meant that the locus of responsibility for delinquent behavior rested within the individual young person, and as such, treatment was targeted to remedy the potential medical or psychological defects presumed to be the root cause of problematic behavior. This paradigm conflicted to some extent with the original child-saving view that implicated the family, poverty, and the larger community in youths' problematic behaviors but nevertheless did not directly contradict the child savers' commitment to treating young offenders differently than adult criminals.

The science of mental hygiene was also connected with the American eugenics movement. From the perspective of race progress, American and European eugenicists were politically invested in finding a biological basis for criminality. Key eugenic thinkers of this era proclaimed a strong scientific link between genetics and deviant or aberrant characteristics such as crime, prostitution, disability, and disease (McGloin, Pratt, and Maahs 2004). Following this logic, the eugenicists maintained that so-called degenerates should not only be removed from mainstream society, but also prohibited from reproducing (Luker 1996; Schlossman and Wallach 1978). In a pattern not so different from Progressive Era conceptualizations, sex differences were assumed to be inherent in the origins of delinquency, with young women's problems being of a sexual nature and young men's, of inherent violent or deviant traits (Abrams 2000). This assumption and the eugenic philosophy underpinning the medical model led to some extreme interventions, such as forced sterilization of delinquent young women (Kunzel 1993).

Throughout the following decades, the medical model of delinquency departed from eugenics and became more heavily influenced by advances in psychiatry and, later, psychology to become an individualized treatment model. The prevailing view considered delinquency to be a symptom of deeper individual problems and internal conflicts that, if left untreated, would become progressively worse (Shoemaker 2009). Accordingly, insight-oriented therapies, such as those based in psychodynamic theory, emerged as the dominant strategy to rehabilitate incarcerated youth. In practice, this meant that work with youth offenders became focused on their individual psychological makeup, rather than their inherent deviance per se. Yet still, the focus remained on understanding and treating the individual in institutional care for the sake of minimizing risk of reoffending. And although none of the purported treatments stemming from the medical model ever proved successful (Krisberg and Austin 1993), the legacy of this orientation persists even in contemporary discourse on the causes of and remedies for juvenile delinquency.

Children's Rights and Deinstitutionalization: The 1960s and 1970s

Juvenile delinquency returned to the center of public discourse with the political upheavals and reforms of the 1960s and 1970s. A sense of frustration with an ineffective individual treatment paradigm and a renewed emphasis on children's legal rights resulted in pivotal Supreme Court lawsuits that substantially influenced trends in juvenile justice and corrections (Kent v. United States, 383 U.S. 541 1966; In re Gault 1967; In re Winship 1970). As a result of these key cases, accused minors were granted federal entitlement to legal protections once absent from the juvenile system, including the rights to receive notice of the charges, to obtain counsel, to confrontation and cross-examination, and to exercise the privilege against self-incrimination. These changes caused some to fear that the juvenile court would become more like an adult, criminal courtroom rather than a humanitarian effort. These fears were partially realized, as the implementation of more regularity in juvenile justice processing, sentencing, and confinement blurred some of the established lines between the juvenile and adult judicial systems (Krisberg and Austin 1993).

In the wake of these landmark decisions, two congressional acts also reflected a new way of thinking about juvenile offending and incarceration. Fueled by the deinstitutionalization movement in mental health, the prevailing idea was that youth should be treated within their families and communities, reserving out-of-home care (including correctional confinement) as a last resort. Youth advocates pressed the federal government to pass two major prevention bills: the Juvenile Delinquency Prevention and Control Act of 1968 and the Juvenile Justice and Delinquency Prevention Act (JDDPA) of 1974. These two pieces of legislation provided federal and state funding for community-based prevention efforts, initiated a national clearinghouse on juvenile delinquency (now the Office of Juvenile Justice and Delinquency Prevention), and launched the development of community-based prevention programs for youth considered at risk of delinquency. The emphasis of this era was on diversion and prevention, as faith in either individual moral or medical rehabilitation had gradually eroded (Bernard 1992). And although deinstitutionalization and due process legislation had large-scale effects on how youth were processed within the courts, these changes did not actually reduce the number of youth who fell under the purview of the juvenile correctional system (Krisberg and Austin 1993).

Getting Tough on Crime: The 1980s and 1990s

By the early 1980s, public perception of the juvenile justice system substantially shifted once again. In a departure from the former era's commitment to due process and fairness, social attention shifted to concern about rising crime among young people. Part of this fear was fueled by a steep rise in juvenile crime, and violent crime in particular, that occurred between the late 1980s and mid-1990s, reaching a peak in 1994 (Snyder, Sickmund, and Poe-Yamagata 1996). Although adult violent crime rates also increased during this same time period (Office of Juvenile Justice and Delinquency Prevention 2000), statisticians and the media paid disproportionate attention to violent crime rates among youth. In response to mounting public fear of youth crime and lack of confidence in either rehabilitation or diversion as solutions, state legislatures across the United States enacted policy measures designed to "get tough on crime." Reflecting these changes, the federal Juvenile Justice and Delinquency Prevention Act was amended to include provisions that permitted states to try juveniles as adults for certain offenses and to enforce minimum detention standards in juvenile court (Bernard 1992).

Public support for these measures was enhanced by increasingly negative public representations of urban young men of color, sparking widespread panic about the spread and severity of juvenile crime. Dr. John Dilulio, a distinguished political scientist, played an influential role in advancing the argument for stiffer punishments and stricter sentencing laws for minors. His writings, published in both academic and popular venues, argued that violent youth were capable of responding only to the threat of severe criminal sanctions. In an article written for the *Weekly Standard* (1995), he coined the term "super-predators" to refer to "morally vacant" urban young men lacking "impulse control or empathy." In the same article, Dilulio described the looming threat of these dangerous super-predators:

> On the horizon, therefore, are tens of thousands of severely morally impoverished juvenile super-predators. They are perfectly capable of committing the most heinous acts of physical violence for the most trivial reasons . . . They fear neither the stigma of arrest nor the pain of imprisonment. They live by the meanest code of the meanest streets, a code that reinforces rather than restrains their violent, hair-trigger mentality. In prison or out, the things that super-predators get by their criminal behavior—sex, drugs, money—are their own immediate rewards. Nothing else matters to them. So for as long as their youthful energies hold out, they will do what comes "naturally." Murder, rape, rob, assault, burglarize, deal deadly drugs, and get high (1995, 23).

In spite of these pejorative and incendiary statements, the super-predator theory held major sway over public opinion and the cascading policy responses that ensued (Scott and Steinberg 2008a). Other well-known economists and political scientists did not endorse the super-predator label outright, but tended to agree with Dilulio's contention (1996, 16) that "if the penalties for crimes could be made more swift, certain and severe, then, undoubtedly, we would have less crime." High profile violent crimes committed by youth, most notably the 1999 shooting massacre at Columbine high school in Littleton, Colorado, and media portrayals of youth gang culture in urban hubs, supported the need to implement an adult-like criminal justice system for juveniles as a means to achieve public safety. Suppression gradually replaced rehabilitation as the main strategy to combat what the public perceived as a wave of uncontrollable violence, particularly among urban African American and Hispanic young men.

As faith in rehabilitation and diversion strategies eroded, so did the century-old Progressive Era legacy of a juvenile justice system that aimed primarily to rehabilitate, rather than strictly punish. In this sense, the 1970s Supreme Court cases establishing due process rights for youth also catalyzed a trend wherein juvenile court proceedings would increasingly come to resemble those of adults (Feld 1993). The lines between systems were further blurred by a wave of legislation allowing individuals under the age of eighteen to be tried in adult criminal courts and sentenced to adult facilities. By the late 1990s, all US states and the District of Columbia had provisions in place to waive or transfer youth to adult court, including fourteen states that had mandatory waivers to adult court for youth as young as sixteen. Moreover, thirty-four US states had passed laws that once a youth had been waived to an adult court, any subsequent cases would automatically be transferred to the adult system (Sickmund 2003). Juvenile justice scholars Elizabeth Scott and Lawrence Steinberg (2008a, 17) describe the progression of this get tough on crime trend: "As youth crime rates rose during the 1980s, conservative politicians ridiculed the juvenile system and pointed to high recidivism rates as evidence that rehabilitation was a failure. According to some observers, the juvenile court may have met the needs of a simpler time when juveniles got into school yard fights, but it was not up to the task of dealing with savvy young criminals who use guns to commit serious crimes."

By the turn of the twenty-first century, just a hundred years after the system's inception, mounting concerns over juvenile crime, gang violence, and public safety had trounced any remaining romanticized notions of wayward youth in need of supportive adult guidance. As a result, by 2005 the number of minors serving time in adult jails more than doubled, and over 2,000 juveniles had been sentenced to life without the possibility of parole (LWOP) in adult court (Back and Calvin 2008). Clearly, the juvenile justice system had departed from its original mission of providing moral guidance and a second chance for abandoned youngsters.

THE CURRENT SYSTEM

Twenty-first century juvenile corrections can be seen as a product of the tensions that have unfolded over its one hundred plus years of operation. The current system is fractured by ideological clashes regarding the most effective means of curbing youth crime, and by most indicators, it is failing to substantially fulfill the goals of either public safety or rehabilitation. In order to understand these ideological clashes, it is critical to appreciate the practical complexity of the current system and its constituent population. To that end, we now present the role and functions of the current system, a demographic profile of youth who are housed in these facilities, and the major yardsticks used to measure the success or failure of these institutions. This background information provides the necessary context to present the two dominant positions in the current debate about juvenile corrections reform, the advocacy view and the public safety view, and the ways in which each differentially influences public discourse, policy, and practice.

Youth Behind Bars: Demographics and Outcomes

Despite the major changes that occurred beginning in the 1970s, the juvenile justice system is still distinct from its adult counterpart in its stated mission and goals. For example, the Office of Juvenile Justice and Delinquency Prevention (OJJDP), a division of the US Department of Justice, has a stated mission of "serving children, families, and communities." By contrast, the mission of the US Bureau of Prisons, which is geared to adult federal offenders, is "protecting society and reducing crime." These statements are emblematic of the long-standing paradigmatic differences between the two systems, distinctions that are not just ideological but also procedural. As the founders of the juvenile justice system originally envisioned, youth who remain under the purview of the juvenile court are entitled to hearings with specially designated judges, and are likewise held in juvenile-only facilities while awaiting trial. Court proceedings are typically confidential and juvenile crime records are not made public. In addition, youth crimes have different classifications from those of adults, and judges are afforded far more discretion in their sentencing decisions.

The majority of youth who appear before the juvenile court for delinquency petitions are not in fact sentenced to correctional institutions or other out-of-home placements. Of the 1,666,064 youth in the United States charged with formal delinquency petitions in 2007, 148,603, or 8.9 percent, were formally placed in institutional care, and the majority were sentenced to probation services and/or home supervision (Sickmund, Sladky, and Kang 2010). Typically reserved for violent or repeat offenders, these court-mandated out-of-home placements can be set for a specified or unspecified period of time. In many states and jurisdictions, judges can order young people to serve time in a correctional facility until they are determined to be rehabilitated or until they age out of the system, which ranges between ages eighteen and twenty-four per state laws (Sickmund 2003).

The OJJDP Census of Youth in Residential Placement counts the number of youth (aged twelve to twenty-one) in juvenile correctional placements on a given day. Although its counts do not provide information on the total number of youth who serve time in correctional placements annually, the database is nevertheless instructive. In 2007, for instance, 86,927 youth were confined on a given day, spanning a variety of placement types and including 75,101 young men (86%) and 11,826 young women (14%) (Sickmund et al. 2011). Clearly, the system has retained some of its historic emphasis on the behaviors and problems of young men; the overwhelming proportion of males to females in juvenile correctional placements has remained stable in the past two decades, even given disproportionate increases in young women's arrests for violent offenses compared to young men during this same time period. According to the FBI Uniform Crime Reporting data, while rates of all violent crime decreased significantly for young men between the years of 1991 and 2005, they decreased much less significantly for young women (rate of change of -10.2 compared to -27.9). Only one type of offense—simple assault—increased for young women during these years at a rate of 24 percent, compared to a decrease of 4.1 percent for young men (Federal Bureau of Investigation 2006).

While the interpretation of these data is complicated by the steep decrease in youth crime overall since 1994, the increasing proportion of young women arrested for violent crimes remains noteworthy. Some have suggested that as gender norms have loosened, young women have become more aggressive (Garbarino 2006). Yet others have attributed these arrest trends to policy changes, particularly in school settings, that have reclassified girls' formerly innocuous behavior as violent (Chesney-Lind and Okamoto 2001). Along these lines, an OJJDP expert study group examining the FBI arrest trends alongside other national data on violence and victimization concluded that policies concerning family violence reporting and intervention have likely contributed these arrest patterns, as opposed to actual changes in girls' behaviors (Zahn et al. 2008). Regardless of the cause of these gender variations in arrest patterns, young men still comprise the vast majority of youth sentenced to out-of-home placements, and these figures have remained stable for decades.

Racial disproportionality is also endemic in juvenile facilities. According to the OJJDP National Disproportionate Minority Databook, racial disparities are evident in all levels of juvenile justice processing—from arrests, through to trials, convictions, and sentencing. For placements specifically, 31 percent of minority youth have adjudicated cases that result in an out-of-home placement, compared to 25 percent for white youth (Hispanic youth are grouped in with white youth in this database) (Puzzanchera and Adams 2011). Racial disparities for African American youth are most the most pronounced; African Americans represented roughly 16.5 percent of the nation's youth population (ages 12–18) in 2007, yet an overwhelming 40.8 percent of youth in correctional placement (Sickmund et al. 2011).

Undeniably, the American juvenile corrections system is a costly enterprise. The average cost per youth for a state-funded youth correctional facility in 2006 was $241 per day, or approximately $88,000 per year (American Correctional Association 2008). By comparison, the average cost for an adult correctional stay in 2006 was approximately $65 per day, or $23,876 per year (Pew Center on the States 2008). These costs vary widely by state; Wyoming, for example, spent $24 per day while daily costs for youth in Connecticut were approximately $726 (American Correctional Association 2008). In total, the United States spent approximately $4.7 billion on youth correctional facilities in 2006. When these facilities become overcrowded or have unacceptable conditions, lawsuits cost taxpayers millions more.

Despite the relatively high costs of juvenile incarceration, research has consistently found that the majority of young people who spend time in correctional facilities will experience new arrests, convictions, or stints of incarceration in the juvenile or adult system within a few years of their release. While very few states accurately track long-term recidivism rates beyond the youth's probation period (Snyder and Sickmund 2006), existing evidence is not all that promising. A longitudinal study of nearly 2,500 juvenile offenders who had served time in a juvenile correctional facility in Texas found rearrest rates as high as 85 percent over a five-year period (Trulson et al. 2005). Similarly, the California Department of Juvenile Justice found that 81 percent of youth paroled from its state institutions were rearrested within three years of their release (California Department of Corrections and Rehabilitation 2010). Rates of new convictions (a more conservative recidivism measure than new arrests as many arrests to do not lead to a conviction) tend to be slightly lower, with eight states (Arkansas, Florida, Georgia, Kentucky, Maryland, North Dakota, Oklahoma, and Virginia) reporting an average twelve-month reconviction rate of 33 percent, accounting for both juvenile and adult system dispositions (Snyder and Sickmund 2006). Overall, these high recidivism figures have rightly raised public and mass media concern that taxpayers are wasting their money on costly programs and even exacerbating the potential for future criminality among detained or incarcerated youth (Holden and Zeidenberg 2007; Szalavitz 2009).

In addition to high rates of repeat offending, youth with histories of incarceration fare poorly in regard to educational and vocational attainment and other indicators of well-being. Youth who fall into the hands of the

corrections system tend to have histories of educational neglect, learning dis-
abilities, poor school records, and school transience (Bullis and Yovanoff
2002; Coffey and Gemignani 1994; Moffit 1990). These cumulative disad-
vantages, coupled with time spent away from a mainstream school setting,
all contribute to low high school completion rates, estimated to be less than
20 percent (Osgood, Foster, and Courtney 2010). Both low educational
attainment and incarceration are associated with higher rates of unemploy-
ment and decreased earning potential (Hagan and Dinotziver 1999). For
example, Bullis and Yovanoff's (2006) longitudinal study of over 500 youth
exiting the Oregon Youth Authority system found that only 28 percent were
employed after one year of their release. Youth with histories of correctional
placement also tend to have poor outcomes on a range of other social indicators, such as housing stability and receipt of public assistance (Clark and
Robertson 1996; Hagan and McCarthy 2005).

As these studies have collectively indicated, juvenile incarceration has
largely failed to either rehabilitate youth or to protect society from future
crime. While public systems spend a great deal of money on these programs,
once released, these young people are highly likely to reengage in criminal
activity and to fare poorly in measures of adult well-being. For these reasons,
the social and economic value of juvenile incarceration has been increasingly
called into question, particularly in light of sharp disagreement about what
that incarceration should entail, and toward what end. Examining current
perspectives on juvenile corrections reveals these deep divides, ones very similar to those that have encumbered the system since its inception. The liberal
advocacy paradigm and the more conservative public safety model continue
to dominate the discourse on the value and demerits of the juvenile justice
system, invoking different narratives and constructions of young offenders in
their attempts to influence public opinion, policy, and institutional practices.

The Advocacy View

In the wake of the major changes that occurred in the 1980s and 1990s, a
strong advocacy voice emerged to demand a reversal of the punitive juvenile
justice policies and practices ushered in during this time period. Advocates
blamed the tough on crime approach with eradicating a fair system of justice
for youth offenders and essentially eclipsing the rehabilitation or public welfare aspects of juvenile justice. The Sentencing Project, a liberal criminal
justice research and advocacy group articulated this position: "The transfer of
increasing numbers of children from juvenile to criminal courts is continuing
in the face of mounting evidence of the harm it does both to the children and
to public safety—once again 'tough on crime' politics undermines good public policy" (Young and Gainsborough 2000, 10). Armed with a wealth of new
research to back their claims, advocates have argued for an approach to

juvenile justice that includes reverting to a separate system of juvenile justice, diverting all but the most severe offenders from deeper involvement in the system, and implementing proven, evidence-based practices in order to interrupt a more severe criminal trajectory among incarcerated youth.

One of most prominent arguments for the advocacy view stems from emerging research on adolescent reasoning and brain development. In the late 1990s, the John D. and Catherine T. MacArthur Foundation funded a series of studies seeking to understand the developmental aspects of cognitive maturity. Countering a prevailing belief that brain development is effectively completed by at age sixteen, these studies suggested that higher order cognitive functions such as reasoning, impulse control, and the ability to resist peer pressure often continue to develop well into adulthood (Grisso et al. 2003; MacArthur Foundation Research Network on Adolescent Development and Juvenile Justice 2006). Based on this research, the Foundation adopted the stance that juvenile brains (and the young people housing them) deserve treatment in accordance with their unique development and level of cognitive maturity, because "the same factors that make youth ineligible to vote or to serve on a jury require us to treat them differently from adults when they commit crimes" (MacArthur Foundation 2006, 3).

This viewpoint is not all that dissimilar to G. Stanley Hall's construction of adolescence as a developmental stage distinct from both childhood and adulthood. But in the twenty-first century, advocacy and children's rights groups have increasingly leaned on an emerging body of neuroscience to bolster these claims. Parallel to research conducted on young people's reasoning, a series of brain imaging studies found that several components of younger brains are structurally and functionally different than those of older brains (Giedd et al. 1999; Gogtay et al. 2004; Sowell et al. 2001). Liberal advocates have used these studies as a basis to argue that young people are biologically and universally predisposed toward impulsivity, unreasoned judgments, and susceptibility to peer influence, all amounting to a rationale for why young people may be less responsible for their behavior than adults and therefore deserving of a separate system of justice.

Prominent (and politically unaffiliated) professional groups such as the American Medical Association, the American Association of Child and Adolescent Psychiatry, and the American Psychiatric Society have endorsed this view, which has seen widespread traction in the public policy arena. Indeed, these professional associations and others collectively filed a brief in *Roper v. Simmons*, a 2005 Supreme Court case that overturned the constitutionality of the juvenile death penalty. Relying on this research, the brief argued four central points: 1) adolescents are inherently prone to risk-taking behavior and less capable of resisting impulses because of cognitive and other deficiencies; 2) brain studies have established an anatomical basis for adolescent behavior; 3) research shows that adolescent brains are more active in regions related to aggression, anger, and fear, and less active in regions related to impulse control, risk assessment, and moral reasoning than adult brains; and 4) adolescent brains are not fully developed in regions related to reasoning, risk taking, and impulse control (McLaughlin et al. n.d.). Clearly, many advocacy and professional groups have relied on this recent brain imaging research to influence law and policy concerning juvenile justice; in particular, providing a legal rationale to maintain the separation between the juvenile and adult justice systems. Yet important questions remain about the potential implications such discourse holds for public policy and the day-to-day lives of young people.

Some researchers and legal analysts, for example, consider this research too new to use as a basis for public or legal policy (Aronson 2007; Bower 2004). Others have questioned the consequences of this research for public perception and subsequent policy making. A *New York Times Magazine* feature focusing on the implications of recent brain imaging studies argued that this research has major and potentially unforeseen consequences for the future of both juvenile and adult criminal justice (Rosen 2007). For example, the claim that young people are biologically and universally less culpable than adults for their crimes introduces significant questions about responsibility and punishment. Will this research be used to show at what age rehabilitation may not work? Or, on the flip side, can the misuse of this science paradoxically lead the public to conclude that youth are not biologically capable of rehabilitation due to fixed developmental deficits (Cox 2009)? Further, the argument that some young people's behavior (irresponsibility, poor impulse control, and other socially recognized tropes of adolescence) can be ascribed to biological deficiencies and immaturities—as indicated by the successful arguments invoked in *Roper v. Simmons*—bears striking resemblance to the medical model's adherence to notions of delinquency as rooted in the biological or genetic make-up of the young person.

Still others have challenged many scholars' and policy makers' interpretations and implications of these studies' findings. Scholars of youth work including Howard Sercombe (2010) and others (Paus 2005), for instance, have readily ceded the point that neuroimaging has revealed interesting findings related to brain structure and function. However, they cautioned against the essentialist and biological determinist arguments that follow, namely that these differences in structure constitute inherent biological deficiencies in the young adult brain. Such claims assert that behavior labeled by adults as impulsive or risky can be attributed to young people's immature brain functioning, and contrary to much of what is known about experience as a fashioner of neural pathways, they largely disavow the impact of environment and experience on how brain functioning becomes patterned. In other words, these scholars argue, "the brain as a structure is shaped not only by genetics, by biology, but also by environment, by experience. The brain does not only determine experience. Experience also determines the brain" (Sercombe 2010, 34).

Mike Males (2009, 2010) has also challenged the biodeterministic implications of adolescent brain research, focusing his critique on the implications of a discourse centering on adolescents' fundamental deficiencies. Citing a wide range of statistics often invoked as evidence of young people's impulsiveness and poor executive reasoning, Males has argued that young people's risk-taking behaviors are seldom presented alongside meaningful comparisons with similar behaviors among adults or within the economic and environmental contexts that help explain them. Absent these comparisons or context, a narrative of the cognitively deficient adolescent risk taker reigns unexamined. Far from serving young people's interests, the conventional interpretations of emerging brain science simply reinforce a dominant paradigm in which adolescents are uniformly pathologized: "Teens' higher rates of car wrecks proves adolescents' inner recklessness; adults' higher rates of suicide reflects adults' outer environments. A 16-year-old robber represents a crime-prone class; a 46-year-old embezzler represents only himself [*sic*]. If teens and parents fight, blame contrarian teenage development and neurons" (Males 2010, 59).

For these and other reasons, a few advocacy voices have argued that brain research must be used with caution and does not in any way establish absolute lines on when maturity occurs—or even what social and cultural markers constitute maturity—nor does it absolve youth of responsibility for their crimes (Scott and Steinberg 2008b; Steinberg 2009). Still, based on this notion of brain-in-formation, the advocates' position suggests that youth are inherently more deserving of the opportunity for rehabilitation than adults (MacArthur Foundation 2006). In this sense, juvenile offenders should be treated humanely, in facilities designated for youth, and with proper care and attention to their unique developmental and cognitive needs (Ryan and Ziedenberg 2007; Young and Gainsborough 2000).

Advocates have further argued that trying and sentencing youth in adult criminal courts and institutions does more harm than good, both for the general public and for youth themselves (Scott and Steinberg 2008a). In regard to public safety, a number of studies have found that youth who are tried in adult courts and who are sentenced to adult facilities are more likely to commit further and more serious crimes than equivalent groups of offenders who remain under juvenile court jurisdiction, regardless of their sentence (Bishop et al. 1996; Fagan 1996; Redding 2003). Research has also consistently reported that youth are needlessly harmed by their experiences in adult jails and prisons as they are highly susceptible to abuse, rape, and violent victimization by older inmates and by correctional staff (Beyer 1997; Forst, Fagan, and Vivona 1989;

Ziedenberg and Schiraldi 1997). For example, a twenty-year longitudinal study in Pennsylvania concluded that youths held in adult jails and prisons are five times more likely to be sexually or physically abused than adults, and thirty-six times more likely to commit suicide (Deitch et al. 2009).

Collectively, these studies have undermined the tough on crime premise that trying and sentencing youth as adults is socially beneficial, and ample evidence has shown that youths' lives are negatively impacted by the trend toward adult sanctions for juvenile crimes. As the idea of adult time for adult crime has clearly been rejected by a chorus of advocacy voices, it is important to consider the current advocacy view on the promise (and perils) of facilities designed for youth. On this matter, opinions are somewhat less consistent.

To begin, at the same time that advocates have labeled adult prisons as abusive, harmful, and ineffective for youth, similar criticisms have been lodged at juvenile facilities. Recent developments in the New York State juvenile justice system provide an excellent case example for this argument. In December 2009, the *New York Times* headline story began with the following statement: "New York's system of juvenile prisons is broken, with young people battling mental illness or addiction held alongside violent offenders in abysmal facilities where they receive little counseling, can be physically abused and rarely get even a basic education, according to a report by a state panel" (Confessore 2009). In response to four separate incidents of excessive force by staff, including one that resulted in death, New York State Governor David Patterson appointed a task force of experts to conduct a thorough review of New York State juvenile correctional facilities. What they found was an extremely deteriorated system of care for youth to live in, let alone to be rehabilitated. The task force documented an absence of adequate mental health, health, or educational services, and concluded that youth are unjustly subject to violence, substandard living conditions, and unnecessarily harsh practices such as shackling and restraints. In response to these deplorable conditions, the report called for the implementation of community-based programs to keep lower-risk offenders on home supervision, and the transfer of bureaucratic oversight of juvenile correctional facilities to the state child welfare agency (Vera Institute of Justice 2009).

Unfortunately, the New York case is not an isolated story. Scores of research reports and investigations of state and county run juvenile detention and correctional facilities have found similarly poor conditions of confinement, an absence of quality rehabilitation programs, and the failure of programs to prevent injury and/or death from victimization or self-harm. In the mid 2000s, advocates called for California to dismantle its entire state-run system of juvenile corrections due to persistent reports of abuse, suicides, assaults, and murders committed on the premises. In response, the state has closed most of its state-run juvenile facilities (Macallair, Males, and McCracken 2009) and in 2011, Governor Brown signed Assembly Bill 109, a realignment bill that among other provisions, authorized the gradual transfer of nearly all state juvenile detainees to county probation systems (Criminal Justice Alignment, *Laws of California* 2011). In New Orleans, a class-action lawsuit recently filed on behalf of youth in the state run juvenile detention center charged that the facility "has rats and mold, lacks adequate educational services and trained staff and keeps young people in their cells for at least 20 hours a day" (Evans 2009). The list of these lawsuits is quite extensive, all essentially charging that juvenile correctional facilities are mismanaged and abusive to the point that they fail in both their rehabilitation and public safety missions.

At the same time that many juvenile systems are the subject of lawsuits and ardent demands for reform, one US state, Missouri, has earned nearly universal praise from advocates. Over the past two decades, Missouri closed its only large training school and moved to a system of regional, small-scale, community-based treatment programs. The state also dramatically reduced the number of youth waived to adult court. For fiscal year 2010, the state reported that just 16 percent of committed youth recidivated within the year following their release (Missouri Department of Social Services 2010). Advocates are enamored with Missouri's successes for various reasons, not the least of which is the real life evidence that treatment and compassionate care in a juvenile-specific system can simultaneously help youth and promote public safety.

So what about the Missouri model is presumed to work so well? The state has presented a near perfect combination of elements to appeal to juvenile justice advocates. The first is the use of small, homelike facilities that can be seen to resemble a return to the Progressive Era ideal of caring for wayward and abandoned youth. The notion of cottage dormitory living for juvenile offenders stands in stark contrast to the images of rat infested cells, shackles and restraints, and prison guard abuses associated with larger institutional settings. Another major piece of the Missouri equation is the implementation of interventions that have been empirically shown to reduce repeat offending. In this sense, the Missouri model gets at the heart of the newer science of youth offender rehabilitation: evidence-based practice.

Evidence-based practice is not necessarily a new strategy, but in the past decade it has emerged as a captivating buzzword for programming in juvenile corrections as well as other social services targeting young people. Evidence-based correctional practices rest on the assumption that empirically definable and testable interventions, when applied with fidelity, can reduce thinking patterns and behaviors associated with criminal offending. In juvenile corrections, advocates for evidence-based practices have praised such strategies such as multi-systemic therapy (MST), various cognitive behavioral therapies (CBT), and aggression replacement training (ART), among others (Greenwood 2010). These treatment methods, often involving a short-term focus on changing the thoughts and impulses associated with criminality, have been tested in repeated experiments in order to establish themselves as proven programs (brand name programs shown to reduce delinquency and recidivism, with at least two randomized clinical trials), proven strategies (generic strategies shown to reduce recidivism in meta-analyses of the research, that are not branded), or promising programs (brand name programs without the backing of repeated, randomized clinical trials). The evidence-based practice movement has a major influence over current policy and practice goals for public correctional facilities. States and counties are under increased scrutiny to show that the programs they employ conform to evidence-based standards, and the language of evidence-based practice permeates expert recommendations on systems reform (Crime and Justice Institute 2009). Subsequently, the treatment of youth in corrections has moved toward branded and manualized treatment modalities that are often rooted in cognitive-behavioral therapies. In many ways, one might view the evidence-based movement as the modern scientific paradigm for correctional care, this time not seeking to identify and grapple the root causes of delinquency (as in the early medical model), but rather striving to identify the most efficacious ways to cure antisocial thought patterns and behaviors.

Not all reform-minded thinkers, however, universally focus on the development and implementation of evidence-based practices. Dr. Jeffrey Butts, a highly respected researcher in the juvenile justice field, has cautioned against the assumption that most youth charged with crimes are in need of highly specialized therapeutic interventions (Butts 2008). Rather, Butts has argued that the majority of youth offenders benefit from the same types of programs that help all youth thrive, which are related to solid education, positive relationships with adults, and the development of pro-social talents and interests. A similar line of thinking can be found among proponents of alternatives to detention, largely associated with the Annie E. Casey Foundation's efforts in this area. Referring to studies showing that the deeper youth are involved in the system the more criminal they become, proponents of alternatives to detention suggest keeping all but the most violent youth out of institutions and instead providing alternatives that are home- and community-based, with Butts's positive youth development as a core principle (Mendel 2010; Stanfield n.d.). While diversion is already a routine practice in most probation systems, the idea has resurfaced as a potential remedy for correctional and institutional inefficiencies.

Thus although youth advocates and reform-minded thinkers are not fully united in their focus, they are in agreement on a few main points. The first is that the juvenile justice system, including corrections, must conform to the unique (and scientifically rooted) developmental needs of young people. Related to this argument, trying and sentencing juveniles in the adult criminal system is, with few exceptions, not sensible public policy. The third major point is that to the extent that youth corrections continues to resemble the conditions of adult facilities, the results won't be promising and will likely even make system-involved youth worse. These arguments have been backed by a wealth of scientific reports and highly publicized investigations of juvenile facilities, and partly for these reasons, have emerged as the most visible perspective on juvenile corrections in the past decade.

The Public Safety Model

In the wake of such a strong advocacy movement, the question remains, what has happened to the more conservative, tough on crime voice? While some of the earlier super-predator discourse persists to this day, it is not all that visible, and even the original architect of this theory, John Dilulio, has publicly retreated from his position (Becker 2001). Only some of the most conservative public commentators still publicly refer to youth offenders in starkly pejorative terms that indicate a lack of potential for rehabilitation and a culture of nascent, incurable criminality.

Although academic and scientific support for these arguments has eroded and public expressions of their sentiments no longer appear on the front-page or evening news, one can nevertheless find these and similar arguments in the new media domains of popular opinion: online discussions, blogs, and similar forums in cyberspace. And in spite of its tempered withdrawal from the social spotlight, the public safety view still has a large impact on policy-making; liberal advocates still fight an uphill battle in regard to less restrictive and more rehabilitative oriented policies and funding.

This observation gives rise to a perplexing social question—one taken up directly by journalist Dick Mendel (2010): Why does the conservative public safety model reign over juvenile justice in a time when the juvenile violent crime rate is lower than ever, and when this position lacks articulated public mouthpieces?

> From 1994 through 2005, a period when youth homicides and other serious juvenile crimes declined dramatically, the number of youth adjudicated in juvenile courts increased sharply for virtually every class of minor offense: liquor law adjudications up 57 percent, adjudication for "public order offenses" up 70 percent, simple assault adjudications (typically fighting) up 80 percent, and adjudications for "disorderly conduct" up 109 percent. This, despite growing evidence that informal responses to routine adolescent misbehavior yield far better outcomes. So why does the public safety model still dominate?

According to opinion polls, the public generally endorses the view that youth should be treated in juvenile facilities where the primary goal is rehabilitation. A 2006 national survey of over 1,000 adults using a representative sample found that a nine-to-one majority of respondents believed that for youth, rehabilitative services and treatment help prevent future crimes. Further, 80 percent believed such services were cost-effective, suggesting that spending money to provide these services will save tax dollars in the long run. Nearly 70 percent of those polled reported that they believed housing youth under eighteen in adult correctional facilities makes them more likely to commit future crimes, and they also overwhelmingly disagreed with the premise that such punitive consequences teach youth lessons that deter them from criminal activity (Krisberg and Marchionna 2007).

Despite voters' expressed opinions, punitive policies still dominate. For example, the State of California, which currently houses 16 percent of all youth in correctional confinement in the United States (Sickmund et al. 2011), has long professed liberal attitudes regarding juvenile offenders. A 1988 survey of California voters' attitudes revealed very similar themes as the 2006 opinion poll cited above: a preference toward rehabilitation and treatment, keeping youth in juvenile facilities, and separating juveniles from adults (Steinhart 1988). Yet as an exemplar of this paradox, California voters and politicians have nearly consistently approved more punitive measures for juvenile offenders over the past two decades. In 1988 (the same year that voters reported preferring rehabilitative approaches), Californians passed the California Street Gang Terrorism and Enforcement Act, a sentencing enhancement that can add from two years to life to a convicted violent felon's sentence if prosecutors prove the crime was done to benefit, in association with, or at the direction of a criminal street gang. The law includes cases involving minors. In 2000, voters passed Proposition 21, which among other provisions, required more juveniles to be tried in adult court and increased penalties for gang related crimes. And finally, in 2007, 2009, and again in 2011, three California Assembly bills that would have effectively ended the practice of assigning life without the possibility of parole (LWOP) sentences for juveniles died before reaching the floor for a full vote. The evidence is compelling: In spite of contradictory social preferences, public policymaking in regards to juvenile corrections continues to favor harsher penalties and punitive orientations over rehabilitative approaches. What factors might explain this disparity?

We suggest three explanations for the persistence of the public safety model despite the public's stated endorsement of alternatives. The first relates to the role of the media in perpetuating myths about youth crime. Juvenile justice scholar Barry Krisberg and colleagues (2009, 2) have argued that despite the sharp decline in youth crime since the mid 1990s, newspapers continued to spread widespread fear with "articles about 'kiddie car thieves,' homegrown terrorists, and youth who 'just wanted to kill.'" They also suggested that very few media outlets ever report on the decline in juvenile crime rates or programs that successfully help youth, leaving the public with a distorted and fear-based view of the current climate. A 1997 report by the Berkeley Media Studies Group substantiated these claims. This study found that more than half of local news stories on youth involved violence, and more than two-thirds of the violence stories concerned young people under age twenty-five, even though 57 percent of violent crime was committed by people aged twenty-five and over and 80 percent was committed by adults over eighteen (Dorfman et al. 1997). Communications experts have further argued that the mass media jumps upon any opportunity to showcase the violence and brutality related to youth crimes, but does not follow up with any context to help the public make sense of such events. This media fixation on the violence itself then sets the stage for public policies (McManus and Dorfman 2002).

The sensationalism associated with youth crime and violence has also increased in recent years with the advent of YouTube, cell phone cameras, and social networking Internet sites. For example, in October 2009, a cell phone video recording of the brutal beating of a white seventeen-year-old high school student on a Chicago school bus by two African American students became so widely circulated via YouTube that even President Obama commented on the incident. Throughout the blogosphere, commentators charged the perpetrators with a racially motivated attack (without any context or evidence) and suggested that the attackers would not respond to a minor punishment such as school suspension. One radio show posted the following notice on its Web site, inviting a public response regarding how to best punish the perpetrators: "School officials haven't said how long the students, 15 and 14, are suspended for as a result of the Monday beating. Authorities at first labeled the attack as racially motivated, but have since backed away from that description. The Ron & Don Nation is left to wonder: Is a suspension enough? Why haven't these thugs been expelled already? And police have yet to file charges against the pair, so should they? Given their age, would they even face appropriate punishment in a court of law?" (The Ron & Don Show, n.d.). Statements like these draw attention to the brutality of youth crime without any context for understanding the violent acts, leading the public to question if the punishment will fit the crime. From the attention drawn to this case, one would not logically conclude that youth violent crime has in actuality declined in the last decade. Rather, images of the super-predators or thugs come to mind, even if this more overt language is no longer publicly acceptable.

In addition, new social media permits individuals to voice feelings about youth crime and violence that are no longer stated in more public arenas. With the anonymity afforded in the blogosphere, people are more likely to write pejorative, racist and otherwise socially unacceptable comments likely to promote hatred and fear. On New Year's Eve, 2009, a public transit safety officer apprehended Oscar Grant, a young African American man, for fighting. Grant was shot dead in the back, although unarmed, in front of hundreds of transit riders, many of whom recorded the shooting on their cell phones. The next day, these cell phone videos spread rampantly across cyberspace. Many community groups rallied behind Grant and his family, and in an extremely rare ruling, the officer was found guilty of involuntary manslaughter. Yet although Oscar Grant was the victim of the shooting, many anonymous statements on YouTube and news Web sites revealed a public unsympathetic to his cause. Using racially denigrating terms, commentators assumed that his life was "wasted anyhow" and applauded the officer for getting yet another "degenerate" off the street. Although certainly extreme, this example showcases the power and potential of new social media to incite public fear about youth crime and violence that both covertly and overtly reinforces the benefit of the public safety model.

Our second potential explanation for the persistence of public safety policies despite the public's stated preference for rehabilitation is that there may be broader support for victims' rights groups among politicians and the general public than is publicly acknowledged. Arguments for the rights of victims of juvenile crimes have been voiced in opposition to recent attempts to ban or curb the use of juvenile life without the possibility of parole (JLWOP) sentences through modifications to state or federal laws (National Organization of Victims of Juvenile Lifers n.d.). With few exceptions, advocacy attempts to overturn state JLWOP provisions have largely failed. The victims' rights argument is compassionate to the perpetrators yet firm, taking direct issue with many of the tenets of the advocacy movement. They do not view juveniles as biologically or developmentally different from adults, and they directly attack the plea to consider the children's backgrounds, rather than their crimes. One such victims' rights group articulated this position:

> We note with great interest that the legislative efforts to end JLWOP are not going well for the advocates. Granted their movement is a very young one, and it may only be a passing effort—only time will tell. Despite their general mishandling of the "victim issue," most of them are well-meaning human rights advocates . . . But they have all made a significant fundamental mistake. They have started their efforts to reform the JLWOP sentence with only one argument: "Oh, these poor killers, they were just children." . . . Of course, they don't like to talk about the fact that most JLWOP killers nationally were 17 at the time of the crime, many just days or weeks from their 18th birthday. And all of them are guilty of not just "routine" murders, but aggravated capital level or near capital level offenses that could have resulted in death sentences in many cases, had they been weeks older. . . . That is our question to these advocates: Why

is it that none of your websites and glossy reports about these "poor kids" ever talk about the crimes they committed? The victims they killed? The families and loved ones they left behind with lives irretrievably damaged? (National Organization of Victims of Juvenile Lifers n.d.)

In 2009, the Supreme Court heard arguments in the *Graham v. Florida* case to consider banning JLWOP on the constitutional grounds of cruel and unusual punishment. In 2010, a six to three ruling banned the use JLWOP sentences in the absence of homicide, affecting just a handful of individuals serving these sentences but nevertheless laying the groundwork for further reform (Liptak 2010). The advocacy voice took center stage throughout media coverage of this case, arguing that the time had come to put an end to this violation of the constitution and of international human rights decrees. Only one major think tank, the Heritage Foundation, joined the victims' rights groups in favor of upholding the constitutionality of JLWOP sentences and arguing the merits of this practice in regard to promoting public safety, retribution, and justice (Stimson and Grossman 2009). Thus while victims' rights and conservative groups have retreated to the margins of public debates about juvenile crime and incarceration, when it comes down to policies dealing with the most violent youth, their voices may hold more sway among policy makers and the general public than is detected in public opinion polls.

Our third explanation for the prevailing juvenile law and order policy ethos lies in America's movement over the last several decades toward mass incarceration. The number of people currently incarcerated in the United States is the highest of any industrialized country in the world. In 2008, the Pew Center on the States revealed even more stark statistics on this topic, finding that the United States leads Western countries in its incarceration rate at 750 per 100,000 people, with Russia coming in second at 628 per 100,000 people. So why might this trend matter for the fate of juvenile corrections? Critics have argued that although rates of youth incarceration have declined in the last decade, our societal addiction to imprisonment may prevent the development of true community-based alternatives for youth incarceration. In response to a 2009 case in which three Pennsylvania judges were found guilty of reaping financial reward for sending juveniles to long sentences in private, for-profit facilities, a columnist in the *Wall Street Journal* noted that locking up youth is, in many ways, an American tradition:

We the people say it loud and clear every Election Day, in high-crime periods as well as peaceful stretches: More of our population needs to be behind bars. We love retribution so much we make hits of TV shows in which society's ne'er-do-wells come in for lectures not only by stern, righteous judges, but by tattooed, mulletted bounty hunters as well . . .

And over the years we have embraced all sorts of instruments ensuring that more people got locked up for longer and longer stretches: Three strikes laws, mandatory sentencing laws, zero-tolerance policies. Maybe they aren't "fair," but they've helped to make the U.S. number one in percentage of population in the clink—in fact . . . America has an amazing 25% of the world's prisoners (Frank 2009).

Scholars and advocates have proposed that both economic and racial motivations have fueled the mass incarceration trend. In particular, some have argued that the mass incarceration of adults and juveniles serves the function of keeping African Americans and Hispanics incapacitated from making social gains in the post–civil rights era (Williams 2009). As suggested earlier in this chapter, these disparities are indeed of significant concern, particularly for African American youth.

Moreover, some prison rights advocates have argued that there is a profiteering prison economy that benefits from our continuing reliance on the incarceration of low-income adults and juveniles (Herivel and Wright 2007). For example, commentators have invoked this argument to describe law enforcement union resistance to the closure of New York State juvenile correctional facilities: "The [state] Legislature will finally have to put the needs of the state's children ahead of the politically powerful unions and upstate lawmakers who want to preserve jobs—and the disastrous status quo—at all costs" (A Better Chance 2010). This *New York Times* editorial suggests that economic motives—specifically the unions protecting correctional workers' jobs—are effectively blocking the closure of the state's juvenile correctional facilities. Theories of mass incarceration are well beyond the scope of this work; nevertheless, this trend remains one explanation, along with media influence and sympathy for victims, for why the public safety model reigns when public opinion consistently favors rehabilitation strategies for juvenile offenders.

CONCLUSION

A century after the institutionalization of courts and separate correctional facilities for juveniles, the public is still engaged in heated debate about the potential for incarceration to rehabilitate youth and protect the public from future harm. In the past decade, despite a strong advocacy voice and an abundance of scientific evidence to refute the notion that stern and swift punishment works to deter youth crime, public policy is still oriented to be punitive toward youth offenders, particularly those accused of violent crimes. Rates of violent youth crime have steadily declined since the mid-1990s, and in 2010 they reached the lowest rates on record since 1969 (YouthFacts 2010), yet public perception of youth violent crime does not mirror these realities. And although the advocacy voice has certainly dominated public discourse in recent years, the future course of juvenile correctional policy and practice is yet to be determined.

Contemporary juvenile corrections institutions rest, therefore, at the intersection of these divergent perspectives. On one hand, the advocacy view—emboldened by research evidence supporting treatment as the institution's primary obligation—argues in favor of facilities that stress individual and group rehabilitation through evidence-based practices. On the other hand, such institutions are still fiscally and socially answerable to the public that funds them and therefore must respond to the public's ongoing call to facilitate accountability and punishment. Consequently, juvenile correctional facilities have resorted to blended responses; those that offer treatment and rehabilitation within the context of individual accountability and the enforcement of consequences for criminal behavior. As our study of Wildwood House illustrates, while these blended systems of care may allow institutions to appease (in the short term) multiple audiences, the strategy also introduces specific challenges for the youth and staff most directly impacted by these competing demands.

CHAPTER 2

The Setting

Driving past a small collection of mid-1970s split-level private homes just off
the main road struck us as odd, given our destination: one of the county's
only juvenile correctional facilities. Leaving the neighborhood behind, we
turned up a tree-lined driveway and drove another quarter-mile or so up to
the facility. Passing the facility's welcome sign and large, open recreation
fields including one with a baseball diamond, we noted the absence of the
customary cultural markers associated with prisons. With no encircling fence,
security booth, or visible means of surveillance, the setting spoke more to a
residential school than a juvenile jail. Leaving the car in a small visitors-only
parking lot, we took note of the surroundings as we approached the main
administrative building for our first introduction to the facility. One large,
brick-faced administrative building with a tiny and claustrophobic secure
foyer dominated the upper part of the grounds, with two wings, clearly added
in subsequent remodels, which housed the dorms and school facilities. We
were buzzed through the secure front door into a small lobby as we waited
for the head of the institution who would lead us on our first tour of
Wildwood House. Our year in the life of Unit C had begun.

Wildwood House is a contemporary juvenile correctional facility for
young men located just a few miles from the downtown core of a major urban
center. Founded in the early 1900s as a community response to truant and
incorrigible youth, the facility has a longstanding history in its community.
Over the course of the twentieth century, the institution passed through several incarnations and transformations, most often paralleling larger national
trends in the management of youth offenders. In the mid 1970s the program
adopted its current treatment model, combining features of rehabilitation and
insight-oriented treatment with personal and collective accountability for
criminal conduct. And although the mechanisms and programs used to
achieve these goals have evolved in the thirty years since the program's
implementation, it has remained largely consistent in its orientation toward
rehabilitation. Interested in understanding more about the experiences of

youth and staff inside such an institution, we were fortunate to be allowed entry—and eventually welcomed—into Wildwood House.

At the time of our study, Wildwood House served up to seventy-five young men at any given time, ranging in age from thirteen to eighteen and divided into three age segregated units also referred to as dorms. Accountable to the courts that sentenced these youth, the institution housed young men with criminal histories that deemed them unfit for less restrictive placements (such as group homes or house arrests), but who were also determined to be good candidates for a treatment-oriented correctional program rather than a more punitive state facility. Generally, residents' criminal histories included charges ranging from serial misdemeanors and probation violations to felonies such as crimes against persons or property. Wildwood House residents remained under the legal custody of the juvenile court during their four- to six-month stay and their additional three months of aftercare status upon their release. One of only a handful of publicly funded juvenile correctional institutions in a major urban area, the institution filled a specific niche in the system because of its explicit commitment to blending the system's twin goals of rehabilitation and punishment. The facility director described Wildwood as more of a residential treatment center than a correctional facility, and spoke with pride about the institution's successful rehabilitation and school programming.

PHYSICAL STRUCTURE

Physically, Wildwood House's exterior bore almost no resemblance to the caricatures of juvenile jails popularized in contemporary media. Far from wire fences and barred windows, the institution's exterior shared more in common with a residential school than a prison and was not completely locked or electronically monitored. The facility consisted of a complex of buildings set on a large campus, complete with athletic fields, a full gymnasium, and picnic tables set up on the lawn. The institution's central building contained administrative offices, a lobby, and meeting rooms to support its general operations. Immediately inside a small, claustrophobic foyer was a narrow lobby furnished with uncomfortable and industrial chairs, sports- and fishing-oriented magazines, and a reception area where all visitors were required to sign in. With the exception of a mural on one wall, the lobby was sterile and impersonal; with its 1950s-style gleaming asbestos tile on the floor and few windows, it conveyed a utilitarian emptiness in sharp contrast to the warm exterior. Behind the administrative suite and beyond one locked door, accessible to visitors only with a staff escort, was a central lobby with a staircase leading down to the school and cafeteria, as well as halls leading to the communal showers, large gymnasium, and the three residential dorms.

Unit C, which housed the fifteen- and sixteen-year-old residents, was located through one locked door off this lobby. When we entered the unit on our first tour of the facility we were struck by its openness; the dorm's main living area consisted of a large common room with institutional looking couches and chairs, none of which looked remotely comfortable, organized around a large-screen television set. The remainder of the common space was occupied by foosball and ping-pong tables, individual study carrels set up around the room's perimeter, and an assortment of other activities such as board games and model cars laid out on tables and window sills. The walls featured a combination of artwork created by residents and treatment-oriented posters with self-help slogans such as "There is no 'I' in Teamwork," which contributed to an already utilitarian sense of the room's overall décor. Although accustomed to correctional facilities and their typical milieu, we were struck by the uneasy combination of supportive slogans, displays of individual expression, and the dorm's overall institutional tone.

Adjacent to the common room was a very small staff office where the day-to-day administrative tasks of the dorm were conducted and where individual and small group meetings with residents took place. The office appeared typically cluttered, with stacks of paperwork on desks and an array of file cabinets and shelves housing residents' case files and additional binders and logs to track the day-to-day operations of the dorm. A large dry-erase board facing the door to the office publicly displayed each resident's treatment history and progress, including his primary staff member, current standing in the dorm's privilege system, and any conduct issues pending staff attention. Such public demonstration of individual residents' status served as an unspoken reminder that although Wildwood House emphasized treatment and rehabilitation, these were facilitated through a process of public accountability and surveillance.

A short distance from the common room, in a hallway leading to the sleeping area, was a small bathroom. The bathroom door remained locked at all times (we had to ask staff to unlock the door for us each time we wanted to use the restroom—a clear reminder to us of just how controlled residents' lives were), and a single secure cell called the isolation room consisting of a small window, a concrete bed-slab without a mattress, and an exposed steel toilet and sink. The locked door of this room had a narrow observation window through which the entire room was visible. On our first tour of the dorm, the head of Unit C informed us that the isolation room was used only rarely for youth who were really out of control. Nevertheless, its centrality and visibility (residents walked past the isolation room on the way to and from their sleeping area) clearly made it a looming threat and was perhaps the main reminder to us and the residents that this was indeed a juvenile jail. The only other room in Unit C was a dormitory-style sleeping area consisting of many bunk beds lining the walls surrounding a small recreation space in the center of the room. Another small staff office adjoined the dorm, from which the entire sleeping area could be monitored. Within the dorm, residents each had an assigned bunk bed and a small locker for their personal belongings, although they were allowed no other personal items than their own clothing and a few pictures or letters from friends and family members.

Although residents spent most of their nonschool time in their unit, their daily schedules also included three meals in a large main cafeteria. The dorms ate in shifts, such that residents ate all meals with only their dorm-mates, and for some at unconventional times; for one dorm, dinner was as early as 4:45 in the afternoon. The cafeteria was a single large room with many windows looking out on a lawn and individual tables, each with plastic detached chairs. Food was served from a single buffet-style cafeteria window. The facility employed a cook on staff, and the three dorms rotated responsibility for assisting the kitchen staff in preparing and serving the meals. In keeping with its rehabilitative focus, the facility offered on-the-job training credit for residents who volunteered for kitchen preparation and clean-up work. The food was served in institutional section-divided trays with plastic utensils and four or five selections per meal, usually including starchy and fat-laden foods such as lasagna or other meat casseroles, a fruit item or salad, a dessert, and milk.

Connected to the cafeteria by a short hallway was the facility's on-site public school, consisting of several small classrooms and faculty offices. The teachers at the school were provided to the facility by the local school district. Contrary to many correctional facilities' educational offerings, the school at Wildwood House consisted of a largely traditional high school program, with multiple class periods, passing time, and other familiar features of more conventional schools. The program offered full special education services, including continuing individualized education plans (IEP) from public schools, as well as conducting assessments with residents who may have been in need of special education services but not previously identified. Classes were small, often with no more than six to ten students in each, and represented one of the few opportunities residents had to socialize with youth from other dorms. Each classroom was equipped with computers and limited Internet access, and the school had one additional computer lab for students' use. In all, the school had a very conventional feel; with few overt indications of its placement inside a correctional institution, the classrooms could easily have been transplanted to any high school in the country.

The gymnasium and a communal shower were located on the other side of the building, away from the school and the dormitories. Residents showered together as a dorm every evening, supervised for safety from an adjacent hall by a male staff member from their dorm. On our first tour, we were struck, again, by the very public nature of the residents' lives. In spite of the facility's overall feel being more familiar and comfortable than many of the correctional facilities we had each encountered, features like the communal shower reminded us repeatedly of the primacy of surveillance and safety measures within Wildwood House.

Each dorm also had a set daily recreation period in the gymnasium provided that the group behavior in the dorm indicated no major safety concerns. The gym itself was a fairly modern facility with full-court basketball and a separate elevated area with several pieces of weightlifting and exercise equipment, including free weights. During the warmer months, residents were also permitted at times to play sports outside on the large fields and baseball diamond. Overall, both inside and out, the facility had the feel of a large residential school, with scattered visual reminders of the primary purpose of confinement.

PROGRAM DESIGN

Like many contemporary juvenile correctional institutions, Wildwood House combined treatment programs with individual and group accountability mechanisms. Grounded principally in a cognitive behavioral approach to correcting behavior, the program at Wildwood House rested on an understanding of offending as resulting from the distorted or criminal thinking patterns that the youth had learned from their home and peer environments. In other words, the program and its staff assumed that residents engaged in criminal behavior largely because of messages from family members and other central influences that justified or legitimized such conduct. Based on this interpretation of behavior, the program sought to hold young people accountable for their errors in cognition and the resulting criminal conduct while also offering insight-oriented therapies geared toward uncovering the root causes of these problematic thought patterns and values.

To facilitate rehabilitation, all Wildwood House residents were required to participate in ongoing individual and group treatment modalities including behavior modification activities specifically through cognitive-behavioral therapies (CBT), individual counseling, group counseling, and some specialized interventions such as family group, substance abuse treatment, or services for young fathers. Each resident was also required to participate in a weekly hour long check in session with his assigned primary counselor, which consisted of reviewing the resident's progress, updating treatment plans, and addressing any behavioral or other dorm concerns expressed by the staff or perhaps, by the youth. Treatment activities took up a large chunk of each afternoon and evening following school time. For instance, immediately following school dismissal, the residents gathered in the dorm's common room and transitioned into the daily peer group, which often took an hour or more. Every evening, a variety of rehabilitation activities were offered; some were mandated, and others voluntary. The weekends were far less structured, as treatment programs were mostly packed into the weekday schedule to accommodate youth whose privileges allowed off-campus visits and weekend outings.

The institution's correctional orientation was evident in its rigid schedule and emphasis on dorm safety, rule compliance, and near-constant surveillance of young people's interactions and behaviors. Similar to any other correctional setting, Wildwood House staff enforced strict codes of conduct and behavioral expectations to ensure the safety of the institution. Behaviors such as sneakiness, defiance, or threatening one another through gestures or words were swiftly labeled and consequenced. Further, youth sentenced to this facility were quite aware that other more restrictive environments existed in the county; threats from the staff of worse placements or prolonged engagement with the juvenile probation department also served as a deterrent to disruptive conduct and reinforced the need for the program's more punitive orientation.

Mirroring larger trends in juvenile correctional institutions, Wildwood House relied on an elaborate point and level system to hold these parallel and sometimes contradictory emphases (insight-oriented treatment on one hand and enforced compliance on the other) together. Point and level systems in residential placements create token economies, in which individuals receive positive reinforcement (often in the form of points to be traded in for privileges) for desired behaviors and negative reinforcements (loss of those points) to discourage undesired conduct. These token economies and the point systems that support them originated in the 1970s, with their primary application in psychiatric and mental health systems, and have subsequently spread to schools, residential care facilities for young people, and correctional institutions across the country (Field et al. 2004; Kazdin 1982; Kazdin and Bootzin 1972).

The behavioral management system at Wildwood House held youth both individually and collectively accountable for their behavior through a system of rules and expectations accompanied by points and levels with corresponding privileges for demonstrations of desirable behaviors. Residents' behaviors were tracked on daily scorecards, where they received points for pro-social behaviors and lost them for problematic ones. Staff doled out violations based on residents' rule infractions or demonstration of behaviors inconsistent with the dorm's expectations. These violations were processed in small group meetings, during which residents were required to explain their behavior to a group of staff, who then determined an appropriate consequence, such as a loss of points or privileges. In this way, the point system reinforced the facility's correctional orientation; rewarding compliance and punishing problematic behavior enforced accountability and consequences for criminal or inappropriate conduct. Success in the program, and therefore safety from the threat of more restrictive placement, depended in no small part upon residents' behavioral compliance and steady progress through this point and level system.

The level system managed dorm behavior, but it also supported the facility's commitment to rehabilitation. Youth received points for active engagement in the program's treatment offerings, including specialized treatment components such as required and optional peer groups, individual and family counseling, substance abuse treatment, and skills-building programs such as anger management. Residents could then use their earned points to purchase additional privileges in the facility and signal to staff their successful progress in the program. Consequently, residents were encouraged to participate in as many treatment programs as possible, to maximize their purchasing power in the token economy.

In addition to the day-to-day operation of the token economy system, residents also progressed through a series of program phases termed levels before they were approved for release to the aftercare program. Each of the five program levels conferred a different set of privileges—such as later bedtimes and weekend home visits—as well as responsibilities, such as leading peer groups or coaching newer residents. Linked closely to the program's rehabilitative goals, these levels corresponded directly with residents' perceived progress in treatment; compliant behavior alone was insufficient grounds for moving up in levels. Residents moved up and down on these phases according to staff's ongoing assessments of their emotional and therapeutic progress and ability to comply with the program's behavioral expectations, including school performance. Although many of the facility's treatment modalities emphasized group work and process, the staff tended to assess residents' actual treatment progress more through their individual work on a series of written treatment contracts. These contracts included structured topical essays such as "Understanding My Offense," "The Cycle of Crime," "Family Problems," and "Hurt and Loss," through which youth were required to disclose and process their reactions to and experiences with these issues. As subsequent chapters demonstrate, the contracts became a central indicator of youths' ability to comply with the program expectation that they engage fully and honestly with the therapeutic process.

In most cases, residents were required to share their treatment contracts verbally, first with the staff and then again in front of their peers, reinforcing the group accountability model prevalent in many residential and correctional programs for youth. Staff routinely assessed residents' written contracts for authenticity and depth of reflection or disclosure, and then recommended level advancement for those residents who had successfully completed each contract. Upon receiving this staff recommendation, a resident could buy a request for level advancement, provided that he had had accumulated sufficient points on his daily scorecards. The resident then presented his case again during a team meeting before the assembled staff, who reached consensus about whether to approve the level upgrade and its accompanying privileges. In a process similar to how residents advanced in levels, they could also lose levels for significant rule infractions or failure to demonstrate a satisfactory degree of treatment progress. In these ways, the structure and implementation of Wildwood House's token economy explicitly linked residents' program progress with both their perceived level of engagement in therapeutic work and their behavior and compliance with the correctional aspects of the program.

In their daily lives and routines, residents' lives were mostly structured. With few exceptions, the staff consistently enforced wakeup and lights-out times and a time-ordered daily routine. Residents attended school for the majority of the day during the week, and on weekends this time was spent in dorm-wide events or activities. Right after school, the dorm held their peer process group and then enjoyed a brief period of semi-structured free time in the common room or gymnasium between school and dinner. Following dinner, a variety of therapeutic groups, work on treatment contracts, or other structured group activities were required. Showers and lights-out in the sleeping room ended each evening. Reinforcing a sense of collectivity and communal accountability, the residents lined up to move from one activity to the next or from one part of the building to another; typically, a resident on one of the higher privilege levels led the line and another followed the group at the tail.

Even within the context of a structured environment, the program also attempted to maintain and preserve a sense of individual identity and autonomy for the youth. Excluding those who presented a significant escape risk or had been dropped down to an lower level, residents wore their own clothing in the facility, provided that their clothing contained no references or allusions to gangs, violence, sexuality, profanity, or other topics deemed inappropriate by program rules. They were also encouraged to express themselves through their hairstyles, which were also not uniform. Interestingly, styling one's hair was one of the most significant means of self-expression, and styling each other's hair represented one of the few permissible forms of physical contact between residents. Moreover, as they advanced in levels, youth were encouraged to use their daily points to purchase small entertainment or hobby items, such as model cars, cards, or books. And finally, as residents began to near the end of their stay, they started a gradual process of community reentry, typically starting with short off-campus outings supervised by their families and gradually extending to weekend- or even week-long home visits. These visits not only served to facilitate residents' transition to the community, they also provided an opportunity for residents to demonstrate their ability to comply with program expectations, such as calling in to the facility on time for routine check-ins, without the program's immediate reinforcements.

Evidence of program completion generally involved a consensus of dorm staff, therapists, teachers, probation officers, and any other adults who had direct exposure to the residents' progress. When the staff deemed a resident ready for exit and if he was on a high enough level, he began his transition out of the facility. For some, length of sentence and cost of the program forced some youth to leave unsuccessfully. In either case, recognizing that release from the facility often signaled reentry into the same sets of relationships and challenges that likely contributed to their original criminal behavior, Wildwood House provided community-based aftercare supports to youth for up to three months after their release. These supports varied significantly by virtue of being tailored to an individual youth, but they generally included some combination of surveillance and compliance reporting, group support meetings, and ongoing advocacy and support with the young person's family members, teachers, and probation officers.

WHO'S WHO: THE CAST OF CHARACTERS

Over the course of our year in the life of Unit C, we interacted with a wide range of facility staff, including administrators, teachers, support personnel, and residential staff. Through hundreds of hours of participant observation, we built relationships with many of these staff members and with the residents as well. This section presents a general description of the staff of Unit C, as well as brief biographies of the residents who participated most fully in the project. A more complete description of our methods and some of the nuances involved in building and maintaining these relationships can be found in the appendix.

Staff

Wildwood House employed eight to ten full-time residential staff who were assigned exclusively to a given dorm, as well as a few part-time and substitute care workers who floated between dorms. The regular staff of Unit C worked conventional residential schedules of roughly eight hours, with three shifts (day, swing, and overnight) per day. With the exception of the specialized therapists and the supervisors, the dorm staffs' role was consistent across personnel, and their residential work offered little differentiation based on individual expertise or interest. The dorm staff carried out duties ranging from supervision and safety to running peer groups and providing individual counseling. The staff's role extended far beyond routine supervisory or milieu duties, as they were also expected to forge caring and concerned relationships with the youth and their families—relationships that most of the staff considered to be the most rewarding aspect of their job. The residential staff were also responsible for leading recreational activities, shuffling the residents through their daily routines, and reporting to the courts and probation officers on the residents' progress toward release.

Demographically, it is noteworthy that males comprised nearly all of the primary and part-time dorm staff in Unit C. Only two women worked full-time in the dorm during our involvement with the facility; other female staff worked in different roles across Wildwood House, mostly as therapists or as teachers in the school program. Likewise, it should be noted that although the residents were racially diverse and paralleling national trends, youth of color were significantly overrepresented in the facility (38% of residents were African American, 33% white, 15% Asian, 9% Hispanic/Latino, 4% Native American, and 2% other/unknown); the vast majority of the staff were white. Only one regular shift staff member and a handful of weekend or substitute staff were African American, despite that African Americans accounted for the largest single racial group in the facility. There were also no Hmong staff members, although Hmong youth constituted the third largest group. Finally, most of the staff were early-career professionals in their mid-twenties, although a handful of the longer-term staff were significantly older. Most had bachelors-level degrees with educational backgrounds in psychology, social work, criminal justice, or fields related to the helping professions, and a few had education or training beyond the undergraduate level. Many of the younger staff saw Wildwood House as a stepping stone toward their primary career ambition as probation officers, while the few older staff members had dedicated their entire careers to this particular institution.

Residents

As mentioned, the residents of Unit C were mostly fifteen or sixteen in age, and all were repeat or felony-level offenders who often considered the program as their last stop on the way to becoming certified and tried as an adult. Although we came to know and learn from a number of residents during our sixteen months at Wildwood House, twelve youth featured prominently in this project. All twelve of these youth participated in a series of in-depth interviews and granted us access to their facility records. Through these interactions, we built significant relationships these residents; in many ways, they became the primary narrators of life in the facility. While other residents' experiences are included in this book, the voices of these twelve young men are the common thread around which our interpretations are structured. As a result, their stories run throughout the next several chapters, illustrating and highlighting our observations and interpretations of Wildwood House. At the beginning of our relationships with each of these youth, we asked them to choose a pseudonym to use throughout the project and we use these names to refer to them throughout the book. We list them here alphabetically by the first names they chose for themselves.

BRAD. A quiet Native American youth, sixteen-year-old Brad was withdrawn and somewhat shy throughout his time at Wildwood House, engaging only sporadically with his peers and prompting staff to note in one progress report that he had "no positive connections at this time." Content in the pages of his science fiction or fantasy books, Brad frequently commented to us he didn't like the spotlight of having to communicate his treatment progress verbally, and he became visibly agitated when he was put on the spot to talk about his criminal history or his family problems. In one interview, he admitted that he appreciated the thinking and processing he'd been doing at the facility, but that it all came from his own internal motivation and became "dumb" when he had to share it out loud as part of treatment.

Brad's family history was characterized by instability, trauma, and rejection, having lost significant connections with his biological parents due to substance abuse and incarceration. After shuffling through various homes and foster care, he was temporarily living with an aunt and other relatives, one of whom was also placed Wildwood House. Staff routinely commented on Brad's need to build positive relationships with adults but also recognized that his self-isolation and fear of talking about his feelings might be a mechanism to protect him from further rejection. Originally placed in the facility for a burglary charge, he had a history of robbery, substance abuse, and other residential placements. His academic performance was significantly below grade level, except with regard to reading, at which he placed well above his peers. When asked to describe himself, Brad said simply that he was "just a regular kid."

ELIJAH. One of the stronger, more athletic, and conventionally charismatic of the residents, Elijah came to Wildwood House after a history of theft convictions, disorderly conduct charges, threats, assaults, selling marijuana, and a series of probation violations. His current charge was terroristic threats against his girlfriend, who also happened to be the mother of his toddler age son. He was an attractive African American young man, much shorter than many of his peers but still powerfully built, with tattoos covering both arms and more on his body. From the very beginning of our relationship, Elijah's interactions with us had the feel of an elaborate performance. His stories were dramatic and exciting to the point of being occasionally too fantastic to be believable. A note from an early interview with Elijah commented, "it's as if he doesn't really know any more what parts of the story he actually experienced, and what parts he's embellished to make the stories better." His humor and banter was both very engaging and demonstrative, and many staff believed this to be a façade to cover Elijah's insecurities and fears.

Elijah came from a family rife with instability and criminal involvement; his father had been in and out of correctional facilities for most of his life, the other adults in his life were largely unreliable, and Elijah had himself recently become a parent. Records from his intake into the facility reflect a childhood of trauma and violence that forced Elijah to develop survival skills early on, including use of violence, selling drugs, and other strategies for safety and income. Staff identified these coping strategies as problematic, suggesting that he was, in truth, "a criminal thinker with little awareness of others" and needed "to learn that he cannot control his environment and cannot control others around him." For his own part, Elijah saw himself as talented, likeable, and motivated to do right by his one-year-old son. "Mom never paid attention to me," he said, so "I want to be with my son."

ERIC. Fifteen-year-old Eric was, in most ways, an anomaly among the residents of Wildwood House. A self-described "band geek" who engaged very little with his peers in the dorm, Eric was one of a handful of white boys in the facility; he was slender and fairly tall but otherwise unassuming. Unlike most of his peers, Eric had no other criminal record or placement history. His criminality began with the felony theft that brought him to the facility and came as a surprise to his otherwise conventional middle-class family. Consequently, Eric saw himself as different from the other residents in the facility, as though the program worked for "those people" but was a profound mismatch for him and his circumstances. He even went so far as to strategize with his parents on home visits to invent family issues for the sake of fulfilling his treatment expectations.

Among his peers and the staff, Eric was not well liked. Staff progress notes portrayed Eric as "dishonest and manipulative," and justified denied level requests on the basis that "this boy is always in his superior mode," and because his contracts were "very well written but lacked any emotion." The few staff with whom Eric did build affirming relationships found him to be funny and witty, but the general perception of him was that he "needed to take ownership for what he'd done and admit to himself and his parents that his crime was no fluke." When asked how he saw himself, Eric said that he was easy-going and motivated. His criminal behavior, he said, backfired on him because it was originally all about making money and rebellion, but in the end all he ended up with was a criminal record. Upon his release, Eric articulated his commitment to not committing future crimes, but not because he benefited from the program at all. Instead, he said he would stay away from crime "because I don't want to jeopardize my freedom again."

HUMPHREY. Humphrey was a tall, multiracial youth who carried himself with a sense of uncertainty and trepidation that belied his physical size. One of the only overweight residents in the facility, Humphrey said he did not much enjoy physical activity or sports, preferring solitary and quiet activities like reading popular fantasy novels. Consequently, he was often ignored or dismissed by his peers and spent much of his time on the sidelines of the dorm. Even among staff, Humphrey often flew just under the radar, attracting little attention and completing the program's treatment expectations with few interruptions but equally few celebrations.

Placed at Wildwood House following multiple probation violations and prior intensive residential treatment programs, fifteen-year-old Humphrey was one of just a few youth in the entire institution with a history of criminal sexual conduct. Very literal and concrete, Humphrey struggled at times to demonstrate the critical reflection so prized in the facility. In fact, case notes reflected that Humphrey vacillated between taking responsibility for his criminal behavior (a requirement of sex offender treatment programs as well as the program at Wildwood House) and positioning himself as a victim of other people's abuses and mistreatment. He reported that he didn't see himself as a sex offender and would not need to see himself that way; he could change his behavior and leave this chapter behind him.

JASON. The oldest resident in the project at age seventeen, Jason came to Wildwood House with an extensive criminal history that began with an arson charge and continued through several probation violations, fights, gang activity, and a recent felony escape from a different correctional facility. Though quiet and shy when he first entered the facility, Jason eventually made it clear that he was invested in pleasing the adults in his life whom he determined to be worthy of his respect. He talked extensively about the emotional pain and shame his criminal behavior had caused his traditional Southeast Asian (Hmong) refugee parents and his siblings.

Nevertheless, Jason had also adopted a set of beliefs through his criminal and gang activities that his own reputation and posture superseded his desire to please the adults around him. Noting these beliefs, staff reported seeing Jason as "sneaky" and "hard to read." One staff member noted that Jason had received a total of eleven behavioral violations during his stay in the facility, and that in his role as informal ringleader of the other Asian residents, he was "Dirty! Dirty! Dirty! His anger continues to be nestled on his shoulders!" In stark contrast with this impression, just before discharge from the program, Jason said that he saw himself as "likeable," and "as a good kid who sometimes does bad things without knowing how to do anything different."

JOSH. Sixteen-year-old Josh was a short, stocky Caucasian teen with a round face who appeared much younger than his years. His reputation preceded him, given a criminal history that was entrenched in his family system and much longer and more varied than most of his peers, including a series of assaults, possession of weapons, theft, auto theft, multiple probation violations, and more. The staff noted to us on more than one occasion that his father had also been a resident of Wildwood House as a teen. Josh carried himself confidently and assertively among his peers and with staff, relying on street talk and toughness, some bragging about his crimes, and trash-talking more than physical prowess.

Josh's school records ranked him well below grade level in most academic subjects, attributed to the combination of a probable learning disability and negative attitude toward school. Coming from a home environment characterized by substance use and parental criminal involvement, Josh affiliated with a neighborhood gang from an early age and rationalized many of his oppositional behaviors as normative. Perceiving him as "cocky and cynical," staff routinely mentioned that they didn't trust Josh and believed him to be "lying and manipulating" his way through the program. One of the few residents to say he "deserved" to be at the facility, Josh believed himself to be "more criminal than the other kids" at Wildwood House, a perception that brought him status and regard from his peers. Upon release from the program, he said that he "still wanted to have fun" but was also done doing crimes because he did not want to go to adult prison.

KEI. At sixteen, Kei was admitted to Wildwood House following a history of truancy, burglaries, assaults, and probation violations. Growing up in a Hmong refugee family, Kei experienced consistent instability from an early age, having moved homes so many times before high school that he had lost count. Although charming, funny, and quick to smile, Kei struggled academically; he was significantly below grade level in all subjects except math and academic assessments suggested the presence of a learning disability. As a storyteller, Kei was goofy and playful, very easily distracted, and circular in reasoning, commenting that it was hard for him to focus because he always felt so full of energy.

Staff wrote that Kei saw the world in terms of power and control, and that this external drive for power motivated his criminal activity. Kei did not necessarily disagree, saying that if he hadn't been caught, he would have continued criminal behavior: "I would have done worse things. I'm a boy who wants to have fun, not a man yet." Still, Kei's narrative changed significantly by the time he was released; he, more than many of his peers, wound up attributing much of his changed perspective and newfound commitment to a crime-free life to the treatment he received in the facility.

MARIO. Like some of the other residents in Wildwood House, Mario experienced significant transition and housing instability as a child. An immigrant from Central America at age five, Mario lived in another state until age nine and finally settled in the city nearest Wildwood House. Small of stature, with a scant moustache and barely fifteen, Mario was one of the younger residents—and like Humphrey, one of very few adjudicated sexual offenders in the facility. He had been placed in juvenile detention centers many times for gang-related assaults, selling marijuana, and multiple probation violations.

Mario was quiet and unobtrusive in the daily life of the dorm. He was respected by his peers and well liked by staff, who appreciated his willingness to go along with the flow of his peer group without joining in what they perceived to be his peers' negative behaviors. In spite of having received violations for occasionally roughhousing or being "passive-aggressive" with other residents, this positive narrative continued throughout his time in the facility. Mario identified himself as friendly and adaptable, saying he was committed to getting the most possible out of his treatment program, citing his sex offenses and gang affiliations, specifically: "It's in me to accomplish anything I want."

NINO. Nino was a charming and cheerful African American sixteen-year-old father of twin boys who came to the facility with a history of former placements and probation violations originally resulting from charges of theft and weapons possession. He came from a single-mother family as his father had been incarcerated most of his life. Although he possessed a significant rap sheet, Nino was nevertheless engaging and relaxed throughout his stay in the facility. Polite and articulate, he told stories easily and with obvious enjoyment, demonstrating not only thoughtfulness but interpersonal awareness that was rare among Wildwood House residents. Still, his academic levels were significantly below grade expectations across the board and assessments indicated the likely presence of a learning disability.

From the perspective of the staff, Nino seemed too good to be true; he largely complied with rules and treatment expectations, received feedback and consequences easily, and seldom challenged authority. Still, this led many staff to assume manipulation: "Great behavior; I swear he's almost *too* good," and "Never any complaints. Assuming he'll be out of here in no time. Hope he's for real." In spite of these perceptions, Nino himself said he appreciated the facility for helping him not get mad when things go badly, learning instead to "leave it alone until I calm down." He said, just before release, that he most wanted to "be good and not following my dad's footsteps now that I'm a father, too."

TERRELL. In spite of being one of the younger residents, at age fifteen Terrell entered Wildwood House with a lengthy criminal history including auto theft, assaults, truancy, numerous probation violations, and gang involvement. Terrell was a powerfully built and attractive African American youth whom the staff identified as having a "chip on his shoulder." Among his peers, Terrell assumed positions of prominence in the unstated hierarchy of the dorm, particularly due to his athletic skills. Among staff, however, he was often perceived as arrogant and disrespectful; case notes called him "Mr. Slick," "more crooked than a barrel of snakes," and "real proud of the crimes that he has done." Nevertheless, he worked the program easily and pleased the staff with his seemingly "hard work."

Terrell came from a large family with many criminally involved relatives, including his father from whom he was estranged and who had spent most of

Terrell's life behind bars. His most significant support was his mother, whose attempts to support Terrell in opening up about his family's criminal and gang affiliation dovetailed neatly with the facility's treatment program. Terrell himself did not take Wildwood House very seriously but did state that he hoped he could learn something along the way. Still, prior to leaving the facility, Terrell denied his need for this program and deemed it ineffective because he was "too good of a liar."

THOMAS. Thomas, an African American sixteen-year-old, came to the facility following adjudication for weapons possession, the most recent in a series of charges including multiple probation and curfew violations, truancy, and contempt of court. Wildwood House was his third sequential correctional placement, one of which abruptly terminated because Thomas assaulted a staff member there. Athletically talented and strong, Thomas used his stature and physicality to earn respect from his peers and staff, particularly on the basketball court.

In the routine life of the dorm, Thomas spoke little, although when he did speak it was almost unfailingly polite (he articulated "yes" rather than "yeah," or "mm-hmm" when asked questions). Progress notes from the staff contradicted Thomas's initial assessments; at intake, he was identified as antisocial and seeing the world in terms of power and control, while later case notes cast him as "a nice young man to be around" and a "real nice kid." Like many of his peers, Thomas's academic assessments revealed him to be significantly below grade level in most subjects and noted the likelihood of a learning disability. Still, Thomas performed well in terms of the program's written treatment requirements and left the facility with a different sense of self than when he entered. He said, just before leaving the program, "I'm a person who did something wrong, but will make the right choices now. Before? I was bad, violent, a menace. Now? I'm a socialized person."

TREVOR. At one month shy of fifteen, Trevor was the youngest resident in the dorm. One of the only white residents to earn his peers' respect through his athletic ability and street sense, he was tall and slim with a wiry build and tattoos along his arms and back. He was clever and witty, with a quick smile and easy-going disposition. Trevor came from a family with significant trauma and conflict, particularly due to his mother's mental illness and his father's substance abuse and history of criminal involvement. His own criminal trajectory included significant gang involvement, theft, terroristic threats, and the burglary charge that resulted in his placement at Wildwood House. Trevor also faced academic challenges, scoring at fourth or fifth grade level in most subjects in spite of the IEP in place to support him.

During his intake, Trevor was labeled an "immature conformist" and manipulator who engaged in criminal activities without a guilty conscience and saw the world only in terms of power and control. Reports from staff throughout his time in the facility contradicted this initial assessment, uniformly praising Trevor as a model resident and celebrated his thoughtful and deliberate engagement with the program and his own desire to change: "The usual—helpful, pleasant, and compliant" and "pleasure to have him around." For his own part, Trevor felt that the facility and its staff had been instrumental in helping him think differently about himself, his relationship to adults he learned he could trust, and his criminal history. Motivated largely by a desire to be a good father to his own young son and a role model to others, Trevor said just before leaving the facility, "I feel good about myself; I want to teach my friends what I've learned here."

Conclusion

From the first time we entered Wildwood House through our last observations and interviews, the voices and experiences of the staff and youth who lived and worked in the facility provided the lens through which we came to understand not only the program, but the explicit and implicit culture of juvenile corrections within it. The following chapters present different features of that culture. Stories and excerpts from conversations with residents and staff bring to life the conflicts and tensions between treatment and punishment, the ways in which Wildwood House shaped residents' narratives of masculinity and power, how residents themselves responded to the involuntary treatment that often challenged their self-perceptions and identities, and how they integrated these lessons and experiences when they returned to their home communities.

CHAPTER 3

Mixed Messages

"THERAPY SPEAK" IN A CORRECTIONAL MILIEU

Twenty boys milled about the common room of Unit C, the commotion of their interactions filling the room with active and comfortable background noise. A group of Hmong youth sat together at one table, engaged in a competitive card game of Spades, while some of their peers—predominantly white youth—took pity on a visitor to the dorm in a game of foosball. Another pair of youth sat together at a folding table, supporting one another in writing their treatment contracts, brainstorming word choice and selection of examples to illustrate their personal growth. One youth stood by the second-story window, looking out at a parking lot, large grassy field, and the woods beyond. Dorm staff lingered on the periphery of the room, loosely monitoring the boys' activity. In all, the environment, though clearly institutional and somewhat stark, was comfortable.

Suddenly, one of the staff called to another and pointed to the door leading from the dorm to the hallway, and from there outside. The door was standing open—a clear security hazard. Immediately, the mood in the common room shifted. Mr. Robbins, one of the regular dorm staff stood and called out over the noise and commotion to the boys, "Gentlemen, take a seat!" In an instant, chatter and conversation came to a halt. All the youth rushed to the couches and sat, their foosball match ended and the game of Spades interrupted without comment. The staff conducted a head count, revealing three missing youth. Residents chimed in, calling out the names of their absent peers in support of the staff, even at the risk of ratting out their dorm-mates. Within minutes, the missing youth were accounted for (in meetings or taking a sick day), the crisis passed, and the boys were released back to their previous activities.

This scene belies Unit C's central tension, a tension reflected throughout juvenile correctional institutions across the country. On one hand, Wildwood House serves as a site to facilitate rehabilitation; it must offer the youth in its care opportunities for reflection, for the development of new insights into

49

their behaviors and thinking, and for the cultivation of pro-social interaction skills. On the other hand, these institutions must also fulfill an accountability and correctional role, providing consequences for criminal attitudes and behaviors and offering structure for offenders and eventually, protection for communities. Mr. McClatchy, a seven-year employee of Unit C, summarized this central tension well: "I see my job as mostly treatment, but I know that I have to enforce the rules as well." How does the correctional staff manage these competing responsibilities? How do the youth who are placed in these facilities experience and navigate this hybrid system, bouncing between playing cards with their friends in one moment and possibly selling out other peers in a military-style roll call the next?

Like Wildwood House, many residential programs in the US housing court-mandated youth incorporate a blend of treatment and correctional mechanisms to support the overall goals of attitude and behavior change. Treatment approaches with this population are varied, yet share a common mission of addressing some of the empirically linked underlying causes of delinquency, such as mental health issues, psychological traumas, child abuse and neglect, and substance abuse (Thornberry, Huzinga, and Loeber 1995). Treatment modalities used to address these root causes include psychological counseling (group or one-on-one psychotherapy), CBT (short-term focused therapy designed to teach thought control), and specialized therapies, such as for substance abuse or sex offending (Ruddell and Thomas 2009). As described in chapter 2, many of these treatment modalities were a mandatory part of a resident's individualized plan for progress and release, and they required not only individual therapeutic work but also active engagement in what the facility dubbed "positive peer culture." Central to the program's therapeutic efforts was the recognition that shifts in individual conduct and cognition are made possible only within contexts that support these changes. The institution as a whole therefore made a concerted effort to facilitate a culture in each dorm in which residents worked on their own individual treatment and behavioral goals within the larger setting of a therapeutic community involving peer support and accountability.

In support of the more punitive side of the correctional mission, juvenile facilities often use a quasi-military model of discipline, drill, and ceremony in the day-to-day operations of the institution (MacKenzie 1997). Mirroring the adult penal system, programs like Wildwood House enforce systems of penalties, including solitary confinement, to correct offenders' antisocial behaviors and criminal thinking patterns. Moreover, rituals such as lining up, wearing similar uniforms, and adhering to rigid schedule are all part of the standard correctional mode of practice. Although there is scant evidence supporting the effectiveness of a purely correctional approach (Greenwood 2005), it is still used quite widely in detention centers, boot camps, and other public correctional programs for youth offenders, and the structure of Wildwood House also contained elements of this model.

The treatment and punitive goals of juvenile corrections are often fused together in an institution's behavioral management system. The most common behavioral management program for youth residential care in the United States is the points and levels system. Emerging from mental health institutions, point and level systems are presumed to help youth experience the positive benefits of positive or pro-social behaviors and, on the flip side, to recognize the immediate consequences of misbehaviors (VanderVen 1995). More concretely, in correctional institutions, these systems are intended to teach youth how to identify problematic or antisocial thought patterns, develop insight into the origins of these thoughts, and then seek to replace them with pro-social alternatives. At Wildwood House, the points and levels system took the form of a token economy, wherein youth could purchase their next program level through an accumulation of daily points earned through pro-social behavior and rule compliance. Although quite popular in the United States, there is scant empirical evidence to conclude points and levels systems are successful, and they are not widely used in the other countries. Karen VanderVen has articulated various reasons for why these systems may even be harmful to youths' treatment goals, including criticisms that they encourage unhealthy competition among peers, engender a counter therapeutic relationship between youth and staff, and promote inauthentic engagement in treatment programs (VanderVen 1995; VanderVen 2000).

Like Wildwood House, most contemporary juvenile correctional programs operate under a blended paradigm that includes both therapeutic and correctional aspects of care, often fused by an overarching behavioral management system. Scholars have described this dual charge as frustrating for correctional workers as they attempt to form therapeutic relationships with the youth they also have to frequently punish or isolate (Inderbitzin 2009), and also as confusing for the residents themselves (Abrams, Kim, and Anderson-Nathe 2005). And while the failures of this monumental balancing act are well documented and tensely debated, the inner workings of this blended system of care are not. This chapter takes a closer look at the everyday dynamics of this system of compassionate confinement, presenting the main tensions and inconsistencies that permeated the everyday world of the institution. Specifically, we explore three central conflicts between treatment and correctional frames that played themselves out among the staff and residents of Unit C: family history as the source of criminal behavior, individual thinking errors and personal responsibility, and the limits of self expression in a correctional milieu.

IT'S ALL IN THE FAMILY

When I was growing up I lived a vary tuff life. I didn't grow up like eny normal 14 year old did. I had to do everything on my own without eny support
from my parents. I was alway's left alone by everybody it was as if they didn't
care of love me. My parents wood drink, and leve me alone with no supervision. They wood hit me and tretin me with hurtful words. To avoid my pain
I wood do drugs and hurt other people by doing them I would run away so
my parents could not find me. And I wood also have contact with girls I did
not no to make my self fell good. I felt like I had to make my bets friend
happy so I stoled cars and other thing. I also felt I had to get my parints back
for all the hurtful thing's they have done to me so I stoled more and got into
trouble so I could get the attition. I so badly wanted respet and love from my
parents and friends. I awnted evey body to stop using me and like me for
who I was and not what I could do. (Trevor, Family Problems treatment
contract)

Trevor's self-reflection reflects one of the most persistent tensions around
"treatment speak" that residents experienced in Unit C: how to manage an
institutional narrative that identified boys' families of origin as the source of
their criminal behavior, in spite of whether or not this explanation resonated
with the boys' own recollections or impressions of their families. During
treatment groups and activities, program staff consistently imparted the message to the residents that their unresolved anger at their parents, and particularly their absent fathers, formed the underlying foundations for their own
involvement in crime. When we asked staff what they considered to be the
root causes of the residents' problems, they nearly unanimously identified the
family as the primary problem. As one of the unit's most compassionate and
articulate staff members, Ms. Mason, explained, the main the reason these
boys get into trouble "has to do with their environment and how they were
raised. A number of things, parents using chemicals, neglect, any number of
reasons that kids didn't get their needs met when they were little and therefore created a bunch of other problems that as they grew up."

The lens of family dysfunction was unilaterally applied to all the cases in
the dorm, regardless of the residents' individual circumstances or family histories. Indeed, it was an association so taken for granted that exploration of
family pathology and its impacts on the residents' criminal behavior was a
central feature of the treatment program. For example, as part of the series of
treatment hurdles, each resident was required to complete a written contract
titled "Family Problems" and present it to his peers and staff during group
therapy. If a resident failed to identify pathology within his family of origin
and then link that pathology to his criminal behavior, his progress in the facility was greatly hindered. Consequently, the boys' family problems contracts

nearly unilaterally expressed anger at their parents for some combination of reasons, mostly including substance abuse, divorce, violence, or more generally for their neglectful or absent parenting.

The notion that children who are neglected or whose needs aren't met due to substance abuse or parental absence are more likely to engage in delinquent behavior is certainly substantiated in the research literature and theory on the etiology of juvenile offending (Loeber and Stouthamer-Loeber 1986; Loeber 1990). In Trevor's case, this association clearly resonated with his experience. In fact, he considered his Family Problems contract to be among the most meaningful of his treatment experiences. As evidenced in his written work, Trevor willingly identified and articulated associations between his parents' absence, violence, and substance abuse on the development of his criminal thinking and behavior. For him, the link between family of origin and criminality was entirely clear. However, this was not the case for all residents, and consequently we were initially surprised at the extent to which the facility relied on family problems as a blanket explanation for residents' criminal trajectories. In fact, this frame was so pervasive that after having been in the facility for an extended period of time, even the youth themselves pushed each other to own up to family issues that may or may not have been principally involved in an individual youth's criminal trajectory. Caleb's story presents one such example.

During a routine afternoon weekday peer group, the residents' attention focused on the treatment contract of one of their newer peers, Caleb. An awkward white youth with straight, messy brown hair and a sparse moustache, Caleb presented his first major treatment contract to a group of about fourteen peers who had earned higher levels and two dorm staff, including Mr. McClatchy, who ran most of the afterschool peer groups. The first contract in the series, "Details of My Offense," required residents to examine their motivations for the crime or crimes that resulted in their incarceration. In Caleb's case, this crime involved stealing a car, which he attributed simply to boredom. When prompted to explore the thinking that preceded his crime, he had noted in his contract that he was "just bored" and "didn't feel anything other than that." When he got bored, he said, he liked to "destroy stuff" and "raise trouble." His only real regret was that he "got caught"; for Caleb, his arrest is what made the event a significant issue at all.

As he presented this contract to the group, his peers began calling him out on what they saw to be an incomplete examination of his motivation. Although he had made no mention of his family, of tense relationships between him and his parents, or any motivation other than boredom, Caleb's peers began suggesting that he should revise the contract to include feelings of anger toward his father. They even asked, "Why didn't you write about the fact that you were angry with your dad?" in spite of this "fact" never having been mentioned by Caleb himself. Mr. McClatchy reinforced the residents' reframing of Caleb's behavior, motivation, and family relationships, telling Caleb that his "real problem . . . is that you were so mad at your dad neglecting you that you go and destroy things" and insisting that he hadn't even begun to scratch the surface of his criminal behavior. Mr. McClatchy's interpretation is striking, primarily since Caleb had never mentioned anything in this contract about his father, let alone that his father had neglected him. It appeared that Mr. McClatchy and the larger group accepted as a given that Caleb's relationship with his father must have contributed to his tendency to destroy things, rather than boredom, as he described.

This group experience not only reflects how the peer group itself internalized a narrative of criminality caused by strained family relationships, but also illustrates one pathway through which newer residents became socialized into adopting these narratives for themselves. Although the peer group, with Mr. McClatchy's begrudging approval, ultimately supported Caleb's treatment contract enough to advance him to the next level of privilege in the facility, his promotion was accompanied by a clear message that successful engagement with treatment would require disclosures of strained or pathological family relationships at its core. Staff clearly took great liberty in enforcing their frame of reference around family dysfunction, and like Caleb, residents for the most part learned to buy into the philosophy to move up on their program levels toward their release.

It Works for Some

Despite a treatment philosophy that some residents found confusing and alienating, others clearly felt that they reaped great benefits from engaging in a new look at their own family systems. Trevor, whose quoted treatment contract opened this section, greatly appreciated this focus. Having been abandoned by his mother due to substance abuse and mental illness, he had been primarily raised by his father, himself a heavy drinker with a violent temper and not a great deal of time or energy to devote to parenting. In exploring the connections between his family system and lengthy record of arrests and incarceration, he not only expressed that he had gained a better understanding of the relationship between his "messed-up family" and his criminal trajectory, but also felt that his relationship with his primary counselor helped to re-parent him in many ways. He explained: "Mr. McClatchy, he can relate to the stuff that's happened. Because, I don't think it's happened to him, but I don't know. He knows what I need. He knows the kind of stuff that my dad didn't give to me, so he tries to do his best, y'know, as primary, and somewhat of a father figure." Clearly Trevor felt that he benefitted not only from the understanding that his conflicted family relationships had contributed to his criminal behavior, but also from seeing the possibility of a different kind of parental relationship as modeled in his close relationship with Mr. McClatchy.

Jason also felt that he had benefited from the family focus he internalized during his time in Unit C. A small and witty seventeen-year-old from a traditional Hmong refugee family, Jason had an extensive criminal record. His first major conviction was for arson, when he set fire to a neighbor's garage, and after a series of interventions and probation violations he was ultimately placed in Unit C for assaulting a staff person and stealing a car to run away from his previous placement. Although we found him to be a charming and friendly young man, Unit C was Jason's last chance before a harsher sentence in a more secure state juvenile jail or an adult penal facility.

Jason had struggled for many years with his role in his family, seeing himself as the "bad son." His many siblings were all high achievers in school, except, as he sadly noted, for himself. In the course of his treatment work in Unit C, Jason began to more critically examine his relationship with his parents, and most specifically with his father. Supported in many ways by the facility's focus on family relationships as a key influence in the development of criminal behavior, Jason began to explore different possibilities for his relationships with his parents. In other words, he began to see through his individual treatment and family group sessions that he didn't have to see himself in the way he historically had, as "the worstest son."

In our first interview, Jason shared several stories highlighting the many ways he viewed himself as having failed to live up to his parents' expectations. When prompted to share a memory of when he had felt good about himself or something he had done, Jason brightened and told a surprisingly tender story of giving a present to his father, with whom he had a conflictual relationship due to what he described as a history of corporal punishment and feelings of rejection. He said:

> I bought my dad a birthday gift. He always wanted a weed whacker. So I bought him the most expensive weed whacker they had. And I don't know, I never seen a smile in my dad's face before, and then, after I bought him that, he smiled. I was just like, "dang!" Changed somebody's life, too. I made a smile in my dad's life once. Feels good, 'cuz I'm like the worstest son in his family. And every time he talks to me, he would never smile. I never see him smile. And then first time I made him smile is on his birthday. It feels good when you think back on that. Being the worst son is pretty hard. But you just gotta hang through it. Y'know, change myself and show my dad that I've changed.

Through the course of treatment, Jason gradually expressed feeling better about himself and more prepared to repair his relationship with his dad.

The treatment model's emphasis on naming the pathology within and then reconstructing family relationships had resonated with Jason. He explained that he planned to have a better way of communicating with his father: "I'm gonna talk to him more. Like, about my future, like a dad and son talk."

One Size Does Not Fit All

Unlike Trevor and Jason, however, many of the youth in Unit C struggled to accept the family dysfunction paradigm. Some even found it bordering on the ridiculous. Nevertheless, because of the program structure and rules, they lacked the agency or option of rejecting it outright; even newer residents (as Caleb's story illustrates) quickly learned the importance of developing a strategy to work within the assumptions of family pathology. To do otherwise hampered residents' ability to advance through the program and earn their release.

Josh was one such youth. At sixteen, he entered Wildwood House with a longer rap sheet than many of his peers and he took significant pride in being "more criminal" and "harder" than the other boys in the facility. Josh came from an extended family with a longstanding history in the juvenile and adult correctional system, and although he identified himself as a criminal thinker, he resisted all suggestions that his family had caused his own foray into crime. Consequently, he struggled with writing the treatment contracts that required him to associate his parents' negative influence with his own criminal conduct. He resisted these contracts because he found it "pathetic" that staff required him to blame his parents for his behavior. In one interview, he said, "They blame a lot of stuff on my parents. 'Your parents didn't teach you right.' That's a lie. The reason I was doing these things is not because of my parents. I wasn't abused when I was a child. I wasn't neglected when I was a child. So how has my parents had something to do with this? My parents have always cared for me, not neglected me . . . Taught me right, taught me wrong. So, they blame so much of this stuff on your parents. It's pathetic."

This is not to suggest that Josh saw nothing wrong with his behavior; he clearly understood that he had a criminal history, and that much of his previous behavior had been problematic, and even felt that he deserved to be at Wildwood House. He just resisted the facility's default interpretation of the cause for his behavior. For Josh, behavior came from desire and impulse, not parental pathology:

JOSH: Most of the kids that come through here do have family problems, but that's not really my issue. My issue is my . . . I can't really say what my issue is. It's just my way of thinking.

BEN: What's wrong with your way of thinking?

JOSH: When I see a nice car, I think about stealing it. When I see a nice bike, I think about stealing it. Criminal thinking . . . When they say that stuff it makes me so mad. When they try to blame this stuff on my parents, it just makes me . . . it makes me mad. I cannot stand them putting down my parents when it's not my parents' fault.

This reaction to the narrative of parental pathology put Josh in a difficult and untenable situation with regard to his successful completion of the treatment program. In order to advance at Wildwood House, he felt pushed to accept and reinforce representations of his parents that he fundamentally disbelieved. Worse, it felt to him like a betrayal of his parents.

As might be expected, Josh struggled to resolve this dilemma. Ultimately believing the family pathology narrative to be intractable with the staff, Josh decided that in order to move forward in the program, he had to find family pathology to share in his contracts. He said, "I went home and I told my mom this, and she was just like, 'You know what? Play their game. You know we didn't do that to you, so just play their game.'. . . I can lie and act just fine. This whole time with me [in treatment contracts] is just a bunch of lies and making up some tears and crying in front of everybody . . . And I'm just like, 'Man, give it up. Please.'"

Josh's reaction to the pervasive pressure of the family dysfunction paradigm illustrates a dynamic we consider more fully in chapter 5, in which many residents felt inclined to manipulate the system in order to convince staff that they had changed to in order to earn their release. It also highlights some of the potential dilemmas of using a point and level systems in this type of institution. By linking advantage or disadvantage to evidence of treatment progress, programs can indirectly encourage youth to create images of the self that are inauthentic or dishonest, directly contradicting the intentions of the therapeutic programming.

IT'S CRIMINAL THINKING, GENTLEMEN

Tensions were running high in the facility. Rumors had been circulated by some of the youth that Mr. Robbins, a staff member, had inappropriate sexual contact with the residents during one-on-one time. The unit head, Mr. Lund, was called in to address the issue. He stood at the top of the stairs outside Unit C's main door and watched as the youth came upstairs from the cafeteria in a somber, single-file line. As the residents disappeared, one by one, into the dorm's common room, Mr. Lund addressed the tension in the air: "You think it's bad now? I'm about to make it much worse."

Following the residents into the dorm, he strolled calmly but purposefully to the front of the common room, blocking the TV and looking directly at the assembled youth, who—in contrast to their typical posture and relaxed tone in the common room—were lined up, nearly at attention in rows on the couches. Mr. Lund interrupted the nervous silence in the room with a confrontation, stating that he knew about the "negative talking" among the residents and called the rumors damaging and hurtful. He added, "I do know some of you who've been spreading the rumors, and I know some of you who knew the rumors but hadn't spread them—but also didn't come to staff about them." Taking a deep breath and moving one step closer to the assembled boys, Mr. Lund said, calmly, "this is criminal thinking, gentlemen. The way you set each other up and let yourselves be set up, not to mention what you're doing to the staff, is pathetic and sad. You guys talk to each other worse than you talk to your dogs at home. It's time to get with it."

The boys looked shocked, clearly struck by the impact of Mr. Lund's words. He continued, calling boys by name who had been implicated in spreading the rumors and assigning them violations. He shared his intention to continue issuing violations—or even bigger consequences—as the staff continued digging through the rumor mill in Unit C. The meeting ended with Mr. Lund's reminder that "it's up to you to stop these behaviors. Those of you who didn't know anything about the rumors—and I don't think that's very many of you—are the only ones with no responsibility. If you had even just heard the rumors and allowed them to continue, that's criminal thinking. Criminal thinking will be consequenced!"

While the family dysfunction paradigm had a dominant presence in Unit C, it was awkwardly juxtaposed with a discourse reflecting correctional accountability. In this framework, residents were presumed to engage in criminal thinking patterns that formed a foundation for their delinquent attitudes and behaviors. Residents routinely received direct statements from staff that mirrored those that Mr. Lund spoke: that they had poor impulse control, a tendency to manipulate others, and destructive thought patterns. Underlying these statements is a cognitive-behavioral view that youth justify their criminal conduct by defaulting to thought patterns that make this type of behavior acceptable. These thinking patterns must be changed in order for behavioral shifts to take hold, and criminal thinking must be called out and recognized before it can be shifted. Sometimes direct and pointed to individual culprits, and sometimes directed toward the group as a whole, these messages pervaded the milieu—in the day-to-day interactions with the staff, during recreational activities, and even some part of their therapy and group work, but were strikingly seldom explained to residents. Instead, staff would simply name "criminal thinking" or "manipulation" and leave it to the youth themselves to infer what exactly was criminal in their thinking. In many instances, the boys were reminded as a group that their criminal thinking landed them in the correctional system in the first place, and that it would bring them right back to Wildwood House or a worse situation if their thinking was not property corrected. Mr. Connelly was one of the staff members who stood by this philosophy in his day-to-day interactions with residents, suggesting to us that, "anyone in this facility under eighteen is a criminal thinker; that's why they're here!"

The narrative of criminal thinking, with its emphasis on individual responsibility, stood in stark contrast to the family systems discourse that suggested the boys' behavior resulted from unhealthy familial relationships and overall neglect. We suggest that this observed conflict between paradigms is illustrative of the fundamental tension in juvenile corrections; in this case, the family pathology narrative reinforced the system's treatment and rehabilitation goals, while a discourse of criminal thinking and accountability reflected the more punitive side of the spectrum. Staff relied on these contradictory frameworks at different times to suit different needs, and residents were simply required to follow their lead and respond accordingly. This code switching—a concept we borrow from the field of linguistics, referring to the ability or necessity of bouncing back and forth between discourses or languages—required that the residents anticipate and differentiate when they would be expected to assume responsibility for their own actions, and when they would be expected to account for their behaviors based on their family problems.

Go It Alone or Are We In This Together?

Within the criminal thinking paradigm, tensions were also apparent, particularly in the domain of individual versus group accountability. That is to say, youth in Unit C often received messages that they would be best off concerning themselves only with their own behavior—a narrative common among many behavior modification programs, because the only behavior over which one has any real control is one's own. Many residents grasped this lesson fairly quickly, as they routinely received consequences for individual rule violations or misconduct in the facility, including getting overly involved in another resident's business. They were frequently reminded that they needed to "work their own program." However, residents were also regularly exposed to the facility's expectation—as demonstrated by staff interactions and interventions such as Mr. Lund's collective warning—that as a group, the boys were also accountable to one another and responsible for the safety of the facility as a whole. Standing in contrast to the narrative of individual responsibility and "minding your own business," the concept of group accountability is central to many residential treatment programs, including correctional ones. For over thirty years, programs have used group accountability to promote desired behaviors in residential settings, including peer support and accountability models like positive peer culture (Vorrath and

Brendtro 1976), through which groups of youth form norms that enforce adherence to desired behavior and gradually extinguish negative conduct. In these programs, individual conduct is influenced strongly by community norms. Nevertheless, residents were not often supported in reconciling the inconsistencies between individual and group accountability messages.

In one instance of conflict in the larger peer group, Mr. Lund facilitated a discussion with the residents about what he called the "getcha-gotchas," meaning circumstances when residents deliberately and covertly set one another up for violations from staff. In this intervention, Mr. Lund high-lighted the importance of personal responsibility and encouraged the youth to focus on their own treatment and let go of the need to be in their peers' business. He then went around the room, asking all the upper level residents to add their comments on the discussion. Those residents who had been in Unit C for the longest time and who occupied the highest levels of privilege talked about looking out for one another, being responsible for their own programs, and not getting caught up in other people's issues.

Of course, these goals appeared contradictory; it is difficult to look out for one's peers if one is also expected to stay out of issues or concerns that don't immediately concern one's own treatment. As one resident suggested, if one person got too involved in another person's business or failed to be accountable for his own behavior, he made it hard on the dorm, and the whole dorm suffered as a result. While the getcha-gotchas reflected individ-ual behavior, the entire dorm wound up suffering consequences in the form of reductions in privileges until these behaviors stopped. Accountability for criminal thinking errors was thus shuffled between personal responsibility and group process in a way that was neither clear nor consistent.

Ultimately, staff were responsible for deciding when the criminal think-ing discourse (as opposed to a more therapeutic tone) was invoked in Unit C; residents were simply expected to respond to whichever narrative dominated in a given context or situation. Thus, in the group confrontation described in the vignette that opened this section, criminal thinking was coupled with collective accountability. Mr. Lund's second intervention promoted personal responsibility as a pathway toward the collective good and a reduction in criminal thinking. What unites these illustrations of the framework of crimi-nal thinking is the need—as perceived by staff and in the moment—to favor a punitive orientation over a more therapeutic one.

Often, the staff's prompt demands for group or individual accountability occurred when residents' behavior had compromised the safety of the dorm and staff needed to reassert control, as in the case of the residents' rumors of sexual misconduct by Mr. Robbins. During treatment groups and activi-ties, the staff would nearly always invoke the family pathology lens. But the day-to-day operations of the dorm mostly concerned the rank and file safety issues well-served by a correctional paradigm that held the boys individually and collectively responsible for their thoughts and actions. This clash of philosophies was not only confusing; it also influenced the way that treatment was delivered and experienced. Residents were held responsible for anticipating and responding to the code-switching on the part of staff, and consequently had to intuit what type of response was required of them in a given situation. One of the more confusing instances of this need to adapt to conflicting staff expectations concerned residents' emotional and self-reflective expressions.

EXPRESS YOURSELF (BUT DO IT ON OUR TERMS)

On a crisp autumn day in September, Eric was called in to meet with one of Unit C's classroom teachers to resolve a conflict that threatened his ability to advance to the next level in the facility. Eric was placed at the facility on account of a property crime involving computer misconduct, and as a result, his behavior plan clearly stated that he could not use any computers in the facility. Even so, when a classroom teacher asked him to use a computer to complete an assignment for her class, Eric complied. He was given a rule violation for breaking the condition of his behavior plan, and he seemed genuinely confused about what he should have done.

Sitting with the classroom teacher, Ms. Frucht, Eric explained that he didn't understand his particular rules concerning the use of computers; he was not allowed to use them, but his teacher asked him to. Didn't that mean he had been granted temporary permission? Clearly straining to contain his anger and frustration at this contradictory message, Eric started to lose his control when Ms. Frucht turned the conversation toward Eric being dishonest, emotionally "closed off," and therefore hard to read. She demanded clarifying information from him about the event, why he hadn't reminded his teacher about the computer ban, and what prevented him from simply admitting his culpability and apologizing. Leaning across the desk to him, she said, "Eric, you're just so closed off. You can't express yourself from the heart—what are you afraid of by being honest?" Rhetorical or not, the question signaled the end of that conversation.

Later Eric met with another teacher, Ms. Kohl, to discuss the same issue. Sitting across from her in the facility's small classroom, Ms. Kohl reiterated Ms. Frucht's impressions: "You just tell partial truths; you're not honest. You haven't learned anything here, and unless you open up, you won't be able to clear your violation, which means you'll be here longer."

Leaving the school wing to walk back to Unit C, Eric shared his genuine confusion with us; from his perspective, he had been honest. He knew about the rule restricting his computer use, but he also knew better than to question the teachers' authority in the classroom. Therefore, when he was given permission to use the computer for an assignment, he saw no need to remind his teachers of his restricted access. He "came clean" when confronted with the violation, and could therefore find nothing wrong with his conduct. He did not understand how *not* telling the teacher something he believed she should have known constituted dishonesty or manipulation on his part. In his view, all of his comments to the teachers had been factually correct; he had not lied, and if the staff had allowed him to get away with his actions, that reflects a failing on their part, not his.

Stepping momentarily out of his role as researcher, Ben attempted to help Eric interpret the interactions with his teachers. Using the metaphor of a connect-the-dots picture, in which a person can either see a collection of unrelated dots or draw a line between them to reveal a complete picture, Ben reframed the conflict. Eric had been accurately describing dots on the page, but his teachers wanted him to draw the line between them and describe the entire picture. What he saw as honest expression (laying out the collection of dots), the staff understood as manipulative and dishonest on account of his failure to connect those dots in a comprehensive whole. Eric was being required to express himself consistently with the facility's expectation of honesty and communication (and accused of manipulation and emotional distance when he failed to do so), without a clear sense of what that requirement entailed.

The teaching of appropriate ways for the residents to express their emotions was a pivotal part of the treatment philosophy and it was explicitly woven into the everyday practices of the institution. Many of the staff regarded this opening up process as a hallmark of their work, and they put a lot of effort into facilitating this goal. Ms. Mason, for example, said that the most rewarding part of her job was "when you have one-to-one time with the kids and you can help them think of new ways to look at their issues. And the look on their face when you see that they get something you have talked about and you have connected." Consequently, emotional expression, honesty, and an emphasis on healthy relationships were highly valued in all of the treatment groups, contracts, and the milieu of Unit C.

The flip side of teaching new modes of emotional expression in a correctional facility is that in this type of setting, youth are not fully entitled to display their feelings in an open way for several reasons. To begin, the staff at Wildwood House possessed the ultimate authority to decide whether youth were effectively "buying into" their treatment goals and plans, awkwardly joining treatment progress to the points and levels system in ways that seemed to directly counter treatment goals. As we saw in the example of Caleb's family group contract, and again with Eric and his teachers, threats of punitive action were used to pressure residents to own up to their feelings in a way that was consistent with the staffs' impressions of what form that emotional honesty should take. This forces some level of inauthentic engagement on the part of the youth, and also leaves open much room for manipulation or words and ideas for program gain. Additionally, as the next section will illustrate, residents' displays of emotions were subject to a high degree of monitoring, in the sense that staff were not permitted not tolerate anger or other emotions that might threaten dorm overall safety or sense of staff control. For both reasons, activities that may be considered therapeutic in a voluntary setting were potentially undermined by the interconnectedness of apparent treatment progress with a gradated system of punishments and rewards.

Sincerity is in the Eye of the Beholder

It is not surprising that a treatment program would maintain a significant investment in supporting and evaluating the degree to which its participants take treatment messages to heart. In the context of an institution such as Wildwood House that emphasized accountability to the community, staff evaluations of residents' progress were necessary. Nevertheless, how staff evaluated the residents' shifts in emotional expression and treatment engagement remained problematic. In Unit C, youth quickly learned that they needed to display some shift in emotional expression consistent with staff's expectations. However, in spite of knowing that these expectations existed, some youth were simply ill equipped to perform the desired emotional expression. In some cases, this reflected the reality that a resident had actually not changed his self-perception during his time at the facility or was resistant to such treatment. In others, however, residents simply lacked the skills to demonstrate their changes in the language that staff hoped and expected to see.

Eric was one such resident, fifteen years old and from a white and working-class suburb and a two parent home. His self-described Goth mentality, suburban roots, and noncriminal background made him stick out like a sore thumb in relation to the more street-wise urban residents. His educational scores revealed an intellect far above his age and grade, scoring extremely highly on all academic tests and at the twelfth grade level or beyond in most subject areas. Eric had no rap sheet or criminal history, yet his felony-level offense earned him a four to six month stay in Unit C. His second week there, staff noted: "He's going to struggle: He hasn't been around these types of kids, *ever*."

While Eric acknowledged to us and to the staff that he deserved some type of punishment for his crime, his posture at the facility was very shut down. He typically kept to himself, did the minimum of what was expected of him, and stuck by his stance that he didn't need to be "therapized," as he was not like the other, "really messed-up guys" here. This seemingly superior attitude consistently frustrated the staff and his teachers. In his records, staff routinely referred to him with phrases such as "antisocial behavior" and a "history of being manipulative." Verbally, staff described Eric as a "mastermind criminal" whose code they had yet to crack. This image of Eric persisted, as throughout his records staff expressed concern about his propensity for manipulation and lack of responsiveness to the treatment program. Staff wrote that "Eric needs to take ownership for what he's done and admit to himself and his parents that this crime is no fluke and look within himself to better understand that history may repeat itself if he feels no remorse for what he's done." Other records reveal in concrete terms how Eric's progress in the facility was hindered by "lack of sincerity and emotional openness." His interim evaluation, for instance, noted:

> Request for level advancement was denied due to lack of sincerity. Staff noted that he only talked to a few residents and rarely talked to staff. The team requested he come back on in a couple of weeks with a more sincere request and better staff reports and his openness to all residents and staff. He has presented contracts to peer group and they were accepted. The contracts were very well written but they lacked any emotion. He is very intelligent individual and he is bright enough to jump through hoops in the program. This fact causes many staff to question his sincerity and willingness to change and be introspective.

In spite of a nearly perfect behavioral record at the facility (with the exception of the computer incident at school), Eric consistently encountered criticism and redirection from staff who characterized him as too emotionally shut down to be sincere. In Eric's case and others, a resident's failure to demonstrate to staff that he was doing the emotional work often translated into punishment through violations, fines, level drops, and extended stays at the facility. Central to this observation is that whether a resident actually did the emotional work became secondary to his ability to demonstrate his effort to the staff. Because of this entangled relationship between emotional expression (therapeutic progress) and punitive action (correctional management), residents were often forced to display sometimes even inauthentic emotions simply in order to avoid consequences. In interviews and during observations, Eric routinely shared with us the work he was doing and some of the (admittedly minor) shifts in self-perception he had experienced at the facility. Due to his inability or reluctance to display these changes to the staff, his progress in Unit C was consistently hampered and subject to skepticism.

If You Aren't Angry, You're Not Doing Your Work

Nino's case provides another telling example of how blending treatment expectations into the rules of a correctional milieu can potentially undermine the goals of the treatment itself. Nino was a tall and cheerful African American young man from the inner city. At sixteen, he was already a father of one-year-old twin boys who were in the care of their mother's family. He had a history of criminal offenses ranging from minor (leaving the scene of an accident) to more major (the possession of a weapon). He was admitted to Unit C after a series of probation violations. Nino always presented himself to us in an upbeat manner and was very open during his interviews. Staff, however, were consistently suspicious of him, describing Nino as a kid who seemed innocent but was actually a mastermind manipulator. In fact, his primary counselor, Ms. Breuer, noted in the case records that he was a "passive aggressive manipulation master" and another staff member, Ms. Mason, wrote in a case note, "I also think he is faking it, *he's way too happy!*" The behaviors most consistently cited by staff as evidence of manipulation were Nino's cheerfulness, politeness, big smile, and acceptance of consequences without emotional outbursts, anger, or defensiveness.

On one gloomy winter day, we observed a series of level review meetings between the staff and individual residents. Nino's violation was the last to be heard; he had failed to call in on time or attend an Alcoholic Anonymous (AA) meeting during his weekend at home. When Mr. McClatchy and Mr. Lund pushed him to explain why he didn't make his AA meeting, Nino claimed that he intended to go but just didn't make it. Staff interpreted his explanation as resistance to treatment, and Mr. McClatchy pushed the issue further, asking whether Nino agreed with the findings of his substance abuse assessment. Although he was asked to give his honest opinion, when Nino disclosed that he actually disagreed with the assessment, he was challenged to explain his reasoning: "What makes you think that? Why do you think that the whole team can be wrong, when you're right? You think these people [the Chemical Dependency counselors] don't know what they're talking about?" Nino remained calm, but did not appear to know how to answer these questions.

Finally, as result of his rule infractions, he was consequenced with the loss of a weekend home visit and a failed home visit, thus pushing back the time that he could request his next level upgrade. He didn't appear shaken by the outcome of the meeting and even told the staff that he understood what they were doing and why. Nevertheless, Mr. McClatchy pushed him to show his anger, assuming that Nino must certainly have been angry at the staff for imposing this set of consequences. As Nino continued to deny that he felt angry about consequences he felt to be fair, staff's frustration with him increased.

It is precisely this type of contradiction that residents in Unit C were expected to navigate and reconcile. On one hand, Nino was assuming personal responsibility for his actions, which in other circumstances might be applauded as a demonstration of interrupted criminal thinking. At the same time, however, he failed to do so with the expected emotional discharge, which called his assumption of responsibility into question. Nino was caught in a dilemma where meeting one treatment expectation necessitated failure at another.

We recorded a similar experience with Nino nearly fourth months later as he was preparing for discharge. The staff had recently dropped Nino down to the lowest level, meaning that he would be discharged from the program unsuccessfully, "without having done much work on himself or his family issues," according to his official progress report. The level drop was a consequence for throwing socks in the sleeping room, and staff attributed his sock throwing behavior to "really being mad about other things." Staff shared their perception with us that Nino had been too emotionally closed during his entire time in Unit C, maintaining a façade that everything was okay, as a smokescreen and defense against honest emotional expression. The notion that Nino might actually not have felt this range of emotions was simply not open for consideration.

Nino did finally leave the program, shortly after a team meeting during which staff believed he finally showed some honest emotion. Mr. Lund reported that during the meeting, staff had finally "broken him down" to the point where Nino had cried; the staff viewed his tears as a sign of emotional honesty. It is ironic that this demonstration was received by the staff as emotionally honest, while his previous statements of appreciation for Unit C providing him the opportunity to reflect on his past behaviors and make different decisions in the future were seen as fundamentally suspect because they lacked outward emotional impact.

Sometimes, It's Better to Keep Your Mouth Shut

Residents' feelings were also subject to correctional control in other ways. In some instances, staff tended to discount or silence residents' emotional expressions when they appeared to threaten or challenge the rules. In these instances, the residents were rendered silent and the message was clear: It is better to keep your feelings to yourself. Of course, this message stands in stark contrast to the competing expectation, as experienced by Eric and Nino, to express everything—including anger at staff—for fear of being labeled closed off. For Josh, honest expression became taboo in his relationship with staff, simply because his reactions and emotional displays often contradicted staff's expectations.

Josh, who as we described earlier fully rejected the family facility's pathology model, seemed to genuinely struggle to understand the rules and structure of the dorm. He was open about his confusion, often seeking explanations for the rules or clarification on conflicting messages from the staff. During one conversation with Mr. Lund, he explained that he thought he was doing okay in Unit C, in spite of his recent rule violations, and he tried to offer some explanations for some of his poor conduct. Mr. Lund interrupted Josh's disclosure, telling him to stop explaining himself: "You need to learn how to listen. Just listen to what people have to say, don't explain. When people get hung up on explaining themselves, they stop listening." When Josh attempted to clarify his intention, that his interest was explanation and not excuse, Mr. Lund told him to "just stop talking and listen."

Perhaps as a result of these mixed messages around the use of emotional expression, some of the residents felt closed and shut down with staff, expressing the sentiment that it is better to "keep their mouths shut" than to practice the expressive tools they were learning in their therapies. Jason, for example, said to us: "Staff don't care about our feelings, so I just don't show it anymore." Other residents agreed with this sentiment, suggesting: "You just deal with it if you get upset. You're not allowed to yell at staff or do anything like that. You just keep it inside." Another resident reported that "if you disagree with staff or express your opinion to them, they're just going to punish you. So you can't act out if something's not fair. You just have to take it. You can't grieve it; you can't say that's not fair. If they give me a fine, I'm just like, 'Okay.' I won't try to fight back at all. 'Cause I notice, the other kids, they'll fight back, they'll get sent to time out." Clearly the youth perceived some risk of punitive action in expressing their feelings, particularly if they involved feelings about the rules or the staff.

In this blended system of care, the staff clearly attempted to teach residents new skills regarding emotions and openness that could potentially be useful in a therapeutic sense. Yet due to the correctional context of the facility, staff exerted a great deal of control over residents' emotional expressions. Even when residents received permission—explicitly or indirectly—from staff to express their emotions in appropriate ways, such as crying or other displays of grief, sadness, or fear, these displays had to conform to conditions that staff deemed acceptable. For instance, feeling sad one day about family and personal matters, one resident went into the bathroom without permission so that he could cry in private. The staff gave him a warning for violating the rules about bathroom use, and encouraged him express his emotions in what they deemed a "healthy way," by crying and allowing himself to experience that sadness without transforming it into more destructive demonstrations of anger. Even so, the alternative that they offered was to cry alone in the locked isolation room where residents were taken in response to aggressive, unsafe, or otherwise inappropriate conduct warranting punishment. The implicit message was clear: Expression is okay, but only when private and contained, and even then may be subject to the stigma associated with other displays deemed inappropriate (and therefore suitable for the solitary time-out room).

Thus in many ways, staff discouraged residents' expressions of emotions when those emotions contradicted staff expectations of how youth "should" feel, or appeared to pose threats to dorm safety. Juxtaposed with a treatment philosophy that taught the residents to dig deeper into their personal feelings and to openly express them to adults as a pathway toward healing their criminal thinking and behavior, these other responses created a tangle of confusing messages around when, where, and how young people should utilize the expressive tools that their various therapies required of them.

Conclusion

Wildwood House relied on two dominant and conflicting discourses: the family pathology treatment ideology as contrasted with the criminal thinking mentality. These paradigms operated both simultaneously and separately, and were enacted by staff as the minute-by-minute needs of the milieu required of them. Even within the criminal thinking paradigm, attribution of responsibility shifted between individual and group accountability in a way that was neither consistent nor clear. As a result of these competing and sometimes mutually undermining philosophies, youth were taught tools for emotional expression that some felt to be forced upon them by the rules, or in the case of some other residents, felt authentic and meaningful. We also observed that the linking of treatment and emotional expression to a predetermined set of privileges and consequences through the facility's points and level system contributed to many of the same problematic experiences that VanderVen (1995; 2000) identified; in particular, the tendency toward manipulation (one major exemplar, according to staff of criminal thinking), lack of authenticity in treatment engagement, and confusing relationships with the dorm staff. Thus the crux of this clash in these coexisting paradigms was not that treatment program resonated for some and not others, but rather that youth often failed to meet program expectations due to staff's assessment of their authenticity or appropriateness of their emotional work.

CHAPTER 4

"Take It Like a Man"

MASCULINITIES, TREATMENT, AND CRIME

We walked into Unit C during gym time, finding the boys engaged in a heated debate about a volleyball game. One of the boys complained, "every time I miss a shot, they [the other team] say something, but when they miss, we just don't say nothing, like no big deal. They make a big deal when we don't get the ball." Mr. Connelly, one of the regular staff members on duty, assured the residents that it was "just a game, guys! Why would you make such a big deal over a volleyball game? Tomorrow, will you even remember who won the game? You're here to work on yourselves and get out of here, not to win games." When one of the accused culprits in the conflict tried to assert his side of the story, Mr. Connelly deliberately stopped him, saying: "Sampson, you'd argue about the color of the sky; why do you always have to say something?" He replied: "I'm gonna speak up . . . if I see something's not going right, I'm gonna SAY something." Mr. Connelly dismissed Sampson's position outright, telling him that his need to speak up is about "controlling the dorm," not about saying anything important. The conversation ended there.

Less than an hour after this exchange, the group returned to the dorm for free time. The residents began to engage in different games, and a few lined up to play ping-pong against a staff member. One after the other, residents faced off against Mr. McClatchy. During each game, he shouted out "Loser!" when they missed the ball, such as "5–1, Loser; Serve, Loser!" This tone continued as Mr. McClatchy summarily beat all the boys who challenged him.

This scenario contains numerous layers of complexity regarding institutional context and messages about power, the importance of winning and losing, and the value of competition. On the one hand, Mr. Connelly's attempt to diffuse the conflict on the volleyball court by telling the residents it was "just a game" provided the boys with a sense of assurance that they could play a game for fun, and did not need to chide or insult each other for missing the ball. In this sense, he sent a message that everyone could be equally respected during a team sport. In the next moment, Mr. Connelly's prompt dismissal of Sampson's side of the story directly conveyed that his individual point of view was neither important nor valued, thus contradicting the "equal playing field" ethos invoked in his initial comments. The tone of "it's just a game" was further undermined by Mr. McClatchy's ping-pong dynamics, relaying to the boys that competition was more important than having fun, and that victory should be sought at risk of being labeled "a loser."

This vignette speaks not only to competition, but also contributes to understandings of masculinity shaped in part by the value placed on victory and mastery over others. Deriving a sense of self worth through negative comparison characterizes many features of traditional or hegemonic masculine ideologies that are evident in many social institutions, including correctional facilities, and that often contradicted the treatment messages present in other aspects of Wildwood House's milieu. Conflicting discourses of manhood and masculinity add another layer of complexity to the facility's tangled web of messages concerning appropriate behavior and self-expression and comprise the primary focus of this chapter.

MASCULINITY, POWER, AND CRIME

In the past two decades, scholars have produced a robust body of literature on gender socialization, the development of gender identity in childhood and adolescence, and the intersections of multiple masculinities with additional axes of identity such as race, class, and sexuality (Connell 1987, 1995; Mac an Ghaill 1994; Messerschmidt 1993, 2000; Pascoe 2007; Thompson and Pleck 1995; West and Zimmerman 1987). This contextual understanding of masculinity implies that there is no universal, essential way of becoming or being a man. Rather, individuals adopt a range of gendered responses to their social environments, and in turn, the development of masculinity hinges upon the contexts of social institutions such as the state, schooling, the workplace, and the family (Connell 1987, 1995; Goodey 1997; Messerschmidt 1993). Carrie Paechter (2007) has suggested that these social institutions serve as "communities of gendered practice," in which individuals learn and perform expectations of conduct associated as masculine or feminine in a given context. Masculinity, like all gender, is therefore performed rather than ascribed. As such, its expressions can vary widely from setting to setting, but less so from individual to individual within a single setting. Scholars have investigated prisons as one such site of masculinity practice for adult men (Levant and Richmond 2007; O'Neil and Luján 2009), but only a few have examined masculinities as they are constructed in juvenile facilities (Abrams, Anderson-Nathe, and Aguilar 2008; Cesaroni and Alvi 2010; Reich 2010).

Although juvenile correctional facilities have not been widely theorized as a site of gender formation for young men, there is a strong theoretical relationship between masculine identity formation and criminality, particularly for young men who are marginalized by race and class (Cesaroni and Alvi 2010; Jewkes 2005). Part of learning masculinity in a given environment depends on role modeling. Paechter (2007) describes this as "apprenticeships in gender performance" in which younger members of a community of gendered practice learn the tropes of their (and others') genders by observing and modeling the performances of their elders. In this sense, the types of role modeling men have at their disposal plays a significant role in creating individual pathways toward their eventual expressions of masculinity (Majors and Billson 1992; Messerschmidt 2000; West and Zimmerman 1987). Following this idea, young men who have learned to aspire toward hegemonic or traditional masculine identities, such as those linked primarily to competition, power, and aggression, face barriers in developing gender identities that value cooperation, communication, or emotional expression (Chu, Porche, and Tolman 2005). On the contrary, their route to manhood is likely to include demonstrations of violence, competition, and power.

This is not to say that all hegemonic or traditional masculine performances are criminal and fundamentally in need of transformation or critique. Rather, the unmitigated acceptance of hegemonic masculine traits of competition, power, and violence as legitimate expressions of and means to secure masculine status are often implicated in the formation of criminal masculinities. Researchers have pointed to significant associations between conventional masculine ideologies and problem behaviors among young men, specifically citing school suspensions, arrests, and perpetration of coercive sex among the associated behaviors (Pleck, Sonenstein, and Ku 1993). Given this understanding of the correlation between some expressions of hegemonic masculinities and criminal conduct, scholars have suggested that the worst excesses of masculinity that contribute to criminality may result at least in part from the attempts of men from marginalized backgrounds to access social power and significance (Gibbs and Merighi, 1994). For example, one study of black masculinity found that African American young men learned to enact a "cool pose" as a means to negotiate intersections of race, gender, and power (Majors and Billson 1992). Although the racial marginalization these young men experienced had denied them many of the opportunities and resources needed to effectively fulfill masculine ideals of wealth and power, they nonetheless strived to embody these very traits in other ways. In this sense, men who face major structural barriers to attaining the social statuses associated with traditional manhood may overcompensate with demonstrations of masculinity, such as violence, that are often linked with criminality.

There are strong theoretical links between the social construction of masculinities and the development of criminal identities and behaviors in adolescence and young adulthood, particularly for marginalized young men. Even so, limited research has examined how facilities like Wildwood House, with an expressed commitment to supporting residents' identity change and reform, contend with questions and dynamics around gender among the young men they serve. As the previous chapter laid out an array of paradoxes associated with the delivery of treatment practices within an involuntary correctional system, this chapter similarly delves into the complications associated with masculine identity construction within the facility. We first look at the masculine biographies (meaning identities and learned ideologies) that the young men brought with them into Wildwood House, and then examine how the institution both maintained and disrupted these biographies, particularly as they related to crime.

The Masculine Biographies of Unit C

You gotta be tough to be a man, you gotta have responsibility and y'know, jus' know how to treat women. (Jason)

Before examining the facility as a site of masculinity practice, it is critical to understand the gendered lenses through which residents were inclined to experience Wildwood House. Criminologist Jo Goodey (1997) introduced the notion of the "masculine biography" to refer to the impact of a lifetime of gendered experiences on the development of masculine identity. Such a biography is in essence the narrative outcome, or the lessons learned, from socialization in a specific community of gendered practice. Using this concept, we conducted interviews that traced the development of residents' understandings and performances of gender and masculinity from early childhood to the present. Notable commonalities regarding the masculine biographies of Unit C included conflicted relationships with fathers and male role models, a sense of manhood as a tough exterior, a professed respect for women with conflicted responses to femininity, and a frame of aggression and competition as means to achieve personal power and respect.

Conflicted Relationships with Fathers and Male Role Models

Most of the residents described their early childhoods in idealized terms, as times when their families were intact and they experienced joy and familial closeness. They recounted memories of Christmas holidays and birthdays when they received cars, trucks, and GI Joes and cheerfully played with their siblings and extended family members until they blissfully nodded off to bed. This nostalgic and possibly romanticized depiction of childhood tended to dissipate around late elementary or early middle school years. Most of the boys attributed these changes to particularly difficult and fractured relationships with their fathers and other male role models, such as stepfathers, who were often estranged and sometimes physically or emotionally abusive to them. This attribution was likely due in no small part to the facility's discourse around family problems, as the staff typically believed that young men's highly disproportionate involvement in crime was due to poor male role modeling, paternal absence, or troubled father-son relationships. Mr. Croswell, one of the most caring male staff members we encountered, directly attributed the youths' behavior to poor intergenerational male role modeling: "I think they have too much time on their hands, they have no structure. The parents don't have time for them. I have kids in here that say, 'Geez, my dad was here [in Wildwood House], my grandpa was here.' and I look at the way they interact with each other and I see that the acorn doesn't fall far from the tree, you know. People are products of their environment."

As the staff often imparted messages about the importance of fathers and male role models through treatment groups, one-to-one interactions, and contract work, the residents often at least tentatively bought into these understandings. For example, in examining the origins of his own delinquency, Jason explained that his father's repeated use of corporal punishment caused him to gravitate toward hanging out with his delinquent friends in late and early middle school elementary school. He stated: "The belt right there . . . my dad would whoop my ass every single day. He'd be strict like that. He gets on my nerves and, and y'know, they just don't feel it. They just don't feel what I'm going through. And I'm like, 'Alright, baby, if you don't care about me, I will.' And I'll just go hang out, hang out with my boys and stuff. They care a lot about me. They don't whoop me. I'll just go hang out." Until some point during his incarceration, Jason had not told his father how he felt about this type of punishment. As Jason later expressed in this interview, he wished he had a role model or a man to turn to when he was feeling lost and confused during middle school, but he didn't feel that he could ever turn to his dad for help for fear of physical reprisal. The emotional closeness that Jason and others expressed wanting or missing from their lives was clearly not a feature of the masculine biographies they saw enacted around them; rather, the message they received was often that real men don't need this kind of intimacy.

Other residents had partially or fully absent fathers, either due to divorce, paternal incarceration, or never having known or met their fathers at all. These young men described either a lack of or negative male role modeling from relatives or their mothers' boyfriends or stepfathers. For Brad, his father's longstanding incarceration prohibited the development of any substantial relationship between them. Instead, he was mainly reared by his mother, grandmother, and uncle, who were all heavy substance abusers. In one of the more chilling moments of candor in his interviews, he recalled vivid memories of physical fights between these caregivers when he was just seven years old: "Like this one time, she [Mom] rumbled with my uncle, his girlfriend, and my aunt. And they all went to the hospital that night; they were breaking bottles over each other and just fighting. There was hair all over, it was all bloody and I just watched. I couldn't do nuthing. I woulda got hurt too, probably. I was just scared cuz they broke like three bottles. Everyone got hit with one in the head, a bottle."

Later in the interview, he suggested that his best male role models were his older male friends, who offered him the opportunity to earn money through home robberies and other illegal activities. Numerous similar examples were evident in the boys' life histories, with tales of fractured relationships with fathers and male relatives, incarcerated or absent fathers, along with the witnessing of violence in their homes, particularly domestic violence. These formative experiences led to a sense of articulated distrust for other men, yet at the same time a yearning for male camaraderie and protections through peer associations, sometimes in the form of organized neighborhood or larger gangs. We do not have evidence to suggest that closer relationships with their fathers would have altered their trajectories in any substantial way, or that father-absence was the definitive root cause of their delinquency. Rather, in a pattern that others have noted as common-place among young men marginalized by race and class (Paechter 2007), these boys sought out peers and communities where they could model for and learn from one another's demonstrations of masculinity on their own terms.

"Boys Don't Cry"

Ms. Jacobs, the therapist at Wildwood House, attributed the consider-able gender disparities in juvenile corrections to the fact that boys are social-ized to act out their repressed feelings and traumas, whereas girls are more socialized toward self-harm or acting inward. Indeed, another commonality in the gender socialization of residents of Wildwood House was a host of early messages from their parents and other family members, and then later their peers, that to be a manhood entails maintaining a tough exterior. We heard this repeatedly, in catch phrases such as "boys don't cry," as well as through recounted memories of how they were told to toughen up and hide their feelings in order to prove their masculinity. Jason in particular articu-lated this experience:

JASON: When I grew up, my dad told me boys don't cry. My boys [Jason's friends], be like "boys don't cry." So, y'know, sometimes I have a heart, and when you gotta cry, you gotta cry. When it's not time, time to cry, you don't have to cry.

LAURA: So you do cry?

JASON: I do cry, sometimes.

LAURA: By yourself?

JASON: Sometimes by myself. Sometimes just sit, outside or like in the park, with my boys, look at the stars and talk. And relax.

LAURA: Would you cry in front of your boys?

JASON: Uh-huh, never.

In this interaction, Jason both admitted that he wanted to be able to cry and that he "has heart," but in order to save face with his peers, he preferred to do so behind closed doors. Although he came close to admitting that perhaps he would cry in front of his male friends, when Laura pressed him on this matter, he reverted to his original stance that no, in fact, he would never allow himself to do so. The message here is strikingly similar to what Jason's relationship with his father taught him about wanting, yet being unable to access emotional closeness and vulnerability with other males.

It wasn't just the boys' fathers who provided messages about maintaining a tough exterior, but in some instances, mothers as well. After discussing the violent and traumatic events that characterized his childhood, Brad shared his mother's response to his frequent tears and displays of emotion:

LAURA: So crying was okay in your household?

BRAD: Yeah. My mom knew but she didn't like it when I cried.

LAURA: She didn't? Because it made her upset, or?

BRAD: No, she just didn't like it.

LAURA: Would she, like, come nurture you, or?

BRAD: No, no, she'd just sit down and, "Stop crying." And she'd tell me, like, she still tells me, "Don't cry" or stuff like that.

While most of the residents tended to equate manhood with holding back emotions, there were a couple of notable exceptions. Nino, considered by the staff to be a very problematic resident (as relayed in chapter 3), appeared to us to be one of the more sensitive and emotionally expressive young men in the Unit. His father had been incarcerated most of his life, and he was himself in the midst of a battle for partial custody of his twin sons. In one of the interviews, he talked in some depth about a moment he shared with a male friend that diverged from other boys' experiences of a required tough exterior:

NINO: I cried in front of one particular friend, that I know since the eighth grade.

LAURA: A guy or a girl?

NINO: Yeah. A guy. And it's just me and him, sitting in a car. And I was just under a whole bunch of emotions, or we both was, because he was talking about how his grandfather or a family member dying or something like that, and how his family was falling apart. And it just got me thinking how my grandfather was sick and how my family was slowly falling apart, and we both were just crying.

LAURA: Together?

NINO: Yeah. We was just sitting there hugging each other. Like it was me crying on the female's shoulder, hugging him. And it didn't feel no different. It didn't feel no different.

LAURA: Did that feel good, to have a guy's support?

NINO: Mm hmm. It also lets me know that to a certain extent, I can trust him. Because he opened up and showed deeply emotional personal problems with me that I prawly wouldn't even have told none of my friends stuff about my family like that. But that's just me. And ever since he came out in the open and told me how his family, how he felt about his family, made me want to talk more to him about how my family was and how his family was doing.

Interestingly in this interaction, Nino equated his experience with his male friend to his way of relating to females, emphasizing that "it didn't feel no different" from leaning on a woman's shoulders. This story stood out as notable in the sense that one common feature of most residents' masculine biographies included a belief that it wasn't cool to express sadness or deep feelings in front of other men. Even more than simply not being cool, doing so introduced the risk of being seen as womanly or less than appropriately masculine. Here Nino relayed a very tender moment of opening up to and receiving empathetic support from his male friend. Yet in equating this experience with his way of relating to women, he still could not frame it as occurring in the confines of what he understood to be the normative boundaries of male friendships.

Professed Respect for Women Yet Rejection of Femininity

Even given the residents' mostly traditional narratives about their own masculine socialization, they nearly unanimously expressed a profound respect for women and endorsed notions of women's equality in the workplace, the family, and in politics. When asked about innate differences between women and men, many of the boys deemed it unfair that women have to experience discrimination, double sexual standards, threats of violence, and physiological issues such as hormone changes and pregnancy, that men do not. Trevor, for example, suggested that women "gotta protect their selves and stuff, and watch who they hang around and stuff, and watch the time of night they go out because certain people like to rape females and stuff." Humphrey, who was himself serving a sentence for sexual misconduct against a female, asserted his opinion that there are no real differences between men and women except for those due to social role expectations:

HUMPHREY: I don't think there's a real difference, besides the way some people think. Because, you know, some people think that a woman's too weak to do this job or something, but I don't think that nobody's too weak to do any job. Cuz if they can do it, if they put their mind to it, they can do it. And I know they can do it. So I don't think there's a real big difference, but there is people out there that do see differences and . . .

LAURA: So you don't think it's real different to grow up as a male or grow up as a female in this society?

HUMPHREY: I know that job-wise, yeah, I think it's the same. But, like, women live wronged. They go through a lot. I'd be scared to be a woman, I swear.

This dialogue hints at a complicated picture of womanhood, one in which women warrant respect equal to if not greater than that afforded to men, but also with an acute acknowledgement that women's lives are made more difficult due to potential victimization. The fear that characterizes Humphrey's last statement—"I'd be scared to be a woman"—marks another important nuance of this discussion, that although womanhood is to be respected, a sense of femininity in themselves or other men should be feared or otherwise rejected, as it may signal a failed masculinity.

With few exceptions, the boys expressed distaste for visible femininity in all men, and particularly among gay men, even if they themselves had privately "tried on" their feminine sides or personas. Jason recounted what he considered to be an embarrassing story about dressing up as a woman:

JASON: I'll tell you this though, y'know, but just don't tell nobody. One day, they [Jason's female friends] actually put make-up on me and dressed me in girls' stuff. And I was like, "Dang!" I mean I was freaked out. I was like, "Dang!" When I looked at myself in the mirror y'know, I, I mean, I was wearin' like skirt right here, and black skirt, y'know, with my nails like red, my lips red. My eyelashes . . . I don't know what they did. I mean, the little curl thing or whatever, y'know, they just did like that.

BEN: Did you look good?

JASON: The girls, they be like, "Dang! Your butt looks sexy" and all that stuff, but I'd be like, "All right." 'Cause it was tight. And then I wore that for like five minutes and then just took it off. I mean, they still have some pictures of me, but they won't show them to other people.

BEN: Was it fun?

JASON: Uh, it was fun in some way, but it was fun . . . I don't know. I mean it was, like, weird.

BEN: Did you feel like less of a man, nails done and eyelashes curled?
JASON: I felted gay.

Jason was clearly uncomfortable with this whole story; he hadn't disclosed this experience to anyone before, and although his female friends may have retained pictures of him dressed as a woman, they were appropriately hidden. By ensuring secrecy about his gender transgression, particularly from the eyes of other males, Jason kept his masculinity intact and avoided the "fag discourse," a means of gender policing that C. J. Pascoe (2007) noted in her examination of how boys negotiate their own and their peers' masculinities in a high school context. Consistent with other studies of marginalized urban youth (Froyum 2007), the boys at Wildwood House associated most performances of gender that deviated from a traditional masculine script to be demonstrations of homosexuality. In this light, Jason's equating of dressing up as a woman with "feeling gay" illustrated how gay men were perceived by residents as both abnormal and identifiable solely by feminine gender expressions. Although many denied blatant hatred of gay men, they often suggested that public expressions of homosexuality among men (but not women) were abnormal. Trevor explained:

BEN: Would it be normal for you to see two guys your age walking through the mall, holding hands and laughing to each other?
TREVOR: Nope.
BEN: How come? What would that mean that it doesn't mean for two girls?
TREVOR: Naw, some people would think of it as they're gay and stuff, and I just can't imagine two guys walking around holding hands together. That's just not right.

Complicating this discussion, in the same interview during which Trevor suggested that being gay "just isn't right," he also recounted a story of being able to play around with gender, and to some extent, homosexuality with his best friend Jeff.

BEN: So, if you and Jeff are sitting at the mall and some guy can walk by and you can say he's cute?
TREVOR: Yeah. He's a pretty direct guy, y'know, he'll look at me. I mess with Jeff sometimes, y'know, grab his butt once in a while just to play with him. But he, y'know, gets all freaked out. It's not serious, though.
BEN: Is that why you do it? 'Cause it freaks him out?
TREVOR: Yeah. I just like to embarrass him.

Trevor's expressed opinions related to masculinity, sexuality, and homophobia reflected a typical narrative for the young men at Wildwood House. On the one hand, they feared feminine expression in themselves or other men and had a standard mantra that "being gay is okay, as long as they keep it to themselves." On the other hand, they tended to have some experiences where they could feel comfortable stepping out of their gender boundaries, with close friends or female friends mainly, and that was rationalized as a joke or, as in Jason's case, a performance. One notable exception to outwardly embracing the feminine side of himself was Nino, who even described parts of himself as effeminate. In response to a question about how he sees himself on a masculine-feminine spectrum, he stated: "I would have to say that I am both masculine and feminine, because at some points, I like to be that macho type person, and then effeminate because I like doing hair, and I been just dying to cut my hair so I can get my waves back going like I used to have 'em."

Nino stood out as the only resident we encountered to claim or embrace his effeminate or feminine traits. Yet Nino was also able to salvage his masculine reputation with his peers in part due to athletic skill, and also possibly on account of his status as a father, which functioned as an assertion of heterosexuality in spite of these other gender transgressions. In any case, these narratives reflect how residents walked in the apparent contradiction of worrying about and seeking emotional connection, intimacy, and self-expression while also maintaining fidelity to conventional masculine ideologies. This phenomenon of the boys' conflicted valuations of femininity resonates with William Pollack's (2006) work, as well, in which the double-standard of masculinity allows males to publicly espouse egalitarian ideals about gender while still primarily enacting hegemonic masculinities.

Competition and Aggression as Means to Achieve Power

By far the most common experience of masculine socialization among the group involved fighting as a route to earning power and respect among peers. Trevor recounted a story of one of his first fights in the fifth grade, where he admitted to using aggression as a means of asserting his (and his peers') place in the social pecking order: "It was wintertime out, and we were playin' a game. Y'know, pickin' on a big dude, fat stupid guy. And I wasn't even involved with that. Actually, I was just standin' there, laughin,' and the kid came over and he started pushin' me. So I gave him a big black eye."

This and other similar experiences established Trevor as a leader in his peer group and he continued to prove to others, through physical force, that he would not stand to be bullied. Andrew Parker (1996) noted this as a common strategy by which young men develop and reinforce social standing amongst themselves. In Parker's terms, by proving himself in this fight, Trevor secured his position as a "hard boy," having demonstrated competition and a willingness to fight for a role in the top ranks of the social hierarchy. In a later interview, Trevor explained the mechanism by which he could convert the social stature he secured through these demonstrations into

influence among other young men; his physical toughness endowed him with
the ability to persuade others into committing crimes with him when he
entered middle school. This leadership role and sense of power within his
peer group afforded him confidence that he didn't get, as he explained, from
his fractured home environment or school.

Like Trevor, almost all of the residents had experienced the need to fight
with other boys to prove their worth and social standing, and for many, this
trend had resulted in school suspensions, injuries, and potentially even forays
into more risky behaviors such as use of weapons. The need to establish a sense
of worthy masculinity through violence was clearly and intimately related to
trajectories of criminal activity that led to their placement at Wildwood House.

Overall, with a few exceptions such as Nino, the residents at Wildwood
House described their masculine biographies with similarity and consistency.
Although the specific details and circumstances of their upbringing—in Carrie
Paechter's (2007) terms, their local communities of masculinity practice—
varied, they had learned to endorse and perform certain similar features of hegemonic masculinity while affirming their sense of self as young men in no small
part through their repudiation of anything perceived to be overtly feminine.
The residents carried these biographies with them into the facility, where they
were both reinforced and contradicted, often in complicated and inconsistent
ways, by the program's uneasy blend of treatment and punitive orientations.

MASCULINITIES WITHIN THE DORM

We went outside with the group for a softball game in the humid early summer sunshine. Mr. Connelly had complained to us earlier in the day that the
boys had been "wimpy" recently and needed to get outside for some exercise
and healthy competition. The teams split almost immediately, with the boys
sorting themselves by race and athletic ability. Before long, banter back and
forth between and among the teams took a sour and tense tone, with the
boys baiting one another into more and more aggressive demonstrations of
prowess.

Thomas, an athletic African American resident, hit a fly ball directly to
Eric, who was known among his peers as weak and nerdy. Surprising everyone, Eric caught the ball, and Thomas was out. Stomping off the field,
Thomas shouted, "Fucking faggot!" Mr. Connelly jumped on it right away,
"What was that?!" Thomas replied with mocking sarcasm, "I said, 'good
catch.'" Mr. Connelly said, with equal sarcasm, "Then I said, 'Close to a
violation.' Watch your language." As the game continued, so did the boys'
running commentary on one another's manliness and skill. Elijah put on his
best lisp and walked up to bat holding his wrist limply to one side and swing-
ing his hips exaggeratedly. Other residents joined forces to make fun of one
peer for standing near a picnic table, leaning over the table with his legs spread

to his sides while he talked with other youth. One of the other boys called attention to it by pointing out the position to his friend, and they both laughed. When we asked them about why they were laughing, they commented that they had never seen a guy stand like that before.

This vignette illustrates some of the context in which boys' masculine biographies were both reinscribed and contradicted by the culture of Wildwood House. Specifically, the boys' interactions with their peer group and the institutional ethos of the facility reinforced a stratified hierarchy of gender expressions that tended to reify boys' existing narratives of masculinity as the repudiation of femininity and homosexuality. At the same time, however, Wildwood House encouraged the boys in various ways to explore alternative expressions and performances of gender, including learning to value emotional expression, interrupting misogyny, and modeling positive and emotionally intimate youth–adult relationships.

From the beginning of our observations, we were aware that the boys often sorted themselves during routine activities and meal times according to particular hierarchy of toughness. This is not surprising, since several of the youth actually knew one another from their schools or neighborhoods, and these groups tended to mirror their roles in the outside world. The first tier consisted of the most physically strong African American boys, such as Elijah, Thomas, and Terrell. In the second tier were the tougher white boys, such as Trevor, who may have proven themselves on the sports field or due to their extensive criminal history. In the third tier in the dorm were the Hmong boys, who tended to be shorter and slighter in stature, such as Jason, and they were joined by some of the weaker white boys, or the "extras" who were not physically strong, such as Eric and Humphrey. This social stratification was most evident in the context of the residents' recreation time, particularly in the gym. With few exceptions, we observed the boys self-selecting, often with little dialogue or spoken negotiation, into these distinct groups. Prime court space, for instance in basketball, was afforded almost by default to the dominant athletic group; the others occupied the remaining space around the periphery of the gym engaged in other activities.

For the most part, the dorm residents were acutely aware of their place in the pecking order, which was signaled principally—though not exclusively—through physical prowess or some other expression of power. Terrell spoke candidly about this hierarchy, emphasizing status through gang affiliation as one expression of dominance, and how this pecking order played itself out in the underground dynamics of dorm life: "Who has dorm power? Mostly it's the gang-banger people. If one person that's a gang banger says something to somebody who ain't and who's just running off at the mouth, everybody, later on that day, is gonna say something to him and that person just goin' to get real frustrated and not know what to do because he gonna think everybody's after him."

In this specific passage and the dialogue that followed, Terrell described how he and his friends worked together to intimidate those who are "running their mouth." On the receiving end of this intimidation, Jason, who was a central player in the Hmong peer group, described several occasions during which he encountered these types of threats of violence from the more physically dominant group:

JASON: Yeah, there's some peers, they think they're bad, so they show it. They show it, but I mean they talk the talk but when it comes to the walk, they probably can't walk it.

LAURA: What's the talk they talk?

JASON: Y'know, "I beat you up," and y'know, "I kill you," and all that stuff. Y'know, as if they are the only ones that do that stuff.

LAURA: Has anyone threatened you?

JASON: Me? Yeah.

LAURA: And how do you respond?

JASON: Just like, "Alright man, you dudes can do that. Just wait . . . just wait until we get to the outs and I see you down." It's like that.

LAURA: So you threaten them back?

JASON: Yeah, and then I just keep quiet. It's like, "Screw you, man; I'm trying to just make it through this program. But if you think you all bad, just if I see you once in the outs and you wanna rumble, let's get it on."

Although smaller than most of his peers in stature and excluded from the highest of the dorm's social strata, Jason nevertheless employed similar mechanisms, such as the willingness to use physical force to assert his superiority, in order to carve out whatever power and status he could access in the dorm.

By contrast, Eric's peers treated him as an inferior due to his whiteness, suburban upbringing, and the absence of a street-wise persona. Not only did he lack physical prowess, he was also fundamentally inexperienced with and ill equipped to enact the strategies of dominance and assertion that circulated throughout the dorm. He was very aware of his status in the Unit, stating that the boys saw him as "some kid from the suburbs that can't hoop." To manage his diminished standing, Eric mentally placed himself as superior to what he called the "ghetto, rap culture" that dominated the dorm, and professed not to care that others thought of him as weak. He also identified the top tiered boys as "immature" and "not worth his time." Nevertheless, he recognized that this strategy of mental superiority did not serve him perfectly; reflecting on what he had learned from his time at Wildwood House, he remarked: "Well, I've learned to be greedy. If I want something, I go up in the front of the line. Who cares about everyone else? When I came in here, I was polite about that kind of stuff. But here, you can't just be Mr. Nice Guy. You have to fight back. You have to think, you have to outsmart the others. Normally with adults it's not a problem. But with the residents in here, you have to make your stand."

Even Eric, who preferred to internally and privately criticize the other residents for what he labeled as "ghetto" behavior, still believed that he had to learn and practice some of this posturing in order to get what he wanted, or in his words, "to make his stand." Rather than being covert or underhanded, both the dorm hierarchy and the mechanisms of achieving a higher status were readily visibly, and the route to an elevated standing typically involved demonstrations of power and physical intimidation that were learned in the process of male socialization.

SEXISM AND HOMOPHOBIA

A group of residents sat in a semicircle, distracted and only marginally participating in a therapeutic skill-building session focusing on the importance of communication in relationships. Try as she might, the group's facilitator struggled to engage the boys, who snickered regularly to one another and offered only partial answers to the questions and hypothetical situations posed to them. One such scenario involved a boy and girl making out. When the boy in the vignette tried to touch the girl on her breasts, she said, "No." At this point in the session, the facilitator stopped and asked the boys to interpret the scene: What was he feeling? What was she feeling? What could he do? Only a few boys genuinely participated in the conversation; the others all appeared bored, staring across the room as they slumped in their chairs and occasionally threw out deliberately crass or inappropriate retorts. Elijah raised his hand: "He should just tell the girl, 'Why not? We're gonna do it sooner or later anyway. Why not just get it out of the way?'" Although she appeared momentarily taken aback by the masculine posturing and entitlement nested in Elijah's remark, the teacher let his comment slip by unaddressed and other residents chimed in their agreement.

As several examples throughout this chapter have shown, the staff tended to model or endorse values around competition that often reinforced the masculine biographies that youth carried with them into the facility. The vignettes concerning the softball game and the sexual education group also reveal another layer of messages about masculine social roles that implicitly entailed the subjugation of women and gay men. Although the residents professed a high degree of respect for women, we observed many scenarios that reinforced sexist thinking, including men's entitlement to women's bodies and homophobic humor.

Residents' covert and overt sexist or homophobic comments were met with inconsistent responses from staff, as seen in the softball game incident when Mr. Connelly warned Thomas about the inappropriateness of his "fag" comment but then ignored the homophobic humor in the larger group. It is notable that the dorm staff promptly quelled all discussions of past crimes or violence among the boys, explicitly naming this kind of conversation as telling "war stories," or glorifying attitudes that contributed to criminality or delinquency. Yet with regard to sexist or homophobic commentary, the staff often did little to interrupt or intervene in these conversations. The failure to disrupt many of these thought patterns about women or gay men suggests something significant about the facility's implicit support for these same attitudes, and Elijah's role in both the skills group and softball vignettes illustrates the complex relationship between the milieu, hegemonic masculinities, and crime. In case of the skills group, it is worth remembering that Elijah's crime was in fact related to domestic violence against his girlfriend (the mother of his son), clearly part of what the facility would call his "criminal thinking" and the reason for his placement at Wildwood House. Yet the facilitator's reluctance or perhaps inability to confront his narrative about men's physical power over women in this scenario represents implicit approval of his demeaning way of thinking about sexual activity with women. In the softball incident, again with Elijah involved, the staff failed to call him out on inciting homophobia and potentially targeting one or two residents with homophobic taunts, and instead tended to let it slide. In both examples, the masculine biography Elijah brought into the facility—clearly implicated in his criminal thinking and behavior—remained unchallenged.

In addition to this more passive endorsement of sexist and homophobic attitudes, messages about appropriate and inappropriate masculine social roles and responses were also made explicit in the dorm. For example, several dorm activities and interactions stressed expectations for young men to be unflinchingly brave and strong, pitted against being overtly effeminate or feminine. During one of our visits, we witnessed a presentation to the boys by a US Army recruiter. We arrived in time to watch the last few minutes of the mandatory viewing of a recruitment video, after which one Wildwood House substitute staff member answered questions from the boys and offered commentary on his own prior military experience. At one point, he made reference to a female soldier in the video, calling her a "chick." None of the boys batted an eye at this. Later, one of the residents asked a question about war, asking whether the staff member had ever thought about what would have happened if the United States had gone to war during his term of service. The staff replied that he didn't think about it, because he just would have gone to fight for his country. When the resident mentioned his own fear of warfare, the staff person criticized him, commenting that "only a coward would back out of an opportunity to defend his country."

Labeling the female soldier a "chick" and characterizing fear of combat as a marker of cowardice, the staff member in this case explicitly reinforced the importance of one type of masculinity signaled by toughness at all costs. While this example may be more blatant than others, it reflected how "doing masculinity" for boys and men who don't have access to the other hallmarks of the middle-class ideal is intertwined with a sense of bravado typically associated with a traditional masculine performance. It is a particularly striking and contradictory position for the program to reinforce, given our previous observations that while many residents entered the facility with masculine biographies that reflected these very same values, the facility's treatment programs (and intertwined level system) sought and rewarded demonstrations of emotion and intimacy that worked to the contrary of these traditional scripts.

POSING ALTERNATIVES

Wildwood House offered several possible routes for the residents to try on alternative modes of gender expression. This occurred mostly during treatment groups and through activities seeking to help the boys explore and express their authentic selves and to communicate more empathetically and openly with their peers and family members. Close relationships with staff, including the dorm's few female staff and some of the male workers, also presented the possibility of relational arrangements that did not necessarily align with the traditional masculine stereotypes reinforced by other parts of the milieu.

Expression and Empathy

As articulated earlier in this chapter, from childhood to young adulthood, the residents had received mostly consistent messages from their family members and friends that they should repress emotion in order to affirm their masculinity. Yet through the course of their treatment, learning how to express their emotions was for many residents a powerful part of their experience at the facility. For instance, Trevor expressed pride in his evolving ability to express his himself, "Oh, I can talk about feelings, I don't care who it is. I like expressing my feelings. 'Cuz it's helping other people. It's helping myself. It feels good."

Like Trevor, many residents experienced a sense of relief in being able to express sadness, pain, and other feelings through group and individual therapy. In this sense, the facility clearly offered alternatives to the traditionally male attribute of repressing painful feelings that staff believed had led many of these young men into impulsive behaviors and criminal activity. Humphrey directly stated that emotional expression, which he considered a female practice, ultimately felt good:

> When I was living in the group home, I just noticed that the girls in the neighborhood, they show off lots of emotion. If you're doing something wrong, you saying something wrong, they will tell you. And that's just

what I noticed. And guys . . . there's been kids here, and they'll just sit in team meeting and they'll just look at 'em [the speaker]. Like they get a violation or something, just sit there and look at 'em. And they'll be like, "What are you thinking?" "Nuthin." They're just not even showing nothing. So, it's just like they're holding back them feelings for no reason. Cuz I think it's good to let 'em [feelings] out. Then you feel better.

Although Humphrey articulated the benefits of emotional expression and criticized some of his peers for holding back or not feeling anything, he still equated this ability with a feminine attribute. In other words, talking about his feelings was still construed as less than a masculine practice.

For most residents, the treatment groups provided a working laboratory to verbally express their emotions. Further, these settings provided an environment in which youth could work toward developing empathy and support for each other's feelings. Many residents believed that they learned a lot about themselves by listening to the stories of their peers, a process which may mirror the group socialization in the outside world to some extent, but also taught close listening skills and ways of offering support and encouragement to even those residents they wouldn't pay attention to in other circumstances. Although some of the boys remained distracted or disengaged during their group therapy sessions, most demonstrated genuine instances of mutual respect and empathy.

In one notable example, we observed a peer group meeting where the staff (including the head teacher from the school) had gathered to hear a presentation of treatment progress by Mike, an African American resident. He had been working on his Family Problems contract, delving into his problematic relationship with his father and some of the messages and values he had internalized from this relationship. Mike stood in front of the group and presented a request to all the residents and staff that they start calling him by this name, and not Michael, which was his father's name. After the presentation, during which the boys were uncharacteristically quiet and attentive, the residents congratulated Mike and acknowledged the effort it took for him to speak in front of them all. The staff present for this session responded similarly, smiling, almost beaming, at Mike's accomplishment.

In addition to these observations of empathy and support in the group process, some of the boys talked directly about what they learned from peer groups and spending time listening to each other's stories. Trevor explained: "Well, they [they group] have shared some of the similar things I have, so that's good to know I'm not alone. It's not all the same crime, they're not the same lifestyle, but we're all together. I mean, everybody in there has good individual stories and stuff. But just to hear some of the stuff that they went through is like, "Wow! I'm not the only one, y'know, there's other people.""

During the same interview, Trevor contrasted this experience with the sense of camaraderie he had with his other friends, which was a sense of supporting each other through thick and thin, but also in "running wild." What he discovered in the facility was a different type of support—a difference he attributed to the structure of the treatment groups and contracts. In essence, the treatment activities provided a structure through which residents could learn and practice an alternative type of closeness with other males that may have resembled some parts of their past relationships, but that were also unique.

Interrupting Disrespect toward Women

Although in many cases staff failed to interrupt sexist or homophobic comments among the residents, they were quick to intervene in demeaning talk concerning female staff members. Of the two regular shift female staff members of Unit C, both were relatively new to the job, and Ms. Breuer actually began her tenure in the dorm during our observation period. An attractive younger woman, Ms. Breuer was immediately the target of many residents' sexualization and objectification. Elijah in particular commented regularly on her physical attractiveness and began to spread sexualized rumors about her around the dorm. To garner support and encouragement from his peers, Elijah once made a lewd gesture toward Ms. Breuer that included spraying an asthma inhaler behind her backside while she was turned around. He initially denied all culpability and made up excuses about the incident. Later, however, he claimed to us that he "wouldn't do that [sexually harass Ms. Breuer]" because "she is nothing. She's ugly. She wants to be a man. I wouldn't stare at or flirt with someone so ugly."

A week later, Elijah completed a special treatment contract assigned by his primary staff member in which he accepted responsibility for the incident and admitted his sexual attraction to Ms. Breuer. He also related the incident to his criminal offense of domestic violence. In spite of Elijah's confidential statements to us that he had invented his admission of guilt to comply with staff expectations and thereby avoid a greater consequence, the insistence with which the dorm staff acted on the sexism and lewd gesture demonstrated a concerted attempt to teach the boys to respect women. While Elijah's cycle of female objectification was not necessarily fully disrupted by this experience, he was required to take responsibility for his actions and to admit his culpability in front of the staff and his peers.

Positive and Caring Interactions with Staff

In the course of our time in Unit C, we observed many instances of positive interactions between residents and male staff that modeled supportive and caring adult to youth relationships. The director of the facility believed these relationships to be the foundation of the treatment program and an opportunity to resocialize the young men, whose former relationships with adults he described as "neither consistent nor caring in nature." We indeed observed that these types of relationships allowed the residents to experience alternatives to the interactions with other men (adult and youth) they had previously learned to enact. One such instance unfolded during a midday break from the school day, when Mr. Washington, the only regular African American dorm staff, joined a group of residents at the foosball table. Consistently over the course of half an hour together, Mr. Washington commented on the boys' successes and skill at the game, even as Thomas was beating him soundly. At one point, another resident approached Mr. Washington, interrupting the game to give a report on a voluntary chore for the dorm that he had just completed. Mr. Washington apologized directly to Thomas, turned to the resident, and said, "I want you to have my full attention. Good job! Thank you for doing that [cleaning the laundry room]; it's really helpful." Then he went back to the game, continuing his positive interactions with Thomas.

In addition to these day-to-day supportive interactions, many of the residents developed close relationships with the male staff, and for some, even allowed them to feel re-parented, as was the case with Trevor's relationship with Mr. McClatchy. Through these relationships, the boys experienced the emotional closeness and intimacy they had mentioned wanting from their fathers and appreciating about a few other male relationships, but which they were largely prohibited from exploring more publicly. For example, some of the boys talked about feeling safe in crying in front of the male staff. These close relationships imparted new ways of relating to men that represented a departure from their past experiences.

CONCLUSION

During one of our final visits to Wildwood House, Laura sat at dinner with two new residents. Conversation turned to their lives outside the facility, and both talked about missing home, wanting to sleep in their own beds and enjoy their mothers' home-cooked meals. As the discussion progressed, the boys commented on their experiences in the facility; they said they didn't like being there because it was "not normal" to be around all guys all the time. They missed being around girls. Laura asked if most of their friends at home were guys, to which one replied, "yeah, but this is different. There's so much like competition here. Guys are always trying to one-up each other." When asked if he could ignore that, whether he could step outside the competition, he said, "not really. You can't be a punk and just walk away. That's the problem with having all guys here, trying to be tough. It puts you on the edge."

In the context of the multiple dimensions of masculinity explored in this chapter, one major question remains: Can a correctional program change boys' identifications with criminality if these associations are firmly rooted in performances of hegemonic masculinity? As we have illustrated, through a therapeutic discourse and practices, and for some, very close and caring relationships with the staff, the institution offered alternative scripts for masculine socialization and gender identity construction. The boys were aware of the different quality of these relationships and although not named as such, were modeled on empathy and acceptance. Yet overall, while Wildwood House staff believed that gender socialization and father absence were root causes of delinquency and attempted to teach young men new skills with regard to emotional expression, the milieu closely aligned with the boys' more traditional masculine biographies associated with power, competition, and one-upping each other. In particular, the staff often failed to disrupt sexism and homophobia and, in some instances, even reinforced these ideologies. And perhaps most clearly, the boys' ability to earn power and status in the dorm was closely related to their perceived masculine prowess, often asserted through violence and intimidation of one another. In essence, the extent to which boys can truly challenge the roots of their own criminality within these parameters remains questionable.

CHAPTER 5

"Jumping through Hoops"

IDENTITY, SELF-PRESERVATION, AND CHANGE

Late afternoon on a weekday, a resident named Mark was standing near the office door holding a dictionary. This occurred shortly after staff had heard and rejected his appeal in a violation hearing, unanimously assigning him a consequence for manipulation and saying what people wanted to hear, or what staff and youth called "faking it." Since we had observed the violation hearing and were invested in knowing what he was thinking, we approached Mark and asked him what he was doing. "I'm looking up the word 'manipulation,'" he said, "so I can find out what it really means. It's one of them words that everybody uses different." We stood together and looked up the word, and then we talked about which parts of its definition were the most important for him to remember. Mark decided that "control" and "for your own gain" were important, and then—curious because it's another loaded word—suggested that we look up "control." He said that it made sense that control was about having the power to make other people do what you want them to do, and manipulation is having the control to make people do something in your benefit, but not necessarily theirs. They're related, but he struggled because, as he put it, "How can I manipulate in here, if I don't have control?"

We then asked what treatment contract he was working on. Mark answered that it was his Family Problems contract, but that he was having trouble with it because he didn't really want to share those things "with a bunch of people who care, but don't really care." We asked if he had to do it. He said that if he didn't tell "them" something about this family, he wouldn't be able to finish the program, so he's going to have to do it. We asked what issues he would talk about. He said that there are some family issues that staff think are "better" than others—they expect people to have moms or dads who have drug or alcohol problems, so they like residents to write about that in their contracts. He said his parents don't have these problems, but he might have to make something like that up. He said that at some point, you have to decide whether you're just going to "fly on by and fake it out" or get serious and do some work. That point was a few days ago, when

Mark said he decided to quit faking it and start getting busy, "but it's hard, 'cause what am I gonna write?"

Can a treatment-based correctional program significantly shift a young man's identity if he doesn't want his identity shifted? Does the tendency to fake it trump any meaningful changes that a resident might make? Ms. Breuer once said about the residents that "when they make changes, even small little changes, it is rewarding." But do these small changes matter? The prior two chapters have argued that a juvenile correctional institution is rich in its potential to be a salient site of identity work, given the essential mission of reforming young people and its influence on gender identity formation. But how does such a facility fulfill that potential for individual youth? What elements of this type of program support or impede this identity work? Building on these ideas, this chapter addresses core questions about the process of individual change in a residential correctional setting. Specifically, we discuss the general tendency of residents to initially want to "fly on by and fake it out." While some youth carried this response forward throughout their stay, others experienced significant shifts in their identities and future aspirations. Through the residents' narratives over time, we then discuss three major patterns of change in regard to residents' negotiations of their previously held versions of self in the context of institutional messages seeking to reshape their identities and their futures.

FRAMING "CHANGE": IDENTITY AND THE NEGOTIATION OF SELF-IN-CONTEXT

Identity is a longstanding concern in the study of both institutionalized populations and youth. To examine identity construction within a correctional setting, we frame this discussion with the constructivist assumption that youth actively engage in processes of unfolding definition, in which they try on "possible selves" (Oyserman and Marcus 1990) according to multiple axes of identity—such as gender, race, class, age, and sexuality, among others—and in different environments or social settings (Ungar and Teram 2000; Weis and Fine 2000). This view of identity moves beyond the linear, stage-driven approach initially posited by Erik Erikson (1968), as it recognizes the ways in which young people assume agency in their own identity construction based on multiple factors and contexts rather than age or developmental stage alone. Patricia Phelan, Ann Davidson, and Hanh Yu (1993, 7) follow this constructivist logic in laying out their concept of multiple worlds. They define a world as "cultural knowledge and behavior found within the boundaries of students' particular families, peer groups, and school," and suggest that young people are constantly traversing the sociocultural, linguistic, psychosocial, or value-driven boundaries and borders of multiple worlds. They further suggest that these border crossings are influential for youth identity construction. For instance, young people who are able to be themselves at home in the same way they can be with their friends are more likely to experience fluidity and wholeness in their identities than those whose expressions of identity in one setting are pathologized or rejected in another. More specifically, congruence between worlds may shape how a young person adapts to various settings, whereas incongruence may produce difficulties in forging a positive or coherent sense of self. Educational Anthropologist Annette Hemmings (1998) found this to be the case among African American high-achieving students, who were rewarded by teachers for their accomplishments, but then socially excluded by their peers in their neighborhoods on account of these same achievements.

For some urban young men, ethnographic research has illustrated how crime, violence, and a particular "code of the street" comprise the dominant threads connecting their worlds and the self-representations they forge within them (Anderson 1999). Violent events, weapons, and crime can serve as foundational building blocks to accomplish a sense of masculinity and achievement for young men who are marginalized by race and class (Majors and Billson 1992; Wilkinson 2003). In chapter 4, we explained that the young men of Unit C had life stories that exposed them—often from very young ages—to many of the formative experiences this body of literature has linked to criminality in young adulthood and beyond. In particular, many residents were drawn into activities involving violence and crime in order to gain a sense of power and accomplishment as young men. This chapter is concerned with the process through which the youths' professed identities—those they carried with them into the institution—came into conversation with the discourses of the correctional facility. In keeping with a view of identity as dynamic and interactive, we look closely at how the residents responded to the treatment program's attempts to mold their self-perceptions and in particular, how youth managed the border crossing between their worlds outside and inside of the institution.

Studies concerning other institutionalized populations (homeless shelter residents, elder care residents, and others) have identified strategies that residents use to resist or "talk back to" stigmatizing messages in order to preserve a positive sense of self (Juhila 2004; Paterniti 2000). Residents who are exposed, for example, to programs or staff that convey pathologized identities may challenge these constructions with their own counternarratives. In this chapter, we point out similar patterns of resistance and self-preservation that often undergird patterns of response to institutional messages about the self. The implications of these patterns are intimately tied to the core concern about the extent to which young people can benefit from a therapeutic program they did not willingly choose.

JUMPING THROUGH HOOPS, FAKING IT, AND WORKING THE SYSTEM

Ain't nobody change in here. You just say what they want you to say. You act outside how they want you to act. (Resident)

This statement concisely articulates the general sentiment of the boys of Unit C, at least as it captures their initial reaction to being placed at Wildwood House. As we illustrated in chapter 3, the structure of the institution clearly rewarded what staff deemed to be therapeutic progress among the residents, and evidence of personal growth was the basis of advancement in a gradated system of privileges and rewards. As buy-in to a therapeutic discourse—particularly one with such a focus on family problems—was so pervasive in the facility and essentially linked to successful program completion, residents quickly learned what they needed to do to move up the ladder toward their release. For many, this meant going through the motions of the treatment program, making as few waves as possible, and waiting patiently to return home. Brad summed up his view of the treatment program: "Yeah. I think this program . . . might work for like one person every six months, but a lotta people are just jumpin' through hoops."

Early in our fieldwork we noticed that residents who were further along in the program covertly socialized the newer residents to "fake it 'til they make it." In this specific context, faking it meant that a resident could, by using certain language and key phrases in their written contracts and group work, convince the staff and their upper level peers that they had bought into the facility's treatment discourse and its family-rooted understandings of the origins of criminal behavior. Several residents were candid with us about their intentions to lie in order to get through the program. For example, at the time of Eric's first interview, he had spent just two weeks in Unit C. The following excerpt from this interview captures his initial impression of how to work his way through the program:

BEN: What do you think you need to do in order for that to happen [to get out?]

ERIC: Make the staff happy. You have to prove to them that you want to change your life and you want to do all this and that. The truth is I'm not really all that concerned about changing my life. And before I came in here, I told my mom, just one day as I was driving to school, "I'm done with that life. I'm not going to steal anymore. I don't want to do this. It's not worth it. I'm just . . . going to be good." And I came in here with that kind of attitude, and they're assuming that as soon as I get out there, I'm going to get into drugs and stealing and that kind of stuff, which is not true.

BEN: So how do you reconcile those things? On one hand you're saying you didn't come in with the kinds of problems that other people come in with, so you don't really fit the program, and on the other side you're saying make staff happy. How do you put those together?

ERIC: You have to make your background look bad, and you have to pretend. You have to pretend you're doing well and all this stuff.

BEN: So how do you make your background seem bad?

ERIC: Like, in the contracts, you explain the details of your offense, and I pretty much have to lie in all of them saying that I was having fun and all this. During the actual crime, I was ready to back out at any second, I was just like, "I don't want to do this." But I was being pulled into it. But in the contracts I have to write that it was kind of fun and I was getting an adrenaline rush, and all this stuff that's just completely not true. And you start with that, and then you go up the program and more and more prove to them that, no that really wasn't that fun, that was a very stupid choice. Then they'll think that you're improving and they'll let you out.

BEN: But if you started with, "I know it was a stupid choice?"

ERIC: Then they'll just not believe you. They'll just say "redo it."

BEN: So you have to keep redoing the contracts?

ERIC: Yeah. You have to redo it until it's a complete lie and then they'll accept it.

BEN: How do you feel when you're doing that?

ERIC: I'll do whatever I have to get out of here. I don't care what it is. So if they want me to redo it, and they're going to make me lie, then I'll just do that.

Eric's self-image remained consistent with what he described in the above dialogue: He was not a hardened criminal, but rather a good kid who had made a stupid mistake. Consequently, complying with staff expectation to see himself as criminal—even if it meant lying on his treatment contracts—presented an easy alternative to doing the emotional work it would require to restructure his sense of self. In this sense, his identity was not amenable to the changes in self-perception that the facility expected him to make; after all, it was his behavior, not his core identity or values, that he agreed was problematic. Although his well articulated strategy to appease the staff by inventing problems was by no means uncommon, his case was unique in that the program did not appear to be set up for boys whose backgrounds and identities mirrored his: suburban, without a long criminal record, and with a relatively high degree of stability at home.

Other residents relayed a similar strategy of saying what they thought the staff wanted to hear so they could earn their release. Unfortunately, this deliberate deception in the name of program success actually may have made some youth worse, according to the program's definition of antisocial behavior. We repeatedly witnessed a dynamic in which youths' professed identities related to criminal behavior, and to manipulation skills in particular, were inadvertently reinforced by having successfully faked it through the program. The experience of Terrell, who proudly deemed himself a "master manipulator," illustrates this phenomenon:

LAURA: A lot of the contracts made you write about your family issues. How did you pull that off?

TERRELL: Most of it, I just invented it. Cuz it was just going through my head, I was just thinking, and I'd just write down whatever I thought in my head. I'd just look at it, look over it, read it over, and say, "Yeah, that sounds about right," and then I'd just give it to 'em, let 'em check it over and stuff.

LAURA: But you do have some family issues?

TERRELL: Yes.

LAURA: Did you look at them at all?

TERRELL: Yeah, I did on my last contract, but I didn't really write as much as I wanted to write, I just put that I will start talking about my dad more, and talk to my mother about his absence and everything. So I didn't really get into it.

LAURA: Do you see any value in the type of therapy and the programs they have here, to help kids in your circumstance?

TERRELL: Uh, no, I don't.

LAURA: Okay. How come?

TERRELL: How come? Because, it's like if a kid don't wanna learn nothin' you can't force him to learn anything and stuff, and if he don't wanna go to school, you can't make him say, "Here, you gotta go to school and do this and stuff." He's just gonna go there and sit and act like he's doing the work. He's not really doing the work, so what is he getting out of it? Nuthin, if he doesn't wanna do it. You can't help nobody if they don't wanna be helped, that's just the way I see it.

In this dialogue, Terrell freely admitted that he indeed had some problematic family issues, but not ones that he was willing to explore in the confines of the treatment program. With great certainty, Terrell believed that he knew what he needed to show the staff in order to complete the program successfully, and he had no interest in delving any deeper into his issues than what was required to meet his primary goal of release. So even as Terrell expressed quite candidly that his family may indeed have problems, being forced to do the work would not make him want to change unless he chose on his own that such change was desirable. Since he hadn't come to that conclusion, his default response was to jump through the hoops placed before him. By moving him through the program in response to his treatment contracts, the facility essentially rewarded Terrell for simply meeting staff expectations, even if the real treatment work was not accomplished. In this process, Terrell's professed identity as a master manipulator remained unchallenged and to some extent was even reinforced by the conclusion that he had successfully outwitted the program.

As evidenced in the vignette that opened this chapter, Mark initially had a similar response to the treatment program, one that is ripe with contradictions. Mark's story illustrates the plight of a treatment program tied to a system of reward and punishments in which youth felt pressured to jump through hoops, and in doing so worked the treatment system to their own advantage. In Mark's case, he admitted faking his way through the program by appeasing the staff—which they labeled manipulative—but ironically, Mark didn't even know the very definition of the word. Upon learning that manipulation involved some semblance of control, Mark appropriately questioned if a resident was capable of manipulation in an environment that had completely stripped him of control.

So was the treatment program subject to manipulation, or were some of the boys just simply confused? For some, confusion about treatment expectations was present throughout their stay. Whether due to lack of understanding or other factors, the therapeutic discourse did not resonate at all with some youth. This was the case for Josh, who admitted in an interview several weeks into his time at Wildwood House, "I really don't know anything about what this program is about or what it is trying to teach me."

For others, the practice of faking it reinforced some of the skills that had benefited residents in their worlds outside the walls of the institution. Many residents were used to lying and manipulating as strategies to negotiate their lives in school and the family, so the idea of tricking the system mirrored and reinforced these previously developed skills. In the context of Phelan and colleagues' (1993) understanding of identity as negotiated in response to convergence and contradictions in and between worlds, these residents experienced more of a convergence between worlds than divergence. In the absence of friction between the skills they knew from the outside and those they actually used in the facility (manipulation and deception among them), there was little impetus for youth to try on new identities. In some cases, residents experienced the opposite effect. As Terrell explained, he got better at lying in the facility—a skill had had previously honed on the streets.

LAURA: Where did you learn to lie and manipulate like that?
TERRELL: From hanging out on the streets and hanging out with my cousins and stuff, because they're too good of a liars. They lie constantly and stuff, and like my dad used to do it.

LAURA: What do you lie about?

TERRELL: Um, just things. Like if I don't wanna go over to somebody's house, I be like, "Yeah, uh, I'll be over there in 'bout an hour to half hour." You know what I'm saying, I just tell 'em that, and then when I hang up the phone, I forget all about that person and won't even go over there, so.

LAURA: So you had that skill and then you came here, and did it get better?

TERRELL: Yeah, I got better.

Here Terrell claimed that he had seamlessly built upon his street skills to outwit the Unit C staff. But were the staff really that easily manipulated? Were these skills as translatable to facility life as residents believed?

The staff's perspective on faking it was quite varied, but they certainly did not believe that the youth were in any way in control or capable of fully manipulating the system. When asked directly about the extent of the problem, staff's estimations of the proportion of residents who faked their way through the program ranged from 10 to 85 percent, reflecting a lack of a shared acknowledgement or perhaps understanding of the issue. Some staff found it difficult to be certain when a resident was faking his way through the program, whereas others were confident about their ability to detect and confront the issue head-on.

Staff also discussed a variety of techniques they used when they suspected a resident may be faking it, including pushing or challenging the residents to be "more real." For example, one staff member said: "We really push them, really challenge them, to really commit and we will call them on it. And I think they kind of can sense when we're on to that." We observed this type of pushing during some level request or disciplinary meetings, when staff would strongly encourage the boys to drop their façades and start working the program. Still, this strategy of pushing the residents to deeper engagement with the treatment program occurred inconsistently. It was employed in some instances but not others, without great clarity in terms of what warranted the approach in one case over another.

In one routine level and violation meeting, the staff gathered in the small Unit C office to evaluate residents' readiness to move up in the level and privilege system of the facility and to hear behavioral violations and dole out appropriate consequences. Two residents came forward, one after the other, to present their cases to the assembled staff. The first meeting was with Eric, who was requesting to move up a level in spite of a recent conflict and violation hearing for the incident (described in chapter 3) involving his illicit use of the school computers. Mr. Lund was very harsh with him, challenging Eric to be more honest with the staff about what happened with the computer. Eric explained his position and why he didn't "get it" before. Mr. Lund, not satisfied with this explanation, challenged how he could be in the facility for so long and not get it. Mr. McClatchy also admonished him for not interrupting the cycle of family secrets that must have justified Eric's thinking errors in some way. He suggested that Eric needed to start working, rather than just "getting by" in the program. All of the staff who were present in the meeting remarked that Eric hadn't done enough real work in the program, and they unanimously denied his level request.

Eric left the room and Caleb then entered into the office. He was very quiet and withdrawn as the staff outlined the violations he faced on account of his behavior during a weekend visit home. He had failed to call and check-in during the visit, and he also had a late return to the facility. Throughout his violation hearing, Caleb's eyes were lowered, he made virtually no eye contact with the staff, and answered questions in a choppy, abbreviated way, as though nervous or avoidant. Particularly when contrasted to Eric, who had owned up to his behavior and attempted to put it in context for the staff, Caleb demonstrated almost no accountability for the violations, instead citing excuses like "the clock was wrong," "I was busy," and "my dad didn't pick me up on time." Mr. McClatchy suggested that Caleb should be praised for his request to have a one-on-one talk with his primary counselor upon his return to the dorm and for discussing his grief over his father's negligence during peer group (as presented in chapter 3, Caleb had initially denied that his family problems contributed to his delinquency). The staff let him go with a loss of points and a notation of an "unsuccessful weekend," but no level drop.

Both responding to perceived lying and rule violations, these examples provide an interesting contrast. In the first scenario, staff pushed and confronted Eric on lying, his buried family secrets, and his anger at the program. The frustration we observed is that Eric was trying to explain himself, but not in a language the staff accepted. By contrast, Caleb appeared to get off easy on his violation of program rules, simply because he had done some personal disclosure earlier that week. He wasn't confronted on his lying, as he had employed a discourse of family problems that staff took as evidence of program compliance. Here both boys were pushed past their emotional limits, but not in a consistent or seemingly fair way.

Other staff expressed a great deal more indifference to faking it. Consistent with the individual responsibility ethos undergirding Wildwood House's correctional philosophy, a few staff believed that what the youth made of their treatment was solely up to them. As Mr. Lund stated, "Faking it used to bug me a lot. But now, I figure it's on them. We're here. It's a service. If they want it, they can have it. If they don't want it, it's on them. It's like Old Country Buffet; if you walk away hungry, it's your own fault. It still makes me angry when I'm being manipulated, but they run out of hoops to jump through. It's maddening. It's like, 'here's the information—why don't you take it in?!' But in the end, you have to let go." Contrasting sharply with the rhetoric of pushing residents toward honest engagement with treatment, this approach turns the attention back on youth for failing to work the program, rather than on the staff or the program for making greater attempts to make it work.

Some staff even went so far as to say that they were comfortable with faking it, as long as youth were honest about it. Ms. James, a trained therapist, felt that faking it was certainly better than no response to treatment whatsoever. She said: "'Fake it 'til you make it' is fine, as long as you're honest with me about it. Because here's my belief: If you're going fake it 'til you make it, then at least you're practicing new behaviors. And if you're practicing it, then you're going to change." In Ms. James's view, a resident must experience at least some disconnect between the demonstration of behavior and introspection learned inside Wildwood House than they had previously practiced in their outside worlds. To fake it convincingly, residents had to plausibly and at least somewhat consistently try on new performances of self. Thus faking it might actually still require a border crossing (Phelan, Davison, and Yu 1993) into a new type of identity. At the very least, if residents showed buy-in to the program, even if lacking in emotional conviction, they could not avoid learning. Indeed, as we dug deeper into this issue throughout our observations and interviews, we found that Ms. James's perspective was often borne out in practice. Many youths' responses to the program, even those who started from a position of faking it, went well beyond this initial posture.

PATTERNS OF CHANGE

Late one afternoon, Kou, a newer Hmong resident, approached us somewhat shyly, and asked what our job was there. We explained that we were researchers, trying to learn something about what Wildwood House teaches people and how residents change over however many weeks or months they stayed there. His shyness disappeared, and Kou enthusiastically offered his theory, which was that nothing they learn at the facility can help them change at all. What's most important is not really what the facility teaches but rather that they maintain their own desire to change when they leave. He said, "In here, it's easy to be good. There's no temptation. No cars to steal, no drugs, no girls, no gangs." The challenge, he insisted, is when they leave and go back to their old ways.

While the initial tendency to jump through hoops was quite common, it did not necessarily persist throughout residents' time in the facility. Although many of the boys boasted to each other (and us) about their skills in beating the system, what actually unfolded were various strategies to negotiate the messages and expectations of the treatment program in concert or conflict with their own identities and beliefs about themselves. The core of identity work at the facility required the boys to rethink their family system and the origins of their criminal behavior, and through these endeavors to then arrive at an understanding of how to forge different, law-abiding selves in the future. In the remainder of this chapter, we describe a range of responses to this treatment structure, all of which are integral to understanding how change may indeed occur in these settings. These include tenuous transformation, acceptance of the belief that change is possible, and self-preservation of the identities and self-perceptions youth carried with them into the facility.

Tenuous Transformation

"Do kids change while they are here? Yeah, I think they do. The majority have made changes, at least in their way of thinking. Unfortunately, they haven't had enough time to practice it and see enough success with it before we throw them back in their old environment. They can't cut that tie [with family and old habits] because that's all they have, and yet, we can't keep them here forever." As Mr. Lund articulated, change is a difficult process, made even harder to sustain when youth are unable to practice or apply what they have learned from their treatment in a real world situation. In this quote Mr. Lund also implied that the residents' home environments often conflict with or even undermine their individual will to actualize and sustain change. The issues Mr. Lund raised strike at the core of the ambivalence that many youth expressed in regard to identity transformation and behavior change: They wanted to be someone different, but were unsure whether they could translate their new selves to their worlds outside the institution.

Kou's comments from the vignette that opened this section indicate a very real and pressing tension for many residents. As much as the residents stood to learn and practice within the relative safer confines of Wildwood House, many did not feel equipped to handle what might happen when they were sent home. For Kou, what will he actually do when an available car challenged his resolve not to steal? Or when old friends and family ("negative peers" in the parlance of the facility) wanted to hang out? This sense of tenuous transformation, a perceived schism between the self imagined inside the walls of Wildwood and the self well-suited to the world outside, was the most common mode of identity change among the boys who participated in the study, a pattern of thinking particularly noted among Elijah, Jason, and Nino, and was also present among Mario and Josh.

Elijah presents an excellent example of this ambivalent posture. A young man who entered the facility boasting of his ability to make "fast money" and his sexual prowess, Elijah spent a large chunk of time at the facility manipulating the system and complaining about the treatment program. However, as much he wanted to fool the program, he did articulate a tentative rethinking of his criminal behavior over time. In his first interview, Elijah recollected his past self as "a man that's getting a lot of respect from older dudes; getting lots of money; with a lot of women, stay high; always buy his son stuff but doesn't spend time with his son." Yet somewhere in the middle of his confinement, he grew weary of getting into trouble with the staff and began to engage in some deeper thinking about his past, his family, and his future goals.

In the third interview, he also started to imagine the possibility of being a better father to his son, an idealized parent that stood in contrast to his criminally minded (past) self. To Elijah, a good father was, "a man that is willing to go out there to survive for himself and his son and his family. A man that could find a job, go to school, end up being successful in life for his family." In contrast to this good father ideal, Elijah described components of his past life that he deemed to be "headed nowhere." He stated: "I don't wanna be no dad that he [Elijah's son] gotta look at in a casket." The casket image constituted an imagined extreme possibility for his life in the case that he failed to take the program more seriously. Elijah's journey of identity work was particularly illustrative of this pattern of tenuous, or ambivalent, transformation as he clearly struggled to see himself in a different light. Although he adamantly professed himself reformed, he also identified potential challenges to maintaining this new identity such as the influence of his old drug-dealing friends and his need for a decent income.

At the end of his placement, Elijah's commitments to change were even more pronounced; our notes from a late-placement interview with him recorded that: "[Elijah] talked about how he realized he had 'an unmanageable life,' and that he's changed because he used to think he was 'Da Man,' but now he knows 'I ain't the man.'" For Elijah, "Da Man" was the image of who he might have been: powerful, street-wise, and with money to impress and entice numerous women. By the time of his release, he disavowed this former version of self, yet he did not seem to have a firm hold on a substitute image. The transformation remained untested in the real world, and Elijah himself was unable to elaborate on how he might enact his desired change on a day-to-day basis.

This difficulty in anticipating and planning responses to the challenges of the world outside Wildwood House emerged routinely, particularly as residents approached their release dates. As indicated earlier, Mr. Lund suggested that the familiar environments of friends and family, those to which youth were undoubtedly most attached, had to be addressed because of their potential to inhibit or derail the enactment of changes that youth may desire. The residents also raised similar fears as they anticipated bumping up against the familiar trappings of their family members and friends. To negotiate this tension between goals for change and the realities of contending with these influences, many youth adopted a pick and choose mentality about their anticipated associations and activities. Pick and choose, or "selective involvement" (Abrams 2007) meant that youth envisioned hanging out with specific old friends (but not others), using some drugs (but not others) or leaving some, but not all, parts of their criminal selves behind.

Josh, for example, clearly intended to continue some of his prior behaviors. He said, "I plan on smoking weed once I get off probation [because] I still don't think anything's wrong with it." This was a common sentiment among the residents, who considered marijuana to be far less destructive than other harder drugs or even alcohol. The phenomenon of selective involvement extended beyond drugs to other former behaviors and associations as well. Even youth who had expressed an appreciation for the treatment program, such as Jason, had trouble envisioning solid strategies to disassociate themselves from their core peer groups, particularly when those groups included family members. For example, as he was getting ready for his final phases of the program, Jason told us that he planned to simply just leave his gang friends behind and to focus on himself. Yet he could not envision disassociating himself from his cousins, some of whom were still part of the gang. As with Elijah, Jason articulated a strong desire to adopt a new, noncriminal self. Also like Elijah, this commitment to change was tenuous in part due to his inability to envision the reality of its implementation and associated consequences.

Among those residents who engaged directly with questions of how they would maintain their new sense of self in the face of old environments, many expressed fear about the future. They worried that they would not be up to the challenge. Nino, for instance, described an internal struggle between the "good and bad self," represented by the selves in and outside of Wildwood House, respectively. Specifically, he worried that the bad self would convince the good self to return to old behaviors, believing that "I couldn't ever have fun without drinking and smoking. That I should stay out late, hang with my friends, and be drinking or smoking." The bad self contrasted with hopeful images of his future, in which he would be able to get a job, see life differently, and reunite with his twin sons as a father and responsible provider. Nino had indeed worked on these very challenges and he felt mostly confident that his will to succeed would prevail. Despite his impressive ability to be honest about the intensity of these struggles, the staff recorded very discouraging comments in his record, citing him as a master manipulator who was "always holding back." Nino himself agreed with part of this assessment, explaining why he agreed that at times, he didn't do all the work: "Because when I get to talking about my issues, like I was saying, I don't like to be hurt by my family, because I have been hurt for so long. So I would talk about my issues, but I would only go so far. I wouldn't go too deep down with my issues to the point where I'm hurt . . . So I would get basically surface level and talk about my issues, and that way, once I'm done on top, I can go a little bit, and a little bit at a time."

Nino appeared to be grappling with two identity struggles—the internal conflict between his bad self and his good self as represented by his future aspirations for behavioral and identity change, and the struggle to accept a program that both pushed him to the brink of his emotions and also constantly reinforced the message that he wasn't working hard enough. In the face of these struggles, he somehow emerged hopeful about his future and appreciative of the staff of Unit C. His future vision was that of a law abiding, giving, and responsible young man: "Basically, going back to school, doing what I shoulda' been doing in the first place to get my grades back up, to go to college, and be a construction builder, and basically fulfill my dream, which is building a house for me and my mom."

Due to an array of fears and images about what their futures might bring, many youth, like Nino, really wanted to make changes in their lives, yet doubted their ability to translate their the selves they constructed within the walls of the institution to the worlds of their past (and future). This makes sense given the incongruence between the norms and parameters of these worlds, and the lack of time, as they mentioned, to practice their new skills and identities in the presence of real crime temptations and external pressures.

Acceptance: Change is Possible

A core question driving this book is whether meaningful change can occur in the context of an involuntary correctional facility. As the previous section clearly indicated, many even initially reluctant residents expressed a desire to change and even embodied a tenuous transformation of behavior and identity upon leaving the facility. For a minority of young men at Wildwood House, this desire to change was not only considered but also fully adopted. These residents articulated and demonstrated a genuine and not at all reticent self-transformation that they attributed in large part to the treatment program. Although all of the residents struggled to some degree with aspects of involuntary confinement, the narratives of those who accepted this program, most notably Trevor and Kei, and Humphrey as well, had a consistent pattern of change in their self-perceptions as well as their plans and desires for their futures. In a series of stages that progressed over time, these youth developed a critical lens concerning their past, reconciled with some of their past wounds and family problems, and then expressed a seemingly authentic wish to replace their prior selves with alternative identity possibilities, such as a good son, father, or student.

Kei, a sixteen-year-old Hmong resident, is an excellent example of a young person who gradually learned to embrace the need for change in consonance with the expectations of the treatment program. When he entered Unit C, Kei's long rap sheet included truancy, burglary, and numerous police contacts, prompting staff to assess his level of risk for reoffending as "very high" and to label him a "thrill seeker" with "no concern for the impact his misdeeds have on his victims." They considered him a dangerous and manipulative gang member with extremely violent and antisocial tendencies.

Over the course of his engagement with the treatment program, Kei began to describe his past behavior as "bad," coming to the realization that he "can't learn nothing" through crime. He didn't arrive at this position, however, without some internal struggle. Kei explained his initial response to the treatment program and the difficulties of being open to change: "First, I thought it was gonna be bad, a waste of my time, but then after a little while . . . when I was in [another placement], the staff said it was good and all that stuff. And the staff down there [the other placement] was tryin' to help me too. So I was like, 'Yeah. It does seem like it was gonna help.' And the groups helped me a lot too."

Later in this interview, Kei also revealed how he came to accept his prior behavior as problematic and recognize the "wasted time" his criminal history reflected. This awareness allowed him to absorb and benefit the treatment philosophy: "The contracts help a lot, too. They make you realize what's going on in your life. Like, when I wrote that down, it seemed like I wasted my whole life just doin' stupid stuff to get me locked up. Like time is goin' fast, like 'boom, boom, boom.' All of a sudden one year older, I didn't realize that it was goin' that fast."

For Kei, the process of reviewing his criminal behavior through the program's treatment activities pushed him to acknowledge the behavioral trends in his life as negative and launch a process of potentially changing those patterns. Throughout his stay, the staff also noted his very positive attitude toward the program and his hard work. For instance, in response to one of his treatment goals that he examine family influences on his decision to join a gang, staff stated: "Through contract talks and processing his contract work with his parents and his primary, and receiving feedback from peer group members, he has come to a fuller understanding that his surrogate family [the gang] is no substitute for the real thing." Kei's case is an excellent example of how a young man perceived his placement as a major step toward change. As such, he ultimately welcomed the program's philosophy and how it allowed him to rethink his identity in the gang, his role in his family, and his potential for a different future. Upon leaving the facility, staff affirmed his efforts and offered their well wishes: "Hopefully he's ready for the real world."

Trevor, as showcased in chapter 3, also dug deep into his past in order to understand the influence of his family problems on his criminal patterns. Just shy of age fifteen, he was placed in Unit C having already logged five prior charges and three previous correctional placements. One might assume from this record that he would be out of reach; why would Wildwood House's program finally make a difference when the others had clearly failed? Trevor was initially somewhat resistant to the program, and in his intake assessment, the staff wrote that he was wearing "blinders to repress painful feelings and experiences" and noted that he had virtually no strengths or assets. Yet in the end, Trevor felt that he had worked toward full awareness of the blinders he had used to filter out information that could have been damaging to his formerly held self-concept. He stated, "I didn't realize the amount of crimes I'd done. I didn't realize the amount of felonies I have on my record. Here you get the chance to see the stuff that you've avoided, that you've tucked in." Despite the staff's initial assessment of Trevor as prone to avoiding his painful past, he spent a great deal of time writing extensively about these tucked away experiences. Many of his treatment contracts articulated family stories full of parental abuse and neglect, as well as negative experiences in foster homes. From as early as nine years old, Trevor described major trauma in his family. In one treatment contract, he wrote:

> I remember waking up out of a dead sleep because I heard my little brother crying insstancly so I went to see what was going on. He was standing by the bathroom door like he just seen a goast or something. He told me that mom woke him up and told him to run her a bat(h), he said she got in the tub and started screming saying somebody's choking her, help me. He tried to get the door open but he couldn't so I said call the cops. At this time my adrenalin was pumping vary fast and was vary scared because I knew she was drowning. . . . I started kicking the door as hard as I could so I could get in. and it worked. I finally got in and saw my mom's head under water thinking is she dead, what do I do. So I drained the water and lifted her head up out of the water so she would not drowned, then I pulled her out of the tub and covered her up. . . . I thought I will just wate for the cops or the paramedics but then I thought I cant just set here and watch my mom die. So I began CPR on her. Finally the paramedics came and toke her to the hospital an took me and my little brother to a foster home.

Trevor wrote and shared many similar stories of abuse and trauma, about both his mother, who once attacked him with a knife and left him and his brother outside in their underwear in the middle of the night; as well as his father, who had kicked and punched him so uncontrollably at just eleven years old that he ran away from home. In the process of unearthing these difficult experiences and sharing them with staff and other residents, he found a sense of pride in the earnest and hard work he put into making sense of his past and the positive feedback and encouragement that he received from the adults at the facility. As he explained his own process, this knowledge and insight about his past would allow him to forge a different future, one in which he could still be a leader in his group, yet earn respect by doing the right thing this time. Far from being threatened by the shifts in self-concept that this rethinking of self required, Trevor experienced this as a liberating process though which he attempted to forge an identity that still involved leadership, but that would hopefully produce a different outcome.

Staff concurred with Trevor's narrative of transformation. After initially recording that "Trevor seems a little too comfortable here. No one should be that happy," staff comments nearly always reflected his hard work and positive role modeling for other residents: "Trevor has discussed a great deal of his past life with the group and he has always has been very open to advice and feedback from other members, and he has been tremendously supportive toward other members." In other ways, staff affirmed Trevor's perseverance and effort in spite of the emotional difficulty of dredging up and examining the impact of these experiences, even articulating that his work demonstrated the program's completion: "Trevor has been working hard on sensitive issues; he should be proud of himself," and "it is time to let him go!" Trevor indeed carried his new identity with him out of the facility and maintained his goals to keep in touch with the staff, who, he said, had saved him from a life wasted "in the penitentiary."

Kei and Trevor reflect how some residents experienced the right fit and timing with the facility's treatment messages and benefited as a result. Over the course of a few months, both dropped the posture of faking change in order to dig in to the past and trust that the treatment could help them. Consequently, both exited with optimism about creating a very different future.

Self-Preservation

For some residents, a tendency to preserve a positive and preferred view of self persisted throughout the course of treatment. Even a tenuous or fearful adoption of the facility's treatment discourses did not readily occur. Confronted with numerous messages requiring them to reexamine and question their prior selves and their familial influences, these young men consistently employed strategies to preserve their professed identities and in the process, avoided potential opportunities or avenues for change. It is not simply that they faked their way through the program, although that may have been— and was for many—the strategy they selected. Instead, these youth fundamentally disagreed with the treatment program's assumption that something about their identities needed to shift in order for them to succeed upon release. In this way, they resisted not only the program, but its central assumption of their need for rehabilitated self-concepts.

Not surprisingly, Eric was one of the residents who consistently refused to entertain the need to change. He never saw himself as a criminal from the outset, and therefore by the end of his treatment, he felt he was "walking out of here with four months of my life wasted." Similar to Eric but with vastly different backgrounds and criminal histories, Terrell, Brad, and Thomas shared this view that their lives were not headed in a negative direction and as such, there was no need for them to change. Rather, they positioned themselves apart from the other residents who actually needed the help, and smart enough to trick the system entirely.

Terrell's criminal record logged more than ten prior charges ranging from curfew violations to felony theft. His family history included a father who had been convicted of sex crimes and at least twenty siblings or half-siblings in his family system. Terrell's record also noted that he was "blessed into the Crips" gang as a result of his family's longstanding affiliation with this gang. Nevertheless, Terrell maintained a perception of these circumstances as not significantly problematic, or at least not enough to be shared with staff and addressed in treatment. As mentioned earlier in this chapter, Terrell made a conscious choice to conceal personal issues from the staff, both in regard to his family problems and the extent of his substance abuse. Although he admitted to us an extensive history of drug and alcohol use, his facility record noted that "it appears there is not a family history of substance abuse and Terrell is denying ever having used any nonprescribed chemicals including alcohol." Terrell's reluctance to fully disclose the extent of his problems can be interpreted as an attempt to maintain face among counselors and other treatment staff. However, another interpretation of this hesitation to share his past with staff is that he sought to preserve and protect his self-concept and, consequently, prevent recognition of the family problems and influences that likely contributed to his lengthy criminal record and his present situation.

By the end of his stay, Terrell reported to us that his successful manipulation of the program earned him his release in just four months, which was the lower end of his sentence. He described how he accomplished this task: "How'd I convince 'em I changed? Just acting like everybody else who complete the program, because there's somebody out there who completed the program who I'm close to, and I already told him I know how to play programs, because I been in programs before. It's just simple. I just go along with what they say." Essentially Terrell not only won his release, but also played the program so that he wouldn't have to engage in any real work on himself.

The staff did not always record positive opinions about Terrell's progress, but they also did not hold him back from advancing in the program at any juncture. A few comments reflected some skepticism about his record, such as "he has a nice smile—but it often seems fake," and "Mister Slick seems to be getting by in the program. Seems real proud of the crimes that he has done." Yet overall, when it was time for him to proceed through the program levels, the staff did not in any way hold him back. In fact, his interim evaluation noted that Terrell was making progress toward the emotional and behavioral shifts the program attempted to elicit. Specifically, the evaluation cited that Terrell "continued to take emotional risks," "had shown more trust in relationships with staff," "demonstrated willingness to work on his issues," and became a "positive role model for newer residents because of his more positive attitude." Clearly, the staff's view of his earnest attempts to engage in the treatment program conflicted with Terrell's own story of beating the system without ever making any earnest attempts to change. These disparate interpretations of Terrell's progress speak to the fundamental subjectivity of the very notion of treatment progress within a correctional institution such as Wildwood House.

Like Terrell and Eric, Brad managed to keep his identity and positive self-image intact throughout this stay. As mentioned in chapter 4, Brad had an extensive history of family violence and substance abuse, as well as an early induction into criminal activity by older relatives and friends. His committing charge for this placement was a complicated second-degree burglary involving theft from a cemetery. His biological father was listed as incarcerated and his mother, due to substance abuse and mental illness, had abandoned him to live with his aunt, who was also listed as "unstable" and "having substance abuse issues." Without consistent adult supervision, Brad had stopped going to school entirely and relied on theft to make money.

Like Trevor, Brad's record noted that he had suffered consistent and deeply wounding family traumas throughout his life. His assigned treatment goals included looking "more in depth at his family situation" and "at the pain and hurt he is experiencing and try to find some peace." During his exit interview with us, Brad consistently denied that any of these family issues had contributed to his current situation. Admitting that he did at times resort to stealing in order to obtain money for basic needs such as food or rent, he still refused to tie his behavior to his earlier family traumas or circumstances. Rather, he felt "mad" that staff would change his contracts or force him to write down things he didn't believe. As in other interview experiences, Brad had considerable difficulty even talking about what it was like to be at Wildwood House because he believed so ardently that the program had nothing to offer him. Even when he was able to articulate some benefits he experienced at the facility, such as the ability to stop and think about his life, he was clear that these benefits came exclusively from his own time for self-reflection.

Interestingly, Brad even offered suggestions about what kind of program he thought would have helped him. He said that he would have learned more from a program that focused exclusively on discipline; what he wanted was just punishment. Oddly similar to Eric in this way, Brad believed that although his behaviors may have been bad, that did not mean his identity needed fixing. Bad behavior is curbed with punishment, according to his perspective. He added, responding to a question about what might have been more effective for him:

BRAD: Well, if I were to make this place better, it'd be like lockdowns, beat-downs, and stuff. So I would make sure they won't come back. That would make me not come back, getting beat down and just . . . having little cells like down there [in a holding facility] where every room is locked down and you just sit in there all day, come out for like an hour, take showers or something.

LAURA: So you think they're too easy on you here?

BRAD: They're too easy. This is an easy place.

Despite Brad's reticence to admit any benefits of the Wildwood House program, the staff were very positive about the presumed gains that Brad made including his work on his family problems, which they associated with him coming to terms with his mother's substance abuse and overall absence from his life. Staff consistently noted that he was "working hard and opening up." A few comments were logged about his sneakiness, but overall, he enjoyed, as Terrell did, a great deal of support for his release in just four and a half months. In the end, Brad exited with the steadfast opinion that his life was (and had been) fine, and that the program was "a waste of a couple of months."

CONCLUSION

Faking it raises a number of concerns about integrity of a treatment program as delivered in an involuntary correctional institution, including whether this set-up has the potential to make youth worse by reinforcing the value of manipulation. It also challenges the apparent value of tying rewards and punishment to perceived therapeutic progress, particularly when many youth believed that they were able to trick the staff into believing that they had taken the program seriously.

The tendency to fake it, however, was not a universal façade. As time wore on, many of the youth experienced either an ambivalent or more consistent and comprehensive buy-in to the treatment program. In the realm of identity, most residents were selectively or tenuously adapting to program messages seeking to reshape or reexamine the self. In doing so, they simultaneously filtered out messages and treatment recommendations that were distal from their realities, but also sought to accept the need to change their lives for reasons beyond just earning their release. Similar to patterns of identity and change found in other involuntary institutional contexts (Juhila 2004; Paterniti 2000), the young men of Unit C employed a variety of strategies to preserve a sense of self as they encountered threats to their previously held identities. For some, like Brad, Eric, and Terrell, this process eclipsed the possibility for genuine change in accordance with treatment expectations.

Yet more commonly, the residents found themselves in a heated internal struggle between the old and the new, or between the self they had become and the self they wanted to become. This dilemma was well illustrated in both Elijah and Nino's narratives, which provided a deeper view of the struggles associated with this type of identity work. The next chapter illustrates how these internal struggles unfolded once the youth were returned to the community, the juncture at which they were quite happy to be free, yet simultaneously wary of the potentially destructive trappings of their old environments.

CHAPTER 6

On the Outs

Some of the kids are prepared to leave, and some not. A lot of the kids fight
the system, fight the staff, fight the change. And we've got to let them go.
Throwing together supports for aftercare and hoping the tape holds.
(Mr. Robbins)

You see so many kids that fail and go back to their old ways right when
they get out but when you look at these kids have been in the environment
they are from for sixteen years and we get them for six months, so you can
only expect so much . . . it's tough to do a lot in six months. But at the same
time there are kids that do change. (Mr. Morales)

The success of any juvenile correctional program, whether punitive or
rehabilitative in its orientation, is typically measured by what happens to the
youth when they return to society. Will they become law–abiding citizens or
will they continue to commit crimes? Irrespective of one's political position
on how to best address youth crime, the general consensus appears to be that
correctional programs work when they prevent repeat offending, and as long
as that end is achieved, the methods employed along the way are less rele-
vant. As indicated by the persistence of high rearrest and reincarceration rates
among formerly incarcerated youth (see chapter 1), the return to society,
often referred to as reentry or reintegration, is quite challenging for many
young people. The quotes from the staff that open this section both hint at
the central idea that long-lasting behavior change is sorely tested upon reentry, and that perhaps the best that any program can hope for is that something that youth learn during confinement will assist them in successfully
overcoming these challenges.

Research has shown that upon the return to society, youth face an array
of barriers toward successfully reestablishing themselves logistically, economically, and emotionally. Many young people exit correctional institutions
with the desire to complete basic tasks related to school and employment,
but find school reentry or locating a viable job to be out of their reach (Bullis
and Yovanoff 2002). The acquisition of stable housing also presents challenges, as youth whose family relations are strained or who have aged out of

designated foster care or juvenile housing placements may wind up without a secure place to live (Altschuler and Brash 2004).

These logistical and financial concerns can be compounded by some of the emotional dimensions of the reentry experience. Despite the comfort that close family members and friends can provide for returning young people, these connections may also hold potential for emotional strife and other layers of difficulties (Martinez and Abrams 2011). For example, returning to one's family can be experienced as a relief for a young person but may also become troublesome when family dynamics continue to be dysfunctional, or when families even encourage, either tacitly or explicitly, a return to criminal activity (Breese, Ra'el, and Grant 2000; Parkman 2009). Reconnecting with old friends may also challenge a young person's resolve to forge a new pathway, or, on the other hand, may lead to a sense of isolation or loneliness if these familiar friends are avoided (Abrams 2007; Hughes 1998; Fader 2008). In this complex relational playing field, youths' personal goals to achieve a different type of future are often compromised by the temptations and pressures they encounter in their home and community environments.

In chapter 5, we laid out a series of findings concerning the residents' responses to the treatment program, ranging from rejection of all program influences to a genuine embracing of the treatment program's goals and philosophy. As many of the boys anticipated, particularly those who had strong motivation to change, the true challenge of accomplishing the personal work required of them by Wildwood House would be put to test upon their release. This relates in essence to young people's ability to enact a new version of the self when they cross back into their old worlds (Phelan, Davison, and Yu 1993), without the same set of messages, rules, or norms that they became accustomed to in the institution. With this theory in mind, this chapter examines the reentry experiences of several Wildwood House youth to better understand the process of border crossing from the world of the institution into the worlds of their lives "on the outs." These stories are presented according to the three patterns of change described in chapter 5 (self-preservation, tenuous transformation, and acceptance that change is possible), demonstrating that just as experiences of treatment varied widely among these groups and the individuals comprising them, so did their forays into the outside world. This chapter on reentry thus highlights both variations and similarities among the boys' stories and in doing so, provides another layer of critical information about the potential for juvenile correctional programs to influence (for the better) the course of young men's lives.

PREPARING FOR EXIT

As a whole, Wildwood House staff members were very concerned about preparing youth for reentry, and as the statements that opened this chapter indicate, many had major doubts that four to six months of treatment could overcome the external forces waiting to challenge the residents' resolve upon their release. A series of steps were built into the program to help youth get ready for exit, including weekend visits home for those on higher program levels. During these weekends at home, residents were required to make frequent call-ins to the facility, to attend various treatment groups (such as Alcoholic Anonymous) in the community, and for those classified as drug or alcohol dependent, to take a urine test upon their return on Sunday nights. Through these weekend contracts, the supervisory relationship between the facility and the youth was maintained. Staff routinely deemed the residents' weekends unsuccessful for such reasons as failing to make their required call-ins, testing positive for drugs or alcohol, or returning back to the facility past curfew. When weekends were unsuccessful, the staff would call a meeting during which the resident was required to explain the circumstances surrounding the weekend, and after some questioning and discussion, the staff would then dole out appropriate consequences.

For example, after a series of weekends without full rule compliance, Thomas was called into the staff office for such a meeting. Although the staff were friendly, their approach to Thomas's case was characterized by fairly strict rule compliance. They confronted him about having failed to get his mother's signature on his weekend contract. Staff also noted that this was his fourth weekend violation for not doing well at home and suggested that his weekend privileges be halted. They then dismissed Thomas from the meeting. Each unsuccessful weekend was assessed and consequenced through a similar process and on an individual basis. In Thomas's case, he lost points, was written up for violations, and temporarily lost his visiting privileges. Nevertheless, as time (and not always treatment compliance) was often the benchmark for discharge, even residents who had multiple unsuccessful weekends, like Thomas, were still typically released in the court ordered four to six month time frame. Staff noted this apparent contradiction in Thomas's records. Commenting on his criminally involved family members and strong affiliation with a neighborhood gang, they recorded upon his exit: "Real nice kid. Too bad he has to go back to his old environment."

Once discharged from the facility, youth were placed on aftercare status, which kept them connected to the Wildwood House program for supervision and treatment. The aftercare program, typically lasting three months (but sometimes less), was considered the highest program level and an extension of a resident's sentence. During the official aftercare period, residents were linked with specifically designated aftercare workers (who were not the same as the unit workers). Ms. Breuer explained the links between the in-house program and aftercare: "We prepare them the best we can, we hook them up with resources, we talk about what's going to happen when you

leave, and you come up with a plan for each kid. Aftercare helps with this."
The aftercare workers monitored the implementation of individualized reentry plans that often encompassed issues such as school reentry, drug tests, and
overall probation compliance. Aftercare expectations closely mirrored those
related to the home visits; youth were required to call in to their aftercare
workers at scheduled times, abide by a curfew, attend weekly aftercare groups
in the community, and for some, participate in drug testing. If a resident
failed to comply with any of these terms, consequences could include a brief
return to Wildwood House or, in the case of more severe rule infractions, a
referral to the juvenile court for a probation violation hearing.

Clearly, the aftercare workers' primary responsibility was to ensure
youths' compliance with their probation orders. Yet the program was also
intended to provide a bridge from the intensity of the program to life in the
community, offering support to young people as they navigated some of the
untested circumstances that many were nervous about their ability to manage. The reasons to provide the type of bridge are plentiful, and the importance of aftercare support is well documented in the research literature
(Altschuler and Armstrong 1994; Altschuler and Brash 2004). Yet even given
this support and structure, how well did the youth from Wildwood House
adjust to their newfound freedom? Did cognitive preparation for exit translate into real-world success, or were the worlds inside and outside the facility
too incongruous, as some staff and residents feared? Did youth retain the
value and messages of the treatment program as they looked back upon their
stay in Unit C?

In this chapter we provide some preliminary answers to these important
questions. All of the young men who participated in this study faced real-
world challenges and crime temptations, such as the lure of old friends and
influences, the availability of drugs and alcohol, the need to make money,
community and gang violence, and family problems. Still, often following
the patterns of identity change noted in the prior chapter, some youth were
able to draw upon the lessons learned in the facility, while others teetered on
the edge of behaviors that were bound to—or did—land them back in institutional life. Perhaps the most compelling piece of these reentry stories is that
even the young men who had very strong motivation to change felt themselves compromised by the environments that constituted their daily lives.

THE SELF-PRESERVATIONISTS: BRAD AND ERIC

These first two scenarios involve Brad and Eric, who as we saw in chapter 5, steadfastly resisted the facility's attempts to help them to rethink their
identities. As their backgrounds in regard to criminal history and family structure were vastly different, so were their reentry experiences. Despite these
differences, it is interesting to note similarities in their insistence on beating

the system and their attempts to preserve their sense of self and values despite programmatic attempts to change them.

Brad: Skirting the System

As suggested in prior chapters, Brad had very low regard for the treatment program at Wildwood House and often stated that he would have preferred swift punishment, such as sitting in a locked cell, rather than enduring hours of painstaking therapy programs. Although he came from a deeply troubled family system, he returned to live under the supervision of his aunt following his release. While in the formal records staff expressed confidence that Brad had made the requisite changes for exit, we were somewhat skeptical about his chances for success based on his own admission of faking it. Perhaps on account of our suspicions, we asked Brad's aftercare worker about his status just four weeks after his exit. We learned that he was on the run; he had failed to comply with all aftercare rules since the moment he was discharged from Unit C.

We tracked Brad down at the local juvenile detention facility to conduct a follow up interview. The juvenile detention facility was quite unlike Wildwood House. It was a holding tank for youth awaiting trail, locked and monitored, with youth confined to cells most of the day. The setting struck us as more the real deal jail for youth than Wildwood House, which wasn't really even a lock-up by comparison. Comparing the two facilities revealed to us how lucky the boys at Wildwood were, in a sense, to be there and not a more restrictive setting. After the guards located Brad, they led us through a series of electronically monitored doors and let us into a locked meeting room about five feet wide by seven feet deep, with brick walls, a round cafeteria table, and plastic chairs. There was also a window on the door so staff could see in but couldn't hear our discussion.

We first asked Brad how he ended up at the detention center. He reported that after he left Unit C, he simply didn't want to do his aftercare program. He stopped going to the group or checking in with his worker, so the aftercare staff sentenced him to go back to Unit C for a weekend. Because he really "couldn't stand to go back there," he decided to run away to his mother's house. He knew that he would get caught at some point but stated that he "really didn't care." When asked why he didn't comply with aftercare, he stated that he simply "didn't want to do all the stuff," especially the call-ins to his aftercare worker and the weekly support group. Brad boasted that upon release from the detention center (likely to occur within the week) he would have a two-week program at another facility but then he'd be off all monitoring, including aftercare and probation. We asked if spending time in juvenile jail was worth it, to avoid aftercare. He replied yes, he definitely thought it was a worthwhile trade-off.

Brad described what his life was like in the short time he was free. For the most part, he reported feeling "really happy," and spent his time "sleeping, seeing friends, and looking for work." He was on the verge of accepting a job helping his neighbor with a construction business when the police arrested him for violating his probation orders. Although he spoke without much enthusiasm, he did seem more upbeat than when he was at Wildwood House. His general mood was consistent with his prior stance: that he would prefer to be locked up and do his time than endure more therapy. Brad recounted in detail a weekend when he and a friend took their bikes, camping, and fishing gear to a lake and spent the weekend outdoors. Brad had a great time this particular weekend because, in his words, "I finally felt free." It was an odd juxtaposition: this celebration of the feeling of freedom shared while confined in juvenile detention, all as the result of disengagement from a program intended to support his increasing freedom.

In the month since his release, Brad reported that he had avoided using marijuana or engaging in criminal activity. When pressed further, he assured us that "for real," he didn't have the desire to smoke anymore, although plenty of marijuana had been available to him. He described also being bombarded by offers to return to theft in order to make money. He claimed that he had refused all of these opportunities because he didn't want go back to jail (again, in spite of behaviors to the contrary that had landed him back in juvenile detention). Although Brad mentioned a few instances of hanging out with some of his old crime buddies, he insisted that he wasn't at all tempted to go to that life, stating "if there is a job, there is no need for crime."

When asked what lessons he took away from his time in Unit C, Brad replied that he had literally forgotten about being there and "didn't learn a thing." He still believed that all the "therapy stuff was total bullshit" and that one reason he failed to comply with aftercare was that he didn't want to attend the required weekly support groups. Brad reiterated that it was worth it to go on the run and get locked up for a few weeks rather than spending a weekend back in the dorm. He boasted that he had successfully played the game to get out and "jumped through hoops" (his words precisely) to earn his release. Nearing the end of the conversation, Laura asked him: "In the end, what should the story be about Brad?" He simply responded: "Brad was happy to be out, and doing well and just needs a job." Much to our surprise, his statement seemed to be true. Brad was successfully discharged from probation and had not incurred any recorded juvenile or adult charges up to eighteen months after this final interview took place.

Eric: The Narrative Sticks

Shortly after Eric left Wildwood House, he and his parents moved out of state. This move officially ended Eric's probation in the county where he had received his sentence, so he was not required to complete the aftercare program. As mentioned throughout this book, Eric skirted the edges of Unit C's social and treatment worlds for his whole stay, never quite buying into the program, nor receiving any level of acceptance from the staff or his peers. His experience being so unique in our observations, we knew that we would want to check in with him after his release. Fortunately, Eric provided us his e-mail address upon his departure. We wrote to him about four months later, posing general questions about his relocation, his new school, his family, and what he thought of his stay in Unit C once he had some time to look back. A few days later, he responded with a long and very detailed e-mail.

Eric began by filling us in on his new life. He assured us that he was making "all As" in his honors classes, even without putting too much effort into his studies. He was happy to make new friends and described his school life "better than ever." Regarding his family, he described his relationship with his parents as a "sore subject," stating "my parents haven't changed a bit- they still aggravate the hell out of me." In a noteworthy departure from his previous narrative that denied any significant family issues, he opened up more about his family problems, describing his mother as very controlling and restrictive. He also wrote that he deeply missed the company of his older brother, who had not moved with them, and that he was very unhappy being with his parents alone.

Socially, as in his previous school, he found himself torn between two cliques: the "druggie" group ("kids that aren't afraid to be themselves and express themselves however they want to") and the "normal kids," who "had higher morals and brains," but were "a little less fun to be around." He tended to look down on the druggie group but found them still appealing for their expressions of individuality. He wrote: "No offense to the druggies or anything, but sometimes I wish I was dumb so I could fit in better, but having a brain in the group I guess isn't so bad for them." Eric was confident that he was making the right choices with regard to friends and keeping his footing in both worlds.

As anticipated based on his limited criminal history and determination never to return to a facility like Wildwood House, Eric had stayed out of trouble since his departure. As his time away from the facility lapsed, he became even more convinced than he that he didn't learn anything of value from Wildwood House: "I know it was a complete waste of time. I wasn't saying what they wanted to hear, I said what I had to say to get my ass outta there, and to do that I had to make them think that I've changed. I'll take for granted that I have changed in the sense that I'll never do an offense to the degree of the one that I did do, but as for other things, like my personality, how I view the world, etc., I haven't changed a bit."

Still insisting that the program did not influence him in any way, he made it clear that his identity (i.e., the way he views the world, his personality and

values) was completely intact. He next railed against the program for trying
to "cram stuff in his head" that he already knew, since he was indeed "smart
enough to have morals." Maintaining his air of superiority, he wrote:

> I can see where the program would be a great help to somebody that has
> grown up in a broken home or somebody with a low IQ, or somebody
> with drug problems, etc., but the program is just is NOT designed to
> "treat" kids with an IQ above the "legally mentally challenged" level
> and a little brain power. When I first got there I had no idea what I was
> supposed to do, but by the time I left that shit-hole, I picked up on how
> to cheat and beat the system, just like any other. Every system, constitu-
> tion, anything along those lines ever made can be beat. It's not that I
> want to go around and beat up every system I encounter, but in the case
> of the program it was necessary to get my life back. Not to mention, it
> wasn't that hard to beat, either.

From this correspondence, it appeared that Eric steadfastly held to his belief
that he had cheated the system, which he described as "a bunch of crap neatly
tied up with a little bow-tie." He likened his beating the system to playing a
game of chess, where you have to outwit and outplay your opponent. He
mocked the staff for believing that he had changed his criminal ways and
resolved his family issues: "Ha, I laugh at them. I laugh at them hard! I've
come to the conclusion that Wildwood House was just an ideal niche for
morons, gullible authorities, and depressed people to live and work."

Last, Eric asserted that he had changed his criminal mindset, but not in
any way due to the treatment program. Finally admitting that he did actually
have a criminal thinking pattern in the past, he stated that he found new ways
to let out his rebellious streak with less harmful consequences, such as smoking
cigarettes. He considered cigarette smoking to be his assertion of his freedom
and an outlet for the "rebellion that I can't have enough of." He attributed the
change in mindset to being free from the facility, in general feeling mentally
healthier: "When I was in there, my mental health was the lowest it's ever
been. It's the one thing in my life that I look back at and it just hurts. I'm not
going to commit another crime that will jeopardize my freedom."

Even with the many advantages he could claim—a new environment, a
good school record, and a stable family—it is noteworthy how much Eric's Unit
C experiences still informed his identity. It may not have been the influence that
Wildwood House's treatment program intended, but there was an impact
nonetheless; the resentment of the system that confined him and the newfound
appreciation of freedom seemed likely to prevent him from future involvement
in crime. Due to his move to another state, we were unable to track if he had
incurred any new charges. However, despite his self-perception as a rebel capable of beating any system, a life of crime did not appear to be in his future.

Common threads concerning patterns of change emerge from these two fairly dissimilar stories. First, Brad and Eric both claimed that they were motivated to change purely for deterrence reasons, expressing with certainty that they did not want to endure any future involuntary confinement. Second, both were insistent that the program did nothing to change them, and that any changes they had made were due to their own will. And finally, both highly cherished their freedom after their stay at Wildwood House, which bolstered their sense of happiness, or in Eric's terms, his "mental health."

As far as the others who tended toward self-preservation, we know fairly little, since our attempts to follow up with them directly failed. Still, we learned some fragments from court records and conversations with aftercare staff. Terrell apparently managed to stay out of trouble up to sixteen months after his release. We were unable to locate him for a final interview since according to the aftercare workers he often skipped the group and appeared, unsurprisingly, to get away with it. Among this group, only Thomas, who had progressed easily through his time at the facility, had incurred several new felony charges two years after his release, both in the juvenile and adult criminal justice systems. Although the longer-term picture for these youth is unknown, it is striking that regardless of their lack of buy-in to the program, most of these young men averted trouble with the law in the twelve to eighteen months following their release.

BETWIXT AND BETWEEN: REMAINING AMBIVALENT

As detailed in chapter 5, many residents had an ambivalent sense of buy-in to treatment discourses and acceptance of their need to change. This ambivalence was reflected in residents' uncertainty about letting go of their previously held identities, and also in how they tended to bounce back and forth between working to benefit from the treatment program and trying to beat the system. Two residents in particular, Jason and Elijah, continued to experience this ambivalence about change upon their reentry, which became further complicated as they faced their old friends and social influences.

Jason: Dodging Trouble

Although Jason had often expressed to us how much he learned in Unit C, he did not successfully complete the program. In fact, during our observation period, he was one of just a handful of youth who was terminated due to a breach of the rules. Throughout the program, staff consequenced Jason several times on account of gang threats and fighting. After his sixth event, occurring about five months into his stay, Jason was removed from Wildwood House for fighting with another resident. The court subsequently sentenced him to the local detention center (the same one where we interviewed

Brad) for two weeks, after which he was placed on electronic home monitoring and probation. Because he left unsuccessfully and was not mandated to
complete the aftercare program, Jason maintained no connections to Unit C
staff or aftercare workers.

When we reached him a few months after his abrupt departure, Jason had
just completed his house arrest and was nearing the end of his probation period.
Contacting him by phone, we made arrangements to meet him at his high
school. We were somewhat surprised to find that he was attending a large,
mainstream high school, as his record had indicated that he was performing at
a second or third grade level in most subjects, often got into fights in school,
and had a record of extreme truancy. Nevertheless, he was enrolled in the
eleventh grade. Although he did not show up for our first scheduled meeting,
our second attempt proved successful. After a few minutes of uncertainty, waiting outside the main office at the end of the school day, we saw Jason walking
toward us, wearing baggy jeans, a collared shirt and a heavy puffy jacket. He
immediately saw us and smiled. We suggested that we leave the school grounds
to walk around his neighborhood and grab a soda along the way.

Our meeting with Jason was unique among all our visits with former residents in that he had the opportunity to show us his neighborhood and school
environments. Repeatedly, he talked about how happy he was that we
"finally came to [his] school," and that we weren't just "playing him" by pre-
tending we were coming to visit. On our walk around the neighborhood,
Jason took us to his childhood library and showed us the section where he
used to look at books with his brothers. As we continued, he shared memories of growing up in his largely immigrant neighborhood. Jason termed his
surroundings "very ghetto," although the neighborhood appeared to us to be
working-class, with single family and duplex homes and tree lined streets; it
certainly did not strike us as a stereotypical ghetto. Despite this appearance,
the neighborhood was known for gangs and violent activity, particularly
among Hmong youth.

When we walked by his old middle school, Jason noticed a group of his
friends on the corner. He had mentioned earlier that he didn't want to interact with these friends "because they're negative," so when we passed them,
he said to Ben, "block me," and moved aside so they couldn't see him. He
later disclosed that he hid from his friends because didn't want to have to talk
to anyone about who we were. He also mentioned that he didn't want to
have to explain to his homies why, if his electronic home monitoring had
ended, he wasn't hanging out with them anymore. This moment bore wit-
ness to Jason's apparent struggle: On the cusp of being free from home monitoring, his homies literally awaited his return to his old life, as signaled by
their lingering on the corner. To us, Jason appeared to be just barely dodging
trouble.

Jason was teetering on the edge of his old life of gangs and violence while also attempting to hang on to his cherished freedom. He was clearly trying to please his family more (a matter which had become important to him), but was simultaneously flirting with danger. He reported, for example, that he still smoked marijuana and drank alcohol sometimes, but not every day as he had in the past. He also said that he no longer hung out with his "negative friends," but they still came over to his house now and again. Similarly, he talked about ditching class only occasionally at his new school, but then he added that he persuaded his new friends to ditch with him. He was clearly not clean in the sense of following all the rules required by probation, home, and school, but we did get the sense that he was trying.

At one point, Laura asked Jason if he missed Unit C in any way. Although he was still mad about being kicked out and resentful toward a few of the staff, he replied that at times, he missed the structure. Looking back, he remained ambivalent about the whole experience. On the one hand, he felt that it was a "waste of six months of [his] life." In the next statement, he said that it "helped just a little bit." In the end, Jason believed that he had made changes in himself because he wanted to, but not due to the influence of the treatment program. Consistent with his overall ambivalent posture, Jason remained insecure about his ability to change and nervous about what might happen once his probation was fully terminated. Given this ambivalence and lack of confidence, along with his admitted substance use and associations with gang friends, we were surprised to find out two years later that Jason had no further juvenile arrests in the state, and only one adult charge pertaining to a minor traffic violation. Jason had managed to steer clear of trouble, despite the multitude of factors that seemed to be working against him.

Elijah: Still Got the Street in Him

Exactly two months after his release date, we ran into Elijah in Unit C on a Sunday afternoon. Elijah had been court ordered to return to Wildwood House for twenty-four hours for failing to comply with his aftercare plan. We spotted him during recreation time and noted that he seemed very comfortable there, fitting back into the social rhythm of the dorm and playing basketball with the better athletes. When he noticed our presence, Elijah appeared excited to see us and immediately walked over to ask us if we wanted to interview him. Although he was leaving in just a few hours to return home, he wanted to make sure that we got his story on record.

Elijah began the conversation with a broad overview of his life since release. He started by talking about how his relationships had improved: He was getting along much better with his mother and stepfather and had reunited for a short period of time with his son's mother. He explained that he wasn't seeing her anymore in a romantic way, because he found out that she had cheated on him while he was at the facility. He seemed genuinely upset about these events, even though he had often cheated on her in the past, and his expectations of monogamy were fairly ambiguous. Elijah didn't appear to be too open to changing his opinion about either her behavior or his response to it.

Elijah then switched gears to talk about crime. He admitted that he had encountered some temptations to sell drugs, particularly because he needed money to support his son. The lure of making fast money had been hard for him, harder than he had ever imagined. However, he resisted these crime temptations in order to stay out of jail. He felt this decision was simple, explaining: "It's easy for me [not to sell drugs]. I just don't want to, 'cuz I don't wanna be back in here. Or I don't wanna be away from my son no more." Although Elijah had not sold drugs, he did later admit to using marijuana, which, if discovered, would have constituted a probation violation. Twice during the interview, he denied using marijuana, only to admit later in our interaction to having smoked since his release. Once he admitted using, he stated that he felt very confident that had the situation under control, because he was not addicted. To him, smoking once or twice a week was not a problematic pattern like his prior daily habit had been. This was a very similar story that we heard from Jason in regard to marijuana use. Overall, Elijah described feeling still very torn between his old self, the one with "the street in him," and his new self, including the type of responsible father and provider that he wanted to be for his son. This betwixt and between position seemed to be reflected in his twenty-four hour hold at Unit C and his admission of occasional drug use. He was indeed testing the waters of his newfound freedom.

Looking back on his stay in Unit C, Elijah still had mixed feelings about its value. On the one hand, he claimed to have retained skills he learned in his cognitive behavioral skills group, such as "thought stopping." He also learned about the value of attending and completing high school and he had enrolled in a probation school upon his release. On the other hand, he stated that he very seldom reflected on the therapeutic work he did in the program, and that for the most part, he found the written treatment contracts to be of little personal meaning for him. Elijah mainly looked back on his time at the facility as fun, likening his social life in Unit C to "a summer camp." He mentioned that he and his aftercare friends often reminisced about dorm pillow fights and fun times that indeed sounded to us more like summer camp than jail. When he did find time for personal reflection, he simply felt grateful to have his freedom back: "When I think about it with myself, I be like, 'Damn, I'm so glad I'm outta that place.' I got my freedom. I can take a shower without anybody lookin' at me." According to Elijah, his freedom was not worth abandoning just to make fast money.

Elijah was still tied to his narrative of beating the system, boasting to us many times how well he succeeding in manipulating the staff. He talked about the sneaky stuff he did with other residents and the ways he lied to earn his freedom. Still, he suggested many times that he learned things "here and there." Most importantly, he said, he developed a greater sense of caring about his son and his own future. This was consistent with his story as a whole; over the course of his treatment and reentry, his son increasingly came to represent his major catalyst for change.

As for future goals, Elijah proudly related to us that he was recently selected to play for an amateur league basketball team. For this opportunity, he said that he would even quit smoking cigarettes and marijuana. But most importantly, his immediate goals were to stay out of jail and to provide for his son. If nothing else, Unit C had given him the opportunity to "get more serious" about his life. As one of the young men in the study who was the most traditionally masculine in his self-conception and social presentation, it seemed fitting that the idea of becoming a better provider for his son was motivating him to stay out of trouble. He talked about the importance of some staff role models at the facility, notably the African American men, who had taught him these lessons about manhood. Consistent with his previous views, this discussion about manhood centered on his position as a father, but did not reflect on how he treated his son's mother or other women. Nevertheless, his desire to perform a type of masculinity associated with being a better provider and father constituted his main hook toward change.

As always, Elijah had provide us with interesting reflection points: Could someone consider the program a joke but still get something out of it? Might Elijah's attachment to the masculine ideals of the strong provider indeed help him to stay out of trouble, even if a similar sense of masculinity and his quest for power had been a strong entrée into his array of past crimes? Could his fear of being controlled by the system keep him out of trouble? Unfortunately, it seemed not, as records from about twenty-one months after this final interview revealed that Elijah had experienced legal trouble for probation violations and was later convicted in adult court of weapons possession. As much as he professed to want to be an admirable and providing father, the trappings of his street self seemed to have caught up with him in a way that he was unable to avoid. Jason's and Elijah's stories are important, as they illustrate the pressures these young men faced in their outside worlds: of old friends (and gangs), drug use, and the practical need for money. They also both described themselves as living out a particular quandary: wanting desperately hold onto their freedom, but not knowing or necessarily wanting to escape the trappings of their pasts in order to make this happen.

Like Elijah and Jason, other ambivalent youth also struggled with the pressures of the outside world. According to the aftercare staff, about one month after his release, Nino was sentenced to another facility for sixty to ninety days for failing to comply with his probation orders. His longer-term official record was not located when later queried. Josh also did not comply with aftercare. His whereabouts unknown, the aftercare worker at that time said that when Josh was finally picked up, he would face charges for violating his probation. Sixteen months later, official reports indicated that he had incurred at least two new juvenile convictions and was back in a longer-term program at Wildwood House. Only two of the five youth in the ambivalent group (Jason and Mario) had no new charges on their official records at eighteen or twenty-four months after their release. Although we did not have the opportunity to record all these stories, we would surmise that the pressures of the social environment, coupled with ambivalence about change, all amounted to various circumstances and events that led many of these residents back into crime.

READY TO CHANGE: TREVOR

Far from ambivalent, a few youth left Wildwood House with great confidence in their ability to sustain the changes in behavior and identity that they had made in the treatment program. Trevor and Kei stand out among this group, and Humphrey possessed a similar outlook. All three left with the goals of creating a different future and avoiding the triggers that might facilitate a return to past behaviors. Following up in detail with Trevor provides a glimpse into how this will to succeed meshed and conflicted with real world experiences.

Unlike the majority of the residents of Unit C, Trevor wanted to stay connected to the staff upon his departure. He frequently called the staff and visited the dorm on several nonrequired occasions. Trevor was a willing participant in the aftercare program and was attending a probation school. Although we had briefly seen him at the facility during one of his voluntary visits, we hadn't connected with him one-on-one. When we finally reached him by phone about three months after his departure he was eager to talk to us, and we made a plan to meet him between school and his aftercare group.

On a chilly December day, we met Trevor outside his school, where he was standing with a few probation school students who were also former Wildwood House residents. Trevor wore a ball cap, baggy pants, a button down shirt, and a large down jacket. He told his friends he was going to talk to "these guys" (pointing to us) and left his friends behind. We walked over to a small diner where we ordered some soft drinks. In our initial moments of conversation, Trevor was quite distant; he avoided eye contact, sat as far away from us as he could without being rude, and felt generally out of reach. We noted this as unusual for him, in stark contrast to his typically positive and engaged demeanor. Given his visible discomfort, we began with some small talk about his life since release, the research study, and some of the residents we knew in common. He informed us that his father had bought a new house, left the girlfriend Trevor had disliked, and helped him to get a job at his business. When we asked about his son, Trevor said with a smile, "I knew you were going to ask that." This interaction seemed to break the ice a bit, as it reestablished our conversational familiarity.

Before going into detail about his family or his aftercare program, Trevor admitted that staying out of trouble was, in itself, extremely challenging, and "much harder than he had ever imagined." That, with the requirements of aftercare added on, had become difficult for him to manage. The way he contented with these challenges (with ninety-nine percent success, he reported) was to "lay low": meaning not socializing, staying in the house, and "keeping a low profile." Going to a probation school rather than a large public high school had also helped him to stay out of trouble. When asked to identify the hardest component of reentry, Trevor responded that staying in after curfew was the most difficult piece. He admitted breaking the rules by going out after his mandatory nightly call to his aftercare worker, which seemed to contradict his earlier statements about laying low.

Trevor reported that his home life had presented many challenges, which may have accounted in part for why he his broke curfew so often. He told us a story about how he and his father had recently "duked it out" in a nasty fist-fight, one so severe that he had to take his father to the hospital for stitches. Contrary to Wildwood House's lesson that communication is a preferred means of coping with family stress as opposed to violence, Trevor seemed proud of himself for having won the fight. He boasted that on account of these injuries, he didn't think that his father would "mess with him" again. This story raised further inconsistencies. For example, Trevor initially said that he and his father were getting along "really well," but then later told the story of this horrible fight. When asked if his father was caring for him "as a dad," he initially reported that things were better, but then admitted they really weren't better, because his father was "still at the bar a lot." Trevor then added: "I'm doing this on my own, guys. You know that," alluding to his entire life history of basically raising himself without stability or consistent parenting. Near the end of our conversation about his family situation, Trevor softened, saying that he wished he had more adults in his life to care for him. He asked if we would come and see him again the next day, or even on Christmas.

Underscoring his deep longing for adults from whom he felt authentic and genuine care, Trevor also talked about his reaction to the aftercare program, and specifically his perception of the aftercare staff. Unlike his near complete appreciation for the staff of Unit C, Trevor felt that the aftercare workers were "out to bust [him]" for little things, but did not care much about larger accomplishments, such as doing well in school, or getting along better at home. He also complained that the workers got caught up in the minor details, like whether or not he called in on time, and that they turned little mishaps into bigger mistakes. For example, he explained that if he missed a check-in time, the workers "assume you were out doing something ille-gal." He was much more frustrated about his aftercare program than we had expected based on his past feelings toward the Unit C staff.

Trevor shared additional relational challenges that he was experiencing with his "baby mama," Marie. He admitted to still being involved with her, but also having sexual relationships with other women without her knowl-edge. As the talk of girlfriends and sex unfolded, Trevor awkwardly said: "Can I ask you guys a question? Would you be pissed if a friend of yours was sleeping with your baby's mom?" As it turned out, he recently discovered that his best friend Jeff had become involved with Marie behind his back. While he appeared upset about this series of events and the potential drama surrounding them, Trevor also tried to rationalize the situation by criticizing Jeff's ability to "get girls on his own," and claiming the ultimate tie to Marie through their son. Still, underneath this bravado, we detected betrayal and emotional strife in Trevor's relational life.

Given the problems he was experiencing with those closest to him—his father, Jeff, and Marie—Trevor attributed most of the positive support in his life to his friends in the aftercare group. Sticking together as a group after school helped them to stay out of trouble. For example, during the down time in between school and aftercare group, they frequently reminded each other to look the other way if something was "going down" in the neigh-borhood. He said he felt no shame or embarrassment about how much this group of guys relied on one another. In an unexpected extension of Unit C's emphasis on group accountability, Trevor and his peers had formed a collec-tive structure to help one another succeed in the outside world.

It was time for Trevor's aftercare group, so we walked him back to the corner where the former Wildwood House residents had reconvened. The boys stood in a huddle, having what seemed to be a fairly intense conversa-tion about the recent suicide and pending funeral of a peer from a different dorm at Wildwood House. Standing outside the group and observing their interactions reinforced the perception of group cohesion Trevor had previ-ously described; they joked around with each other and genuinely seemed to offer each other support around the loss of their friend. Youth who might have fought or jockeyed for position and authority within the walls of the correctional facility were supporting one another through what appeared to be a very difficult emotional experience.

As it turned out, this was our only aftercare meeting with Trevor, but not due to any problems on his part. Even with all the challenges he described—raising himself, dealing with "baby mama drama," and complicated issues with his father and friends—he still managed to do well. When we checked his official records eighteen months after we saw him, he had no new juvenile or adult arrests or pending charges. Perhaps the support he sought for himself and the work that he did in the treatment program had paid off. In any case, Trevor seemed to genuinely miss the caring from adults that he received in Unit C, and his awkward entrée to our initial conversation indicated to us some of the difficulties Trevor was experiencing in the relational aspects of his life. Trevor's reentry experience had a lot of positives, such as the aftercare group, his more stable living situation, and contact with the Wildwood House staff, but several of the stresses he described could have indeed compromised his ardent determination to change his life.

Although we did not follow up with Humphrey or Kei in person, official reports were also mostly positive. Like Trevor, Humphrey had nothing new on his record and did not violate his probation. Kei had initially gotten into trouble for violating his probation, including a brief stay at the same detention center where Brad and Jason had spent time. According to his aftercare worker, he received the violation for using drugs and hanging out with his gang. But eighteen months after this probation violation, he had no new charges on his record. While it is heartening to see that these youth maintained, in the short run at least, their commitment to change, Trevor's story also illustrates the many challenges youth may encounter in their initial few months of community reintegration. It is important to note that even for the most motivated young person in this study, life after release was experienced as hard, lonely, and at times fraught with emotional turmoil.

REENTRY STORIES: LESSONS LEARNED

Official records relay just one marker of the post-release adjustment of formerly incarcerated youth: recidivism. Rearrest, reconviction, or reincarceration rates are the typical yardsticks used to evaluate the successes of any juvenile correctional program. While this book is not written specifically about reentry, for several reasons the stories presented here are nonetheless critical to building a fuller understanding of the potential for treatment-oriented correctional programs to change the course of young men's lives.

First, it is apparent that regardless of the treatment received, the cognitive reworking, or the motivation inspired by the program, all of the young men that we interviewed faced numerous struggles upon their release. Some of these struggles were easily anticipated, such as how finding a job, or the lure of drugs, alcohol, or fast money. Others were a more nuanced, such as the relational issues, betrayals, and general social strain that some of the young men described in regard to their old friends, the mothers of their children, or their extended family members. Some of these relational tensions have been described in other qualitative scholarship (Martinez and Abrams 2011), but we could not have predicated the extent to which the boys discussed these social and emotional challenges. It is striking that even the most clearly motivated youth in this book, Trevor, found reentry to be extremely difficult and much harder than he ever imagined. Although he had worked hard on processing his past family traumas and their relationship to his criminal behaviors, he nevertheless found himself essentially raising himself in the context of a violent situation with his father, who was still drinking in excess. It appears that even the most motivated youth will to be put to the test when the systems surrounding them remain the same.

Next, it is apparent from these stories that there is not just one route to imparting change. As a program set up with both punitive and rehabilitative elements, youth were capable of responding to either aspect of the program (or both). For example, in the cases of Brad and Eric, who claimed to not have learned anything from treatment, the will to never return to a place like Wildwood House provided motivation to avoid any major criminal activity, at least in the short run. Although the program was not set up to reward those who simply jumped through hoops, it is indeed interesting that only one of these highly manipulative youth (Thomas) got into immediate trouble upon their release. Their self-concepts may not have changed much, but their will to avoid doing time was certainly a by-product of their involuntary confinement.

Of those who returned to patterns of criminal activity in the twelve to eighteen months following release, most were mainly ambivalent about the need to change, or their ability to do so. Jason's and Elijah's stories illustrated the sense of just barely hanging on—faced with old habits, friends, and crime temptations, these youth were navigating a life betwixt and between their old worlds and visions of who they wanted to become. Their stories and narratives were remarkably similar, as both felt torn as to whether they beat the system or got something meaningful out of it. Both also brushed up against dangerous activities on the outs but tried to stay out of jail. Why many of these ambivalent youth in particular got back into trouble, or why some did and some didn't, remain open questions. Still, one can surmise that bumping up against all of these challenges without the full confidence or motivation to avoid them likely allowed some of them to slip back into trouble or at least, to get caught. This doesn't mean in any way that the treatment program was lost on them altogether, but perhaps instead, that the forces of the environment were simply stronger and more tempting than individual will.

These aftercare and reentry stories present a multitude of contradictions and they underscore tensions evident throughout this book. If some residents who fake their way through these programs actually do better upon release than those who undertake tentative attempts to change, what is the value of this treatment in the first place? If some youth are motivated by deterrence and others by treatment, how do we create a system that works for everyone? If youth who genuinely want to change have such little support once they are released, how can these treatment effects truly be sustained? While the answers to these questions are seemingly less clear than when this book began, we intend to examine them and their implications in our concluding chapter.

CHAPTER 7

Rehabilitating Rehabilitation

WHAT WE LEARNED FROM UNIT C

WE BEGAN THIS BOOK by raising critical questions about juvenile incarceration in American society, noting the major paradigm shifts and fractured opinions surrounding the appropriate goals and orientation of this system. If juvenile corrections has indeed—as many critics have charged—failed to fulfill its mission of rehabilitating youth and protecting society, is it worth ongoing investment in relatively expensive facilities purely for the sake of punishment? What balance of punishment and rehabilitation is needed to effectively change the attitudes and behaviors of young offenders? In pondering this concluding chapter, we wish that we could offer the perfect answer, one that would ensure that all youth in the system could be rehabilitated given the right blend of treatment, fear of returning to incarceration, and access to community-based supports upon reentry. Yet we know that if a magic cure existed, it would have been discovered before us. Still, the perfect cannot be the enemy of the better; our inability to offer the ideal solution to the dilemmas facing juvenile corrections cannot unilaterally discredit attempts toward improvement. Therefore, in this chapter we will use the experiences and voices of the youth and staff we came to know at Wildwood House to comment on what we view as pathways to better policies and practices than those currently in place.

CAN YOUTH BENEFIT FROM A SEPARATE JUVENILE SYSTEM?

Chapter 1 presented a broad-brush history of juvenile corrections in the United States and identified some of the antecedents of significant policy changes occurring during the 1980s and 1990s that chipped away at a separate system of criminal justice for juveniles. In a fear-based response to rising trends in youth crime, greatly exaggerated by popular media and academic discourses, all US states ushered in statutes permitting the transfer or waiver of youth to adult criminal courts, and some juvenile correctional facilities began to resemble the punitive orientation of adult prisons. Responding to these major changes, concerned advocates have launched a movement to revert to a system of juvenile corrections modeled after its original ideal: with caring and homelike facilities that first and foremost provide the youth in their care with the opportunity for rehabilitation. Underlying this position is the belief that youth are quite malleable to change, and as such should not be subjected to the punitive orientation or the problems with abuse and violence that are rampant in adult penal facilities.

Although our book did not directly address the transfer of youth to the adult criminal justice system, this very current debate is intermingled with fundamental questions about the ability of the juvenile system to adequately respond to youth who have been charged with crimes of a more serious nature. Is there a compelling social reason to turn youth over to the adult system, when overwhelming evidence has shown that these practices do more harm than good? Based on our experiences at Wildwood House and in consideration of this growing body of evidence (Ryan and Ziedenberg 2007), we argue that young people whose court involvement warrants out-of-home sentencing deserve the opportunity for rehabilitation in a specifically designated juvenile justice system. The adult correctional system, with its focus primarily oriented toward punitive consequence as the means to deterrence, is not the place for youth offenders. Admittedly, this position becomes murkier in cases of severe and disturbing crimes such as murder or rape. But since these represent the overwhelming minority of young people's criminal activity, we will keep our focus here on the larger pool.

Among the Wildwood House youth, Trevor and Brad, even given their significant differences in backgrounds and responses to the program, provide evidence in favor of our argument to not give up on a separate juvenile system. Both had long rap sheets at intake, including felony-level offenses, and extremely poor psychosocial assessments in regard to the potential for rehabilitation. As Trevor described, even at age fourteen, Wildwood house was his last chance before being certified to stand trial as an adult. Both also described family situations warranting other types of early interventions that unfortunately—and for whatever unknown reasons—were not provided. Despite these poor prospects and lack of external safety nets, follow-up at eighteen and twenty-four months after their release showed that neither of these youth had been charged with or convicted of new crimes. Given Brad's very negative attitude toward Wildwood House, his change is much less clearly linked to investment in the treatment program than in Trevor's case. Yet it is still worth noting that for both of these youth, remaining in a treatment-oriented juvenile system gave them yet another chance—one that did not expose them to the stigma of an adult criminal record, or potentially, the rampant violence and abuses associated with the adult penal system.

This is not to say, however, that treatment-oriented correctional facilities such as Wildwood House necessarily benefit all who experience them.

Some youth may not be ready or motivated to change, as was the case with Josh; others face challenges related to individual and family contexts that may be insurmountable upon reentry, as we saw with Elijah. Yet although the dominant yardstick of correctional success wasn't achieved in Elijah's case, he nevertheless made pro-social changes during and after his time at Wildwood House; he became reinvested in obtaining his high school degree and came to greater clarity about his motivation to become a better father. It seems that not all of what he learned through this program was lost on him, even if he failed in the eyes of the juvenile justice system.

Consequently, with the caveats that not all youth will respond ideally to the interventions offered by juvenile correctional facilities, and that success should be measured with multiple yardsticks, we firmly advocate for policy shifts aimed at restoring and preserving the integrity of a separate juvenile system. We see in this separate system greater potential than the adult system to benefit young offenders and support reentry into their home communities. In practice, we support the reversal of policies mandating automatic transfers to adult criminal court on the basis of age or type of crime. As each young person is unique and presents specific circumstances and charges, these automatic transfer statutes fundamentally limit the opportunity for youth to be offered a chance for individualized support toward rehabilitation. From 2005 to 2010, advocates successfully modified or scaled back transfer laws in fifteen US states (Arya 2011), and the Supreme Court decisions in *Roper v. Simmons* and *Graham v. Florida* also found in favor of treating juveniles differently from adults in regard to sentencing for capital crimes. It appears that public sentiment has gradually begun to lean back toward individualized and rehabilitative approaches, and that policies are following suit. Based on our experiences and observations at Wildwood House, we are greatly encouraged by these trends.

Is Rehabilitation Too "Soft" to Make a Difference?

One of the major pillars of conservative criticism concerning juvenile corrections is that the system is too easy on youth. In other words, if youth do not fear going back to "summer camp" (as Elijah retrospectively characterized his experience), it stands to reason that they will continue to cycle back through the system. In contrast to this view, advocates have voiced their support for broader implementation of the Missouri model, meaning smaller, homelike facilities with caring, well trained staff and empirically supported treatment practices. As chapter 1 documented, the majority of youth in correctional institutions will indeed return to the hands of the criminal justice system, either though rearrests or reincarceration as juveniles or adults. But does this signal that the system is too easy on youth, or, on the other hand, that a primarily punitive system cannot effectively rehabilitate youth? Or, challenging both positions, might other, unknown factors come into play?

The young men of Unit C demonstrated a wide range of responses to the treatment program, from buy-in and earnest work to a complete rejection of any need to be treated in the first place. In other words, what may have felt too easy for young people who believed they would have been more deterred by a purely correctional program presented a significant opportunity for personal growth for others who may have become worse in a more punitive environment. Thus our experience at Wildwood House lends weight to both sides of the argument about the softness of treatment-based correctional programs. For example, a young person like Kei may genuinely change as a result of this kind of program, much to their own surprise, and also to the contrary of staff expectations. At the same time, other residents may feel that these systems are too easy to manipulate and hold no regard for their treatment components. Still, as this book demonstrated, even some who found the system too easy, such as Eric and Brad, wound up committed to maintaining their freedom. In fact, in a somewhat ironic twist on the notion of deterrence through fear of punishment, Brad was deterred by the thought of having to comply with any further treatment.

The range of responses to the Wildwood House program that we observed strongly indicate the presence of multiple and unexpected pathways toward change. We view treatment-based corrections as neither too soft nor the perfect solution for all youth. As the Wildwood House stories illustrate, it is possible for treatment-based correctional facilities to have a deterrence effect while also offering possibilities for more pro-active, intentional, and genuine work toward a different future. Some youth may positively respond to one aspect or the other (in the sense of not committing further crimes), and some may respond to both at once. Given the various scenarios we witnessed and how these youth changed in their responses to the program over time, it appears unlikely that one could accurately predict which youth will benefit most from a rehabilitation-oriented correctional facility. While prior research has uncovered key risk factors for treatment failure (Lipsey 2009), and others have sought to discern the most efficacious treatment models (Greenwood 2010), prediction is by definition never perfect, and even those interventions with the greatest potential for success won't work for all. Our fieldwork helps to put some of these findings into context, and that context suggests complicated and unanticipated responses to a treatment-based correctional program.

Rather than taking a strict side on the too soft on crime debate, we offer an alternative perspective. What we view as problematic is not the value of punishment over treatment or vice versa, but rather the intermingling of these often contradictory paradigms in a single setting. In particular, linking treatment progress with a behavioral system of rewards and consequences clearly contributed to unintended outcomes in the sense of achieving the types of changes among youth that the program desired. As we saw most pronounced in the narratives of Terrell and Eric, few would argue that faking change and then taking pride in manipulating the system are of benefit for young people in the long run. To the contrary, learning to cheat the system will likely reinforce similar attitudes and behaviors that landed them in the juvenile justice system in the first place. And although we take the staff's sentiments seriously that faking it is better than no change at all, we still argue that environments in which youth do not feel the need to fake change in order to gain program rewards have a better chance of working than those that do not.

In practice, if rehabilitation is to be restored as the fundamental goal of juvenile corrections, which we clearly prefer to the alternative of an overtly punitive system, then assessments of treatment progress should be disentangled from correctional behavior management systems. Such an approach would reward or consequence youth for following or violating correctional rules, rather than on the basis of perceived treatment progress or personal disclosure. We believe that these program modifications would circumvent many of the unintended paradoxes of mandated "therapy speak" we witnessed at Wildwood House. Ultimately, the disentangling of these components would lead youth toward a more genuine and authentic engagement in treatment in which they—rather than the staff or therapists—can be the primary narrators and interpreters of their own experiences.

Mr. Robbins once said that the main barrier for youth to be honest with the staff at Wildwood House was their fear of reprisal. We suggest that uncoupling treatment and punitive functions would support staff in developing more authentic relationships with youth—allowing youth to see staff in a different light, no longer simply as authority figures with the power to judge or punish their feelings or expressions. For staff, the disentangling of these two functions would also create greater differentiation of their roles, such that primarily therapeutic staff could focus on developing more trusting relationships with residents, and correctional staff would retain the needed authority to enforce the rules and provide safety. Mr. Robbins further suggested that the main challenge of his work at Wildwood House was "juggling roles, trying to be someone who consequences them when rules are broken but also be there to pick up the pieces." Distinguishing staff roles more clearly may also relieve the pressures of juggling and code switching that arise when staff are responsible for both functions simultaneously.

Is "Boys Will Be Boys" Good Enough?

US juvenile correctional facilities were originally designed for so-called wayward boys, often without parents, or whose parents felt they had lost control over their sons. Despite a century of changes in juvenile courts and correctional institutions, young men still comprise the vast majority of incarcerated youth (Sickmund et al. 2011). In light of this gender imbalance, gender-specific programming in juvenile corrections has referred almost exclusively to addressing the needs of young women. In a system largely oriented toward and accustomed to working with young men, the unique circumstances and needs of young women in corrections have been largely ignored (Chesney-Lind and Okamoto 2001). Yet despite a persistent focus on correcting the behaviors of young men, our experience indicated that facilities like Wildwood House pay little critical attention to the links between gender identity and criminal behavior. As others have suggested, a youth correctional facility is a salient site of construction for masculine identity (Reich 2010), yet how these institutions address gender broadly, and masculinity particularly, is undertheorized as an aspect of practice with this population.

At Wildwood House, residents came to the facility with internalized and taken-for-granted messages about masculinity involving a stifling of emotional expression and a propensity to use violence and criminal activity as a means to gain power and a sense of self-worth. Underlying these notions of being a man was a repudiation of femininity that was inseparable from fear of being perceived as effeminate or gay. Although many youth expressed that they had experimented with alternative performances of gender, most notably in Jason's story of cross-dressing with his girlfriends, they knew that these performances would stigmatize or put them at risk if they became public. Very few had access to internal or external resources that supported a deviation from traditional masculine scripts—the same scripts that were often linked to use of violence and participation in crime. We also found that the facility's milieu mostly reinforced these same versions of masculinity, either overtly or more subtly. Although the treatment program clearly offered alternative messages concerning the value of emotional expression and empathy, these were not the dominant lessons that residents learned or absorbed about masculinity.

In light of this context, we recommend that juvenile correctional institutions critically engage gender as performed to suit the expectations of specific relationships and environments; in other words, some expressions of masculinity that may be considered adaptable in one setting may be less well suited for another. Most of the residents at Wildwood House had learned how to be young men in environments where masculinity required aggression, competition, and overt displays of power, many of the same characteristics necessitated and reinforced by their criminal activity. And yet, many of these same young men expressed pain and dissatisfaction with these expressions of masculinity and their associated rejection of intimacy and closeness. We suggest that incarcerated young men could benefit from programming and programs that directly address issues pertaining to gender, critiquing the learned messages of what it means to "take it like a man," and offering opportunities to explore alternate ways of finding personal power and self-worth in their gender identity without relying on violence or one-upping each other as a fallback. Here they may learn that the masculinities that were necessitated in their prior social systems may *not* be necessary in the future; they can create different masculine expressions that are conducive to noncriminal activities and social groupings.

For correctional facilities to specifically attend to masculinities as features of young men's identities, criminal biographies, and possible future selves, much must shift. To start, the masculine biographies and experiences that young men carry with them must be named and acknowledged. Institutions like Wildwood House maintain a close focus on family and criminal histories, but conventional treatment programs rarely examine specific messages about where and what residents have learned about becoming a man. In order to support residents in shifting criminal identities and behaviors, facilities must consider gender as a salient feature of young men's lives. We therefore encourage a form of gender-specific programming that begins with residents' articulation and subsequent questioning of the meanings of masculinity they have inherited and enacted. This focus, of course, must include attention to how their gender socialization may have contributed to their behaviors prior to conviction and how they may play out upon release.

Moreover, in order for individual exploration of masculinity to have traction in correctional facilities, the institutional milieu must support young men in finding a sense of power and self-worth in alternatives. Here we build on Jo Goodey's (1997) construct of the masculine biography, echoing her assertion that masculine biographies can be rewritten in ways that include new mechanisms for the expression and performance of gender. Linking this with the notion of communities of gendered practice (Paechter 2007), we suggest that facilities in which multiple expressions of masculinity are accepted are more likely to demonstrate to young men that the biographies with which they were raised can be shifted and revised toward more law-abiding futures. Through both implicit mechanisms, such as placing more male staff in therapist positions, or explicit ones, such as challenging comments that endorse violence against women or gay men, facilities can support youth in creating new identities in which being a man can include more than the conventional masculine tropes of competition, aggression, power, and repudiation of the feminine.

Rethinking Expectations

The public places much economic and political stock in juvenile incarceration. Expectations from both sides of the spectrum, for punishment and rehabilitation, are often fairly grand. This remains the case despite knowledge that many youth who are sentenced to correctional facilities, and certainly most of the boys we met at Wildwood House, have experienced a host of prior troubles, often ones that necessitated interventions from other human service institutions such as child welfare, schools, welfare, or mental health organizations. Yet somehow public pressures demand significant and abrupt transformation most acutely at and immediately following the period of incarceration, which generally occurs only as a last resort and is often quite short in duration. Here we must ask: is this expectation realistic?

Wildwood House therapist Ms. James once said that "the kids aren't successful the minute they get out of here; it's about planting a seed and for them to use that as they grow up and develop through life. That's as good as it gets." One might feel disheartened to hear that such a profound investment in a young person's life, signaled by a significant disruption from home and school, can really be simply planting a seed for change. Yet perhaps the wisdom in her words is the framing of correctional confinement as one step in a much larger process, rather than as an entity all unto itself. Following Ms. James's advice, we believe that in order to move toward sensible juvenile corrections reform, we must begin to view a young person's experience of confinement as a small piece of a much larger puzzle. And like most complex systems, reforming just one piece—in this case the individual—generally does not change the whole without investment and active engagement of the other parts as well.

Let's first consider the institution itself, and more specifically, the staff who are charged with caring for these youth on a day-to-day basis. Notoriously, residential treatment and corrections work is characterized by high burnout, staff turnover, and low pay. Staff work long shifts, are sometimes victims of violence, are afforded little room for creativity in their work, and seldom receive appreciation or gratitude for their efforts. As Mr. Lund explained, many, but not all, of the milieu staff at Wildwood House considered their dorm shift work as a necessary step to eventually becoming a probation officer, so turnover tends to be routine. He also suggested that the dorm staff have little time for in-depth supervision or training in therapeutic techniques. Considering just this one piece of the puzzle, many structural interventions may improve the therapeutic services offered in juvenile corrections that can ultimately benefit the residents. In Unit C, we met a number of highly motivated staff with a therapeutic and caring orientation toward their work. But as many voiced, they found it difficult to juggle both aspects of their work, and often wished they had more time and training to devote to the therapeutic aspects of their job. Building on our prior recommendation to uncouple staffs' correctional and therapeutic responsibilities, providing additional training in multiple treatment modalities can provide staff with new resources to better support the youth in their care.

The puzzle metaphor leads us also to seriously consider the importance of improving support upon reentry. Our experiences at Wildwood House—in terms of perspectives from the staff and follow-up contact with the boys themselves—echo and reinforce the perception that it is unlikely (although granted not impossible) that a young person can sustain the changes they make during confinement if their outside environment remains completely unchanged. We saw this repeatedly in the struggles of Wildwood youth, both in those who were amenable to change in the facility and those who were not. All shared similar challenges in returning to the people and the institutions that comprised their former worlds. We are clearly not the first to claim that community reintegration is an important part of the spectrum of correctional intervention. Yet the stories we have pondered and presented reveal the complexity and depth of the struggles these young men grappled with in anticipating, and then facing, their lives on the outs. If the juvenile justice system is to improve its results in regard to long-lasting change, its lens must broaden to include young offenders' parents, schools, community-based organizations, and probation systems that support these youth upon their release.

Although imagining the breadth and scope of the specific supports a correctional system might provide to these various stakeholders to facilitate healthy and effective youth reentry and reintegration is beyond the scope of this book, we are nevertheless convinced that such supports must be in place. In many of the boys' narratives—Jason, Kei, Nino, and Trevor among them—we heard concern about what life would look like upon their release. We watched, firsthand, as Jason literally hid behind us from his former life and witnessed Trevor leaning on the only people he believed to know what he was going through—other Wildwood House alumni—for support when things got rough and he felt lonely. Building on the idea of incarceration as one part of a spectrum of experiences, additional supports must be in place to encourage pro-social changes upon release. These supports we believe must extend beyond surveillance, to include helping youth sustain a positive peer culture (as we saw with Trevor and the aftercare group) and to supporting them through the challenges they will ultimately confront. While reentry services are no guarantee for the prevention of reoffending, coupled with a better system of confinement, they are likely to offer youth greater opportunities to achieve their own goals.

PARTING THOUGHTS

By nearly all accounts, juvenile correctional institutions in the United States are not living up to their potential, with successes occurring certainly no more often than failures. In states across the country, young people are funneled through a system that may have once been imagined to suit their needs but has since drifted far afield. Those are the lucky ones; their less fortunate peers are denied access even to this system, channeled instead into an adult system that maintains no illusions of rehabilitation. In our sixteen months at Wildwood House, we came to know many of these youth as well as the staff, teachers, and therapists who committed their careers to living and working with them. And although we encountered examples of real connection, profound transformation, and powerful personal insight, we also witnessed much confusion, mixed messages, and unhealthy interactions that unintentionally reinforced the criminal thinking that the facility so ardently discouraged. Still, we close our experiences at Wildwood House with a sense of hope and optimism.

We believe that even as confinement is sometimes necessary, it can, in fact, also be compassionate. Centering the needs of the young men who come through their doors as their primary concern, correctional institutions like Wildwood House have tremendous potential to facilitate the development of new insights and ultimately, to impart tools for behavior change. They need not simply punish, nor need they just warehouse young offenders until their ultimate release. On the contrary, by resolving the paradoxes of blended treatment and corrections paradigms, attending to gender and masculinity as salient features of young men's criminal identities, recognizing that multiple pathways to change exist, and providing ongoing support and encouragement to facilitate community reintegration, these programs can fulfill the dual mission of the juvenile correctional system. Of course, this is a tall order for a large and complex system. Reforms of this type will certainly encounter challenges and resistance. But from where we stand, the alternatives are unacceptable.

Appendix: Behind the Scenes

Reflections on Field Research in Action

THIS PROJECT WAS BORN out of mutual interest. When we met, at that time as a new assistant professor of social work (Laura) and a dual degree graduate student in public policy and social work (Ben), we discovered a shared concern for the lives of young people, particularly related to their experiences in institutional settings. Our own direct practice experiences—some frustrating, others affirming—left us wanting a more complete understanding of facilities such as Wildwood House, examining them as subcultures with tremendous potential to influence young people's lives. Due to a sequence of fortuitous events, we put our minds together to launch this project, and after some time to ruminate on the findings, compiled the sum of our experiences and insights into this book. In this appendix we describe how we initiated the project, collected data, and made sense of the many layers of findings. We also reflect on the some of the challenges and ethical dilemmas we encountered in doing collaborative fieldwork in an institutional setting. It is our hope that this appendix will offer transparency in the research process as well as guidance for scholars and students engaged in or planning field research projects.

Getting Started

Gaining access as a researcher to any correctional facility, particularly those housing court-supervised youth, is no simple task. We were fortunate to be introduced to Wildwood House by a senior faculty colleague who had a working relationship with the facility director, Mr. Kowalski, who believed in the value of research to inform and improve practice. While at first we assumed that he would endorse only a more evaluative or quantitative type of study, we were pleasantly surprised that he was open to a loosely conceptualized (and for that matter, more intrusive) qualitative project. We presented Mr. Kowalski with our initial research aims and he proceeded to seek buy-in for the study from the head of Unit C, Mr. Lund, and the staff psychologist. Once the study was approved by external reviewers (for seed funding) and the university's institutional review board (for ethical considerations), we began the process of introducing ourselves and the project to the staff and residents of Unit C.

Our first encounter with this larger audience was during a Unit C staff retreat. About a week prior to this retreat, Mr. Lund and the staff psychologist had taken us on a facility orientation tour and explained to us, among other aspects of facility life, the critical importance of bonding with the staff and earning their trust. As such, our initial meeting with the staff felt critical and anxiety-laden. In preparation for this meeting, we constructed a one-page description of the study that included our basic research goals and the methods we planned to use, along with a bit about our own professional and scholarly backgrounds. We included this last piece of information based on our prior experiences of juvenile corrections staff being wary of outsiders, particularly researchers, coming in to assess or observe their work. During this initial meeting, we wanted to position ourselves to the staff as both insiders and outsiders; clearly, we did not currently work in the system and were therefore likely to be seen as outsiders. Still, we both had practice experience with youth residential treatment and correctional institutions that we hoped would grant us some credibility in the eyes of the staff.

After Mr. Lund introduced us to the staff, we delivered a brief presentation about our study and then invited the group to ask questions. Most of the staff appeared to be disinterested in the information, except for a few who inquired about the time burden of the study (for them and the residents), our planned frequency and duration of visits, and whether or not we were going to offer the staff ongoing feedback about our findings. As we left the retreat, we noted that although it hadn't been a particularly easy afternoon, it had been an important first step in building trust and rapport with the staff—which we knew was critical to our acceptance into their workspace and the effectiveness of the project overall.

About two weeks following this retreat, we coordinated a date and time with Mr. Lund to introduce the project to the residents. Given our direct practice backgrounds, we both felt fairly confident in our abilities to connect with the youth, but we were still oddly anxious. Our first meeting with the group occurred on a weekday during after-school free time. Having at first forgotten that we were scheduled to visit that day, Mr. Lund met us in the reception area and brought us back to the dorm living room, verbally halted the varied activities that were occurring, and introduced us as a doctor from the local university and a student who wanted to talk with them about a research project. He then left us to our own devices, and we glanced around nervously, noting that the unit shift staff had seated themselves in the perimeter of the room to observe our interactions with the residents. This seemed to be their first test of us, our ability to connect with the residents, and whether we "got it" about how to function in this environment.

Ben proceeded to lead a team-building activity involving a tarp and a common task for the residents to complete, drawn from outdoor, experiential education and low-ropes course exercises. The activity went smoothly, and Ben debriefed with the group about what they could learn from the activity, trying to elicit lessons he thought would fit with the treatment milieu. Next, Laura talked with the group about the goals and purpose of the study, the process of informed consent, and what they would be asked to do if they signed up to participate. We then encouraged the residents to talk with us in small groups about volunteering for the individual interviews, and informed them that we would be visiting the dorm on a regular basis as observers, and not as new staff.

A number of youth were interested in signing up for the study, which we considered another stroke of good luck as we weren't permitted to offer them any incentives, financial or otherwise. Once we went over the details of the study and obtained their written assent (since they were all under eighteen and weren't able to consent for their own participation), we began the task of collecting their parents' or guardians' written consent to participate in the study. While we had originally planned to gain parental or guardian consent through the mail, we quickly realized that this strategy was destined for failure. We subsequently changed course and decided to visit with parents during routine Sunday visiting hours. This was probably the most awkward task we had to accomplish during our whole fieldwork experience—we felt terribly guilty about interrupting the small window of visiting time parents had with their sons, and even worse about having to approach them without warning. In a few instances, our awkwardness was compounded by language barriers; subsequently, we had parental consent forms translated into Spanish and Hmong. Despite this discomfort, we succeeded in securing consent from about 80 percent of the parents whose sons had volunteered for the study. We were unable to reach a couple of parents who did not visit their sons, and a couple other parents refused due to mistrust or lack of interest in the study. Over the course of the study, we conducted these recruitment efforts in two waves with about six months in between. These recruitment and consent procedures garnered the participation of the twelve youth in the interview and record review components of the study.

DATA COLLECTION

While we started with initial interests in treatment, gender, and institutional context, we didn't have a solid sense of what we might find. In fact, although both of us were experienced in qualitative research, neither of us was well versed in ethnography. There was a strong learning-by-doing component of this project, and the actual methods we used to collect data were a combination of those we had initially planned and those that emerged along the way.

Participant Observation

The core of ethnographic field research is in-depth participant observation (Lofland and Lofland 1995). Along these lines, we conducted observations at least weekly for the sixteen months and took detailed field notes from the beginning of our study, including our initial meetings with the director, staff, and youth. Our methods of observation and note taking were continually refined as we sorted out our role in the facility and developed closer relationships with the youth and staff. At the beginning, we tended to stand on the sidelines of dorm activities and then sneak away to a corner or the small staff office to take some written notes. As we became more familiar with the staff and the youth, we had much more interactive and comfortable experiences, leaving less time for note taking on-site, which we tended to do upon arriving home after an observation shift.

We also experimented with and learned to use a consistent format for our observation notes, which went through a couple of iterations. In the beginning we used a two-column method: In the left column, we wrote rich descriptions of individual observations or exchanges; these were often quite lengthy. We tried to limit our own interpretive commentary on these descriptions, focusing as much as possible on naming and clearly describing behavior or interactions without interpreted meaning. Then, parallel to these descriptions, we used the right-hand column to offer our interpretations and initial formulations of meaning for each section of the description. The right column was also a location for us to comment on our subjective experiences of the observations; here we could reflexively comment on how the research unfolded, noting our questions or concerns, and purging some of our initial gut-level reactions to events in the facility. Feeling that this method of note taking was too fragmented, we moved to recording our observations and reflections in one fluid narrative, yet still used italics to document our more subjective reflections. Throughout the course of the fieldwork, we shared our observation summaries with one another and discussed points of significant agreement or divergence.

Our growing sense of familiarity and ease in the observation routine did not happen overnight. We recall how awkward we first felt arriving at the facility (should we be announced or unannounced before our arrival?), asking the reception desk staff to alert the Unit C staff of our presence, or even asking to use the bathroom, which staff had to unlock every time we needed to use it. Depending on which staff member escorted us into the dorm, we might be offered information about dorm mood or schedule, but at times we were provided no information at all. Some staff didn't even remember who we were or why we were there. Others seemed to want to engage with us, but only to test us and question our presence there with pointed questions that felt loaded with potential impact, such as "What are you finding so far?"

"Are you going write about us, too?" "Remind me again, what makes you qualified to be here?" and at times more subtle questions about how we are getting along so far in the dorm, or how the boys were treating us. Conducting observations on the weekends was even more difficult, as the front reception desk was not staffed, requiring us to call back to the units on an intercom and wait by the front door for a staff member to admit us. Moreover, on weekends the dorm was often staffed by substitutes or floaters, many of whom hadn't heard our initial presentation about the study or had forgotten about it altogether.

There were also initial questions about what we should actually do while observing. Although we had both engaged in interpretive research projects before, this was our first major foray into routine ethnographic observation. What counted as participant observation? How were we to balance participation and observation? Should we play games with the boys, such as cards or basketball? Should we sit in on therapy groups or staff meetings, or was that too invasive? It seemed like we should eat with the residents and staff during dinner (not eating with them felt rude), but particularly given that we were both vegetarians, the food was entirely unappealing to us. Because we conducted observations together most of the time, we weren't sure if we should observe the same activities or split up. Although the facility director had given us pretty much free reign during observation time, all of these questions arose during our first few months of observations, and we frequently wrote about them and checked in with one another about the fieldwork process itself. It was an ongoing exercise in reflexivity, often recognizing the differences in our privileges in the facility compared to those of the residents. We could choose when and how to engage, when to come and go, and whether or not to eat the food; the boys could not.

A few months into our weekly observations, things got a bit easier, at least in the sense of greater familiarity and comfort in our visits. The regular front desk staff finally offered to check out keys for us to make it easier to move around the facility, including use of the bathroom. With these and other markers of our gradual acceptance into the facility, we became ever more regular features of life in Unit C, and less novel to the residents and less burdensome (from our perspective) to the staff. As we got to know the staff and youth better and forged relationships with them, we also felt less awkward about showing up unannounced; we became more participants and less external observers of the subculture within the walls of Wildwood House. Within a few months, we got to the point where we could let ourselves into the unit, find the group in their daily routines, and strike up comfortable conversations with the staff and residents. We were even often let into the office at the beginning of our observation shifts to read the staff log, getting caught up on the dorm and specific residents, and staff often wanted to brief us on shifts in individual or group dynamics since our last visit. Although our initial discomfort dissipated as we became integrated into the unit, being insiders brought with it new challenges related to maintaining our position and ethical boundaries as researchers, with both the youth and staff. We reflect on these challenges later, in our discussion of the complexities of conducting joint ethnographic fieldwork.

Interviews

Conducting individual interviews with the residents was another major pillar of our research methodology. For each resident who participated in the study, we attempted to follow their stay from entry to aftercare through a series of in depth interviews. We initially planned a series of five interviews, all designed to elicit substantive background information and moment-in-time views of their experiences in the facility. We had hoped to sequence the interviews so that each built on the one before it: 1) getting to know one another and life history; 2) masculine biography; 3) peers, school, relationships, and crime; 4) exit interview, reflections, and future goals; and 5) reentry and aftercare. Ideally we wanted to conduct all five interviews with each participant, but the realities of complex scheduling and the difficulties of locating youth for the aftercare interview led to an average of four interviews per youth.

The interviews were conducted in a conversational format, meaning that we had lists of topics we wanted to cover during each interview, but they could be discussed in any order that made sense according to the flow of the conversation. We conducted almost all of the interviews together, with only a few exceptions. On two occasions while one of us was visiting alone, two different residents in the study requested an impromptu interview, which we obliged and recorded, but did not include as one of the five major interviews. For all the other interviews, we alternated between one of us taking the lead conversational role and the other observing and taking notes not only on the interview content, but also on details like body language that might hold meaning but would not be detected in a transcript. The note-taker was also responsible for posing clarifying questions at the end of the conversation, allowing the interviewer to truly follow the flow of the conversation in the moment without sacrificing its integrity for the sake of making it through the interview guide. For the most part, we tried to alternate interviewer and note-taker positions. However, due to our different genders and personalities, we found that some of the youth were more comfortable talking to one of us than the other. In a couple of these cases, we stuck with our roles throughout the interview sequence. The interviews conducted during confinement always took place in one of Wildwood House's private meeting rooms or on-campus, just outside the building. They usually lasted between forty-five and ninety minutes but occasionally lasted longer, and sometimes we had to end early due to meals or other structured transition times. Following the interviews, we took notes on our overall impressions of the interview, questions to ask in subsequent interviews, or ideas sparked that could be woven into our ongoing reflection and accounting of what we were learning. After writing up these observations, we always shared our notes with one another, partially to fact-check but also to identify differences in interpretation that might hold significant meaning for our overall analysis.

The interviews ranged widely in level of comfort level and rapport. Some boys were quite open with us from the beginning and never stopped; in these cases, conversation flowed easily and trust was readily established. In other cases, the interviews struggled in back-and-forth questions, short responses, and other signals of barriers to trust. Some youth eventually opened up more, but a small minority did not. We also couldn't be certain about the extent to which a few of the boys were posturing or lying to us. For many of these reasons, we learned more from some participants than others and this is reflected in the prose of the book as some boys' stories are featured more than others. On the whole, though, the youth who participated in the study looked forward to their interviews and we likewise enjoyed learning from them. Several boys even offered us their treatment contracts when they neared release—most notably, Trevor—and we included these in the book. In presenting the boys' words, whether through interviews or excerpts from their written work, we decided to keep their spelling and language intact with the hopes that this would help their voices speak directly to readers.

Once data collection was well underway, we decided to add two methods to the study: aftercare interviews with youth and interviews with the Unit C staff. The aftercare interviews were difficult to coordinate, and many were not tape recorded due to various setting issues (loud restaurants) or institutional constraints (interviewing in the detention facility). In those cases, we took detailed notes during and after the interviews. We also lost contact with several youth due to transience and disconnected phones, or our own inability to maintain consistent communication given all of the other pressures of our lives and work. Nevertheless, the aftercare interviews and contacts that occurred with five of the twelve youth were some of the most rewarding parts of the whole experience. We regret that we did not have the opportunity to reach all of the participants after they departed.

As we neared the study's end, we sought approval from the institution and the office of human subjects to interview the Unit C staff. Mr. Kowalski and Mr. Lund generously granted us permission to conduct these interviews during paid work time. Since the staff interviews took place on the work clock, we decided they should be brief, between thirty and forty minutes per interview. Based on our initial understandings of our findings, we created a standard template of open-ended questions that would offer us more insight into the staff point of view on the facility, the youth, and the tensions we had observed. To recruit the staff, we placed a notice in their mailboxes inviting them to participate in the interviews. We then approached them directly during our observation visits to set up interview times. None of the core unit staff or other professionals working in the dorm (therapists, teachers, or directors) refused our invitation, and only one staff member asked that we not record the interview. We found the staff at this point to be very eager to share their views and experiences with us, and these interviews most certainly enriched the study as a whole.

Record Reviews

Reviewing the facility's records on the twelve residents occurred toward the end of our time at Wildwood House. Kyoungho Kim, then a doctoral student who was working on the project with us, created a structure for the record reviews and took electronic notes on all the available records. These documents offered an additional perspective on the professional discourses that staff used to assess and describe youth, including how they viewed their progress or lack thereof. We were then able to compare these perspectives with the youths' own view of their progress. The records also helped us check the background information the participants had offered us in regard to school, family, criminal history, and other information. We found few major discrepancies, which suggested that even those youth who did not warmly embrace the facility or its treatment programs still chose to engage fairly honestly with us. We had worried that some residents might present differently to us than to the staff, possibly out of an interest in appearing good in our eyes or manipulating us, but this did not seem to be the case.

DATA ANALYSIS

Analyzing the volumes of data that were collected during this project took several years, as layers of findings and nuances continued to unfold. While we were in the process of conducting our fieldwork, we frequently wrote memos about what we were learning and then continually refined the larger questions we believed the study was capable of addressing. This ongoing process of reflection paved the way for several iterations of our larger goals. About six months into the research process, three of us (Laura, Ben, and Kyoungho) began a more formalized process data analysis, which was a fairly overwhelming task. We decided to start with the field notes. We began by reading a set of field notes and discussing them, often coding in pairs until we had developed a common codebook to work from. At that time, we did not use a computer software program to manage the data, so we coded by hand.

Once the field note coding was mostly complete, we began to code the interviews using a similar rubric. The next task was to make some sense of this extensive body of information, for once data are reduced to such precise coding units, it often became hard to see the larger picture or to conceptualize how these micro-level observations fit together. We thus consulted regularly with Miles and Huberman's book *Qualitative Data Analysis* (1994) and used many of their recommended data reduction and meaning making tools. For example, in looking into each individual case, we constructed charts that portrayed their life histories as well as those that examined how their thinking about the facility progressed over time. We also used matrices and diagrams to locate patterns of response to the program, such as those we described in chapters 5 and 6. We used memos to locate core themes concerning the setting and the institutional context around our central ideas concerning treatment, power, and masculinities. At many junctures we felt puzzled over what to do next and at times, presenting the analysis to a class or a faculty group often sparked new ideas about how to manage and make meaning from this very large amount of data.

These data reduction exercises led initially to several published articles specifically on Wildwood House (see Abrams and Aguilar 2006; Abrams, Kim, and Anderson-Nathe 2005) and also contributed to future comparative studies (see Abrams 2006; Abrams, Anderson-Nathe, and Aguilar 2008; Abrams and Hyun 2009). Yet the idea of compiling the whole picture of this study into a book continued to linger in our minds both because of the richness of the fieldwork experience as well as the timeliness of the public conversation about juvenile corrections reform. When the two of us sat down to formulate our goals and ideas for this book, we used much of the analysis we had previously conducted. Yet we also found ourselves digging back into the field notes, interview transcripts, and record reviews to discover many new and previously unseen insights. As the space for the presentation of analysis in journal articles is fairly limited, the book format provided a much more comprehensive analysis and presentation of the data as whole. While data analysis of this type can be vexing at times, the continual progression of ideas and insights is also part of the true enjoyment of doing this type of fieldwork.

REFLECTIONS ON CONDUCTING A COLLABORATIVE ETHNOGRAPHY

When we have either jointly or separately presented aspects of this project to academic audiences or students, people frequently ask about the decision to do a collaborative ethnography, as traditionally the ethnographer conducts fieldwork alone. Not really recognizing initially that this was indeed a rare setup, it seemed natural for us to do the project together. We felt that our knowledge and skills were mutually beneficial, and for the most part, we worked very well together. Our observations and insights proved to be similar enough to be compatible, but also sufficiently different to learn from one another and to expand the boundaries of one another's thinking. We had very frequent communication throughout the sixteen months (and after), sharing field notes, ideas, interview observations, and suggestions with one another. In the process of doing the work, we also became good friends.

Yet the challenges of working together in this type of intensive field-work were also present. Occupying two different professional roles (newly minted professor and graduate student at that time), we often held and asserted conflicting priorities. Laura was highly concerned with the research methods, IRB protocols, and maintaining a professional distance with the staff and the youth. Ben was (and continues to be) more tied to the practical side of the conclusions, and was also always concerned about cultivating meaningful relationships with the youth. At times, these roles and our prior-ities within them created tensions. In interviews, for instance, Ben was inclined to allow the interview guide to fade to the background and engage fully in whatever conversation emerged, trusting that something useful for the larger research questions would certainly result. Laura, by contrast, held the focus of the study in the foreground and more resolutely attended to the central questions guiding each interview. Although this certainly created ten-sions in the moment, the roles we organically assumed ultimately comple-mented one another and facilitated much more comprehensive understandings of the boys' lives within the conceptual framework of our overarching research questions.

Challenges in negotiating our relationships with the youth and the staff were also present, which we have described as the dilemmas involved in code-switching between researcher and practitioner roles in the process of conducting fieldwork in a social service setting (Anderson-Nathe and Abrams 2005). Although our practice experience benefited us in many ways, it also presented some dilemmas that might not have emerged had we approached the project from nonreflexive research orientation. For example, circumstances arose in our interactions with the residents when we genuinely wanted to help them with our own verbal interventions, such as in the midst of a rough interaction with staff or with family members. Eric's story of frustration with his teachers and Ben's intervention, presented in chapter 3, was one prime example of this conflict. The complication in these situations, of course, was the difficulty of stepping into practitioner role without stepping out of our position as researchers. This is not to suggest that we felt obligated to maintain a purely objective detachment from the life of the dorm; indeed, recognizing our own subjective involvement with the milieu, we located ourselves in the middle of Raymond Gold's (1958) continuum of participation in the field, not full participants but also not detached observers.

Still, some connections we made with the youth presented unique dilemmas that stretched our understanding of what it meant to be a researcher-participant in such a setting. For instance, by the end of our time at Wildwood House, it was not uncommon for youth (or in one case a parent) to directly ask us to help them, either advocating on their behalf to staff, or to help them write their treatment contracts. Unable to always rationalize this direct involvement in the context of our role as researchers, we had to decline these requests. These were among the most emotionally tense and exhausting moments of our fieldwork experiences.

As our relationships with the staff progressed past our early discomfort and their initial mistrust, we found ourselves confronted with an additional layer of fieldwork dilemmas. Given the unique insight our privileged relationships offered into the residents' lives and thoughts, particularly among the youth we interviewed, we often wanted to speak up when the staff made what we perceived to be disparaging, inappropriate, or off-target comments about residents. Doing so would, however, have challenged the integrity of our roles as researchers by pitting us against the staff. It was important for us as participant observers in the life of the dorm to be accessible to people from multiple positions in the facility. In order to maintain that stance, we could not be aligned with any one group or against any other. For the most part, then, we had to listen to these comments, bracketing our own reactions until we could later debrief or record the experiences in our field notes for later analysis. We also experienced some intense personal biases regarding the staff, in that we felt much more invested in getting to know the staff who demonstrated empathy and support toward the youth, and our inclination was to skirt around those who we perceived to be unjustly punitive or negative. Yet since all of the staff members held equally important roles in this study and in the lives of the residents, we reminded one another to make concerted efforts to interact on a similar level with all of them.

We also faced awkward encounters when the staff would ask for our opinions about some of the youth or the treatment program, and we would hesitate in formulating our answers. While we certainly felt that our insights could add some value to the program, we did not want to jeopardize our relationships with the facility (or potentially put residents at risk of retribution) by allowing ourselves to step into the roles of expert evaluator, critic, or informant. Still, it was impossible in the flow of natural conversation to keep our observations and opinions fully to ourselves. Thus we worked hard, and sometimes unsuccessfully, to answer these questions diplomatically, defaulting to social work practice skills of inviting the staff to share their perspectives and listening intently rather than to directly state our own.

TERMINATION

After sixteen months at Wildwood House, the time came for us to end our involvement with Unit C. We had planned to be there for a year and had exceeded our time. In addition, we had seen and learned enough to draw meaningful conclusions from the data we had collected and we were no longer seeing profoundly different or contradictory events. The process of terminating the relationships that we had developed was more difficult with the staff, as most of the youth who we had come to know had already transitioned out of Unit C. We used our one-to-one interviews with the staff to prepare them for our departure, and we also promised to visit and share our results. Our last observation visit was met without much fanfare; we arrived, we observed, we chatted with the staff and some residents, and we left.

About five months later, we returned to present our findings with the staff in a final report on our work with Wildwood House. This was a complicated task, largely because so many of our findings called attention to the tensions, inconsistencies, and other paradoxes we had noted in the facility's program structure and staffs' interactions with residents. Still, we wanted to respect the trust and openness the staff had ultimately shown by welcoming us into their ranks. Ultimately, we submitted a report that began with findings about what worked in the program, highlighting some of the residents' stories of success and support. We nested our more critical comments in the context of what we believed would work in the future and offered concrete recommendations to help the facility move in that direction. Overall, the staff seemed very receptive to our report and thanked us for our time and interest in the facility.

CONCLUSION

Life in the dorm went on, and after our final report to the staff and occasional e-mails with Mr. Lund, we maintained no lasting connections with either the staff or the youth of Unit C. We write this book now, a few years later and from different vantage points in terms of our own lives and careers, with the knowledge that Wildwood House and Unit C are not unique. Across the United States, youth wake up every morning in correctional institutions and adult staff preside over their day-to-day routines with the hopes that when they are released, they will have made the necessary behavioral and identity changes to avoid future incarceration. Unit C offered one glimpse into this world; we offer this appendix in the hopes that students, practitioners, and other scholars may benefit from a look inside our process as they navigate their own fieldwork experiences in juvenile correctional institutions or similar settings.

References

"A Better Chance." 2010. Editorial. *New York Times*, April 25, A22.

Abrams, L. S. 2000. "Guardians of Virtue: The Social Reformers and the 'Girl Problem,' 1890–1920." *Social Service Review* 74 (3): 436–452.

———. 2006. "Listening to Juvenile Offenders: Can Residential Treatment Prevent Recidivism?" *Child and Adolescent Social Work Journal* 23 (1): 61–85.

———. 2007. "From Corrections to Community: Youth Offenders' Perceptions of the Challenges of Transition." *Journal of Offender Rehabilitation* 44 (2): 31–53.

Abrams, L. S., and J. Aguilar. 2006. "Negative Trends, Possible Selves, and Behavior Change: A Qualitative Study of Juvenile Offenders in Residential Treatment." *Qualitative Social Work* 4 (2): 175–196.

Abrams, L. S., B. Anderson-Nathe, and J. Aguilar. 2008. "Constructing Masculinities in Juvenile Corrections." *Men and Masculinities* 11 (1): 22–41.

Abrams, L. S., and A. Hyun. 2009. "Mapping a Process of Negotiated Identity among Incarcerated Male Juvenile Offenders." *Youth & Society* 41 (1): 26–52.

Abrams, L. S., K. Kim, and B. Anderson-Nathe. 2005. "Paradoxes of Treatment in Juvenile Corrections." *Child & Youth Care Forum* 34 (1): 7–25.

Altschuler, D. M., and T. L. Armstrong. 1994. *Intensive Aftercare for High-Risk Juveniles: Policies and Procedures*. Washington, DC: Office of Juvenile Justice and Delinquency Prevention.

Altschuler, D. M., and R. Brash. 2004. "Adolescent and Teenage Offenders Confronting the Challenges and Opportunities of Reentry." *Youth Violence and Juvenile Justice* 2 (1): 72–87.

American Correctional Association. 2008. *American Correctional Association 2008 Directory*. 69th ed. Alexandria, VA: American Correctional Association.

Anderson, E. 1999. *Code of the Street: Decency, Violence, and the Moral Life of the Inner City*. New York: W. W. Norton.

Anderson-Nathe, B., and L. S. Abrams. 2005. "Getting There is Half the Fun: Practitioners-as-Researchers and Vice-Versa." *Reflections: Narratives of Professional Helping* 11 (4): 69–77.

Annie E. Casey Foundation. n.d. *The Casey Foundation's Investment in Juvenile Justice*. www.aecf.org/Home/OurWork/JuvenileJustice/JuvenileJusticeOverview.aspx.

Aronson, J. 2007. "Brain Imaging, Culpability and the Juvenile Death Penalty." *Psychology, Public Policy, and Law* 13 (2): 115–142.

Arya, N. 2011. *State Trends: Legislative Changes from 2005 to 2010. Removing Youth from the Adult Criminal Justice System*. Washington, DC: Campaign for Youth Justice. www.campaignforyouthjustice.org/documents/CFYJ_State_Trends_Report.pdf.

Ayers, W. 1997. *A Kind and Just Parent: The Children of the Juvenile Court*. Boston: Beacon Press.

Back, C., and E. Calvin. 2008. *When I Die, They'll Send Me Home: Youth Sentenced to Life Without Parole in California*. New York: Human Rights Watch. www.hrw.org/en/node/75357/section/1.

Becker, E. 2001. "As Ex-Theorist on Young 'Superpredators,' Bush Aide has Regrets." *New York Times*, February 9. www.nytimes.com/2001/02/09/us/as-ex-theorist-on-young-superpredators-bush-aide-has-regrets.html.

Bernard, T. J. 1992. *The Cycle of Juvenile Justice*. New York: Oxford University Press.

Beyer, M. 1997. "Experts for Juveniles at Risk of Adult Sentences." In P. Puritz, A. Capozello, and W. Shang, eds. *More Than Meets the Eye: Rethinking Assessment, Competency and Sentencing for a Harsher Era of Juvenile Justice*, 1–22. Washington, DC: American Bar Association, Juvenile Justice Center.

Bishop, D. M., C. E. Frazier, L. Lanza-Kaduce, and L. Winner. 1996. "The Transfer of Juveniles to Criminal Court: Does it Make a Difference?" *Crime and Delinquency* 42 (2): 171–191.

Bortner, M. A., and L. M. Williams. 1997. *Youth in Prison: We the People of Unit Four*. New York: Routledge.

Bower, B. 2004. "Teen Brains on Trial: The Science of Neural Development Tangles with the Juvenile Death Penalty," *Science News*, May 8. www.phschool.com/science/science_news/articles/teen_brains_trial.html.

Breese, J. R., K. Ra'el, and G. K. Grant. 2000. "No Place Like Home: A Qualitative Investigation of Social Support and Its Effect on Recidivism." *Sociological Practice* 2 (1): 1–21.

Brenzel, B. 1975. "Lancaster Industrial School for Girls: A Social Portrait of a 19th Century Reform School for Girls." *Feminist Studies* 3 (1–2): 40–53.

Brower, B. 2009. "Teen Brains on Trial: The Science of Neural Development Tangles with the Juvenile Death Penalty." *Science News* 165 (19): 299–301.

Bullis, M., and P. Yovanoff. 2002. "Those Who Do Not Return: Correlates of the Work and School Engagement of Formerly Incarcerated Youth Who Remain in the Community." *Journal of Emotional and Behavioral Disorders* 10 (2): 66–79. doi:10.1177/10634266020100020101.

———. 2006. "Idle Hands: Community Employment Experiences of Formerly Incarcerated Youth." *Journal of Emotional and Behavioral Disorders* 14 (2): 71–85.

Bullis, M., P. Yovanoff, G. Mueller, and E. Havel. 2002. "Life on the 'Outs': Examination of the Facility-to-Community Transition of Incarcerated Youth." *Exceptional Children* 69 (1): 7–22.

Butts, J. 2008. *Beyond the Tunnel Problem: Addressing Cross-Cutting Issues That Impact Vulnerable Youth*. Chicago: University of Chicago, Chapin Hall Center for Children.

California Department of Corrections and Rehabilitation. 2010. *2010 Juvenile Justice Outcome Evaluation Report: Youth Released from the Division of Juvenile Justice in Fiscal Year 2004–05*. www.cdcr.ca.gov/Reports_Research/docs/Recidivism%20Report.FY0405.%20FINAL.DJJ.pdf.

Cesaroni, C., and S. Alvi. 2010. "Masculinity and Resistance in Adolescent Carceral Settings." *Canadian Journal of Criminology and Criminal Justice* 52 (3): 303–320.

Chesney-Lind, M. and S. K. Okamoto. 2001. "Gender Matters: Patterns in Girls' Delinquency and Gender Responsive Programming." *Journal of Forensic Psychology Practice* 1 (3): 1–28.

Chu, J. Y., M. V. Porche, and D. L. Tolman. 2005. "The Adolescent Masculinity Ideology in Relationship Scale." *Men and Masculinities* 8 (1): 93–115.

Chung, H. L., M. Little, and L. Steinberg. 2005. "The Transition to Adulthood for Adolescents in the Juvenile Justice System: A Developmental Perspective." In D. W. Osgood, E. M. Foster, C. Flanagan, and G. R. Ruth, eds. *On Your Own without a Net: The Transition to Adulthood for Vulnerable Populations*, 68–91. Chicago: University of Chicago Press.

Clark, R., and M. J. Robertson. 1996. *Surviving for the Moment: A Report on Homeless Youth in San Francisco*. Berkeley: University of California, Berkeley, Alcohol Research Group.

Coalition Against Institutionalized Child Abuse. 2007. *Abuse and Deaths: Florida Department of Juvenile Justice (DJJ)*. www.caica.org/Florida_Department_of_Juvenile_Justice_2007_CAICA_Report.htm.

Coffey, O. D., and M. G. Gemignani. 1994. *Effective Practices in Juvenile Correctional Education: A Study of the Literature and Research*. Washington, DC: Office of Juvenile Justice and Delinquency Prevention.

Confessore, N. 2009. "New York Finds Extreme Crisis in Youth Prisons." *New York Times*, December 14, A1.

Connell, R. W. 1987. *Gender and Power: Society, the Person, and Sexual Politics*. Stanford, CA: Stanford University Press.

———. 1995. *Masculinities*. Berkeley: University of California Press.

Cox, A. 2009. "Why Brain Science is Bad for Juvenile Justice." *Huffington Post*. www.huffingtonpost.com/alexandra-cox/why-brain-science-is-bad_b_368129.html.

Crime and Justice Institute. 2009. *Implementing Evidence-Based Policy and Practice in Community Corrections*. 2nd ed. Washington, DC: National Institute of Corrections.

Criminal Justice Alignment Bill. 2011. *Laws of California*. AB 109.

Deitch, M., A. Barstow, L. Lukens, and R. Reyna. 2009. *From Time Out to Hard Time: Young Children in the Adult Criminal Justice System*. Austin: University of Texas at Austin, LBJ School of Public Affairs.

Dilulio, J. 1995. "The Coming of the Super-Predators." *Weekly Standard* 1 (11): 23–28.

———. 1996. "Help Wanted: Economists, Crime, and Public Policy." *Journal of Economic Perspectives* 10 (1): 3–24.

Dorfman, L., K. Woodruff, V. Chavez, and L. Wallack. 1997. "Youth and Violence on Local Television News in California." *American Journal of Public Health* 87 (8): 1311–1316.

Erikson, E. 1968. *Identity: Youth and Crisis*. New York: W. W. Norton.

Evans, D. 2009. "Lawsuit against New Orleans Juvenile Detention Center Turned into a Class Action." *Facing South: The Online Magazine of the Institute for Southern Studies*. February 5. www.southernstudies.org/2009/02/lawsuit-against-new-orleans-juvenile-detention-center-turned-into-a-class-action.html.

Fader, J. 2008. "Inside and Out: Community Reentry, Continuity and Change among Formerly Incarcerated Urban Youth." PhD diss., University of Pennsylvania. UMI (3328552).

Fagan, J. 1996. "The Comparative Advantage of Juvenile versus Criminal Court Sanctions on Recidivism." *Law & Policy* 18 (1–2): 77–112.

Federal Bureau of Investigation. 2006. *Crime in the United States, 2005: Uniform Crime Reports*. Washington, DC: US Department of Justice.

Feld, B. C. 1993. "Juvenile (In)Justice and the Criminal Court Alternative." *Crime & Delinquency* 39 (4): 403–425.

Field, C. E., H. M. Nash, M. L. Handwerk, and P. C. Friman. 2004. "A Modification of the Token Economy for Nonresponsive Youth in Family-Style Residential Care." *Behavior Modification* 28 (3): 438–457.

Forst, M., J. Fagan, and T. S. Vivona. 1989. "Youth in Prisons and Training Schools: Perceptions and the Consequences of the Treatment Custody Dichotomy." *Juvenile and Family Court* 40 (1): 1–14.

Frank, T. 2009. "Lock 'Em Up: Jailing Kids is a Proud American Tradition." *Wall Street Journal*, April 1, A21.

Froyum, C. 2007. "'At Least I'm not Gay': Heterosexual Identity Making among Poor Black Teens." *Sexualities* 10 (5): 603–622.

Garbarino, J. 2006. *See Jane Hit: Why Girls Are Growing Up More Violent and What Can Be Done About It*. New York: Penguin.

Giedd, J. N., J. Blumenthal, N. O. Jeffries, F. X. Castellanos, H. Liu, A. Zijdenbos, T. Paus, A. C. Evans, and J. Rapoport. 1999. "Brain Development during Childhood and Adolescence: A Longitudinal MRI Study." *Nature Neuroscience* 2 (10): 861–863.

Gibbs, J. T., and J. Merighi. 1994. "Young Black Males: Marginality, Masculinity and Criminality." In T. Newburn and E. Stanko, eds. *Just Boys Doing Business: Men, Masculinities, and Crime*, 64–80. New York: Routledge.

Gogtay, N., J. N. Giedd, L. Lusk, K. M. Hayashi, D. Greenstein, A. C. Vaituzis, T. F. Nugent III, et al. 2004. "Dynamic Mapping of Human Cortical Development during Childhood through Early Adulthood." *Proceedings of the Academy of Sciences of the United States of America* 101 (21): 8174–8179.

Gold, R. L. 1958. "Roles in Sociological Field Observation." *Social Forces* 36 (3): 217–223.

Goodey, J. 1997. "'Boys Don't Cry': Masculinities, Fear of Crime, and Fearlessness." *British Journal of Criminology* 37 (3): 401–418.

Graham v. Florida, 2010, 982 So. 2d 43.

Greenwood, P. W. 2005. *Changing Lives: Delinquency Prevention and Crime Control*. Chicago: University of Chicago Press.

———. 2010. *Preventing and Reducing Youth Crime and Violence: Using Evidence-Based Practices*. Sacramento, CA: Governor's Office of Gang and Youth Violence Policy.

Grisso, T., L. Steinberg, J. Woolard, E. Cauffman, E. Scott, S. Graham, F. Lexcen, N. Dickon Reppucci, and R. Schwartz. 2003. "Juveniles' Competence to Stand Trial: A Comparison of Adolescents' and Adults' Capacities as Trial Defendants." *Law and Human Behavior* 27 (4): 333–363.

Hagan, J., and R. Dinovitzer. 1999. "Collateral Consequences of Imprisonment for Children, Communities, and Prisoners." *Crime and Justice*, no. 26: 121–162.

Hagan, J., and B. McCarthy. 2005. "Homeless Youth and the Perilous Passage to Adulthood." In D. Wayne Osgood, E. Michael Foster, C. Flanagan, and G. R. Ruth, eds. *On Your Own without a Net: The Transition to Adulthood for Vulnerable Populations*. Chicago: University of Chicago Press.

Hall, G. S. 1904. *Adolescence: Its Psychology and Its Relations to Physiology, Anthropology, Sociology, Sex, Crime, Religion, and Education*. Vols. 1–2. New York: D. Appleton.

Hartney, C., B. Krisberg, L. Vuong, and S. Marchionna. 2010. *A New Era in California Juvenile Justice*. Berkeley, CA: National Council on Crime and Delinquency. www.nccd-crc.org/nccd/dnld/Home/A_New_Era.pdf.

Hemmings, A. 1998. "The Self-Transformations of African-American Achievers." *Youth and Society* 29 (3): 330–368.

Herivel, T. J., and P. Wright. eds. 2007. *Prison Profiteers: Who Makes Money from Mass Incarceration?* New York: New Press.

Holden, B., and J. Zeidenberg. 2007. *The Dangers of Detention: The Impact of Incarcerating Youth in Detention and Other Secure Facilities*. Washington, DC: Justice Policy Institute. www.cfjj.org/Pdf/116-JPI008-DOD_Report.pdf.

Hughes, M. 1998. "Turning Points in the Lives of Young Inner-City Men Forgoing Destructive Criminal Behaviors: A Qualitative Study." *Social Work Research* 22 (3): 143–151.

Hume, E. 1996. *No Matter How Loud I Shout: A Year in the Life of Juvenile Court*. New York: Touchstone.

Human Rights Watch and American Civil Liberties Union (ACLU). 2006. *Custody and Control: Conditions of Confinement in New York's Juvenile Prisons for Girls*. www.aclu.org/files/pdfs/racialjustice/custodycontrol20060925.pdf.

In re Gault. 1967. 387 U.S. 1.

In re Winship. 1970. 397 U.S. 358.

Inderbitzin, M. 2009. "Reentry of Emerging Adults: Adolescent Inmates' Transition Back into the Community," *Journal of Adolescent Research* 24 (4): 453–476.

Jewkes, Y. 2005. "Men Behind Bars: 'Doing' Masculinity as an Adaptation to Imprisonment." *Men and Masculinities* 8 (1): 44–63.

Juhila, K. 2004. "Talking Back to Stigmatized Identities: Negotiation of Culturally Dominant Categorizations in Interviews with Shelter Residents." *Qualitative Social Work* 3 (3): 259–275.

Katz, M. B. 1986. *In the Shadow of the Poorhouse: A Social History of Welfare in America*. New York: Basic Books.

Kazdin, A. E. 1982. "The Token Economy: A Decade Later." *Journal of Applied Behavior Analysis* 15 (3): 431–445.

Kadzin, A. E., and R. R. Bootzin. 1972. "The Token Economy: An Evaluative Review." *Journal of Applied Behavior Analysis* 5 (3): 343–372.

Kent v. United States. 1966. 383 U.S. 541.

Krisberg, B. M. 2005. *Juvenile Justice: Redeeming Our Children*. Thousand Oaks, CA: Sage.

———. 2006. "Rediscovering the Juvenile Justice Ideal in the United States." In J. Muncie and B. Golden, eds. *Comparative Youth Justice*, 6–18. London: Sage.

Krisberg, B. M., and J. Austin. 1993. *Reinventing Juvenile Justice*. Newbury Park, CA: Sage.

Krisberg, B. M., C. Hartney, A. Wolf, and F. Silva. 2009. *Youth Violence Myths and Realities: A Tale of Three Cities*. San Francisco: National Council on Crime & Delinquency. www.aecf.org/~/media/PublicationFiles/Casey%20Youth%20 Report FinES.pdf.

Krisberg, B. M., and S. Marchionna. 2007. *Attitudes of U.S. Voters toward Youth Crime and the Justice System*. Oakland, CA: National Council on Crime and Delinquency.

Kunzel, R. G. 1993. *Fallen Women and Problem Girls: Unmarried Mothers and the Professionalization of Social Work, 1890–1945*. New Haven: Yale University Press.

League of Women Voters California. 2000. "Proposition 21: Juvenile Crime." www.smartvoter.org/2000/03/07/ca/state/prop/21.

Lesko, N. 1996. "Denaturalizing Adolescence: The Politics of Contemporary Representations." *Youth & Society* 28 (2): 139–161.

———. 2001. *Act Your Age! A Cultural Construction of Adolescence*. New York: Routledge.

Levant, R. F., and K. Richmond. 2007. "A Review of Research on Masculinity Ideologies Using the Male Role Norms Inventory." *The Journal of Men's Studies* 15 (2): 130–146.

Lipsey, M. W. 2009. "The Primary Factors that Characterize Effective Interventions with Juvenile Offenders: A Meta-Analytic Overview." *Victims and Offenders* 2 (4): 124–147.

Liptak, A. 2010. "Justices Limit Life Sentences for Juveniles." *New York Times*, May 18. www.nytimes.com/2010/05/18/us/politics/18court.html.

Loeber, R. 1990. "Development and Risk Factors of Juvenile Antisocial Behavior and Delinquency." *Clinical Psychology Review* 10: 1–41.

Loeber, R., and M. Stouthamer-Loeber. 1986. "Family Factors as Correlates and Predictors of Juvenile Conduct Problems and Delinquency." In N. Morris and M. Tonry, eds. *Crime and Justice: An Annual Review of Research*. Vol. 7, 29–149. Chicago: University of Chicago.

Lofland, J. and L. H. Lofland. 1995. *Analyzing Social Settings: A Guide to Qualitative Observation and Analysis*. Belmont, CA: Wadsworth.

Luker, K. 1996. *Dubious Conceptions: The Politics of Teenage Pregnancy*. Cambridge, MA: Harvard University Press.

Mac an Ghaill, M. 1994. *The Making of Men*. Buckingham: Open University Press.

Macallair, D. M., M. Males, and C. McCracken. 2009. *Closing California's Division of Juvenile Facilities: An Analysis of County Institutional Capacity*. San Francisco: Center for Juvenile and Criminal Justice.

MacArthur Foundation Research Network on Adolescent Development and Juvenile Justice. 2006. *Less Guilty by Reason of Adolescence*. Philadelphia: Author. www.adjj.org/downloads/6093issue_brief_3.pdf.

MacKenzie, D. L. 1997. "Criminal Justice and Crime Prevention." In L. W. Sherman, D. Gottfredson, D. L. MacKenzie, J. Eck, P. Reuter, and S. Bushway, eds. *Preventing Crime: What Works, What Doesn't, What's Promising*. Washington, DC: National Institute of Justice, www.ncjrs.gov/works/chapter9.htm

Majors, R., and J. M. Billson. 1992. *Cool Pose*. New York: Lexington Books.

Males, M. 2009. "Does the Adolescent Brain Make Risk Taking Inevitable? A Skeptical Appraisal." *Journal of Adolescent Research* 24 (1): 3–20.

———. 2010. "Is Jumping off the Roof Always a Bad Idea? A Rejoinder on Risk Taking and the Adolescent Brain." *Journal of Adolescent Research* 25 (1): 48–63.

Martinez, D., and L. S. Abrams. 2011. "Informal Social Support among Returning Young Offenders: A Meta-Synthesis of the Literature." *International Journal of Offender Therapy and Comparative Criminology*. http://ijo.sagepub.com/content/early/2011/10/18/0306624X11428203.abstract?rss=1.

Mason, M. A. 1994. *From Father's Property to Children's Rights: The History of Child Custody in the United States*. New York: Columbia University Press.

McGloin, J. M., T. C. Pratt, and J. Maahs. 2004. "Rethinking the IQ-Delinquency Relationship: A Longitudinal Analysis of Multiple Theoretical Models." *Justice Quarterly* 21 (3): 603–635.

McLaughlin, J. T., E. J. Rosenkranz, T. P. Wei, S. M. Clare, and A. Haider. "Amicus Brief in Roper v. Simmons." n. d. www.njdc.info/pdf/death_penalty/ama.pdf.

McManus, J., and L. Dorfman. 2002. "Youth Violence Stories Focus on Events, not Causes." *Newspaper Research Journal* 23 (4): 6–20.

Mendel, D. 2010. "In Juvenile Justice Care, Boys Get Worse." *Youth Today*, February 1. www.youthtoday.org.

Messerschmidt, J. 1993. *Masculinities and Crime: Critique and Reconceptualization of the Theory*. Lanham, MD: Rowman and Littlefield.

———. 2000. *Nine Lives: Adolescent Masculinities, the Body, and Violence*. Boulder, CO: Westview Press.

Miles, M. B., and A. M. Humberman. 1994. *Qualitative Data Analysis: An Expanded Sourcebook*. Thousand Oaks, CA: Sage.

Missouri Department of Social Services. 2010. *Division of Youth Services Annual Report: Fiscal Year 2010*. www.dss.mo.gov/re/pdf/dys/dysfy10.pdf.

Models for Change. 2009. *Research on Pathways to Desistance: A First Look at Emerging Findings.* Philadelphia: MacArthur Foundation. www.modelsforchange.net/publications/239.

Moffit, T. 1990. "Juvenile Delinquency and Attention Deficit Disorder: Boys' Developmental Trajectories from Age 3 to 15." *Child Development* 61 (3): 893–910.

National Center for Health Statistics. 2010. *Estimates of the July 1, 2000–July 1, 2009, United States Resident Population from the Vintage 209 Postcensal Series by Year, County, Age, Sex, Race, and Hispanic Origin.* Prepared under a collaborative arrangement with the US Census Bureau. Released July 23. www.cdc.gov/nchs/nvss/bridged_race.htm.

National Organization of Victims of Juvenile Lifers. n.d. "Legislation Summary." www.willsworld.com/state_legislation.htm.

Newburn, T., and E. Stanko, eds. 1994. *Just Boys Doing Business? Men, Masculinities, and Crime.* New York: Routledge.

Office of Juvenile Justice and Delinquency Prevention. 2000. *1999 National Report Series: Juvenile Justice Bulletin.* www.ncjrs.gov/html/ojjdp/jjbul2000_02_2/chal3.html.

O'Neil, J. M. and M. L. Luján. 2009. "Preventing Boys' Problems in School through Psychoeducational Programming: A Call to Action." *Psychology in the Schools* 46 (3): 257–266.

Osgood, W., E. M. Foster, and M. E. Courtney. 2010. "Vulnerable Populations and the Transition to Adulthood." *The Future of Children* 20 (1): 209–229. www.princeton.edu/futureofchildren/publications/docs/20_01_10.pdf.

Oyserman, D., and H. R. Markus. 1990. "Possible Selves and Delinquency." *Journal of Personality and Social Psychology* 59 (1): 112–125.

Paechter, C. 2007. *Being Boys, Being Girls: Learning Masculinities and Femininities.* New York: McGraw Hill.

Parker, A. 1996. "The Construction of Masculinity within Boys' Physical Education." *Gender and Education* 8 (2): 141–157.

Parkman, T. S. 2009. "The Transition to Adulthood and Prisoner Reentry: Investigating the Experiences of Young Adult Men and Their Caregivers." Unpublished doctoral dissertation, Virginia Polytechnic Institute and State University.

Pascoe, C. J. 2007. *Dude, You're a Fag: Masculinity and Sexuality in Adolescence.* Berkeley: University of California Press.

Paterniti, D. A. 2000. "The Micropolitics of Identity in Adverse Circumstance." *Journal of Contemporary Ethnography* 29 (1): 93–119.

Paus, T. 2005. "Mapping Brain Maturation and Cognitive Development during Adolescence." *Trends in Cognitive Sciences* 9 (2): 60–68.

Pew Center on the States. 2008. *One in 100: Behind Bars in America 2008.* Washington, DC: Pew Center on the States.

Phelan, P., A. L. Davison, and H. C. Yu. 1993. "Students' Multiple Worlds: Navigating the Borders of Family, Peer, and School Cultures." In P. Phelan and A. L. Davison, eds. *Renegotiating Cultural Diversity in American Schools*, 52–88. New York: Teachers College Press.

Platt, A. 1969. *The Child Savers.* Chicago: University of Chicago Press.

Pleck, J. H., F. L. Sonenstein, and L. C. Ku. 1993. "Masculinity Ideology and Its Correlates." In S. Oskamp and M. Costanzo, eds. *Gender Issues in Contemporary Society*, The Claremont Symposium on Applied Social Psychology, Vol. 6, 85–110. Newbury Park, CA: Sage.

Pollack, W. S. 2006. "Male Adolescent Rites of Passage: Positive Visions of Multiple Developmental Pathways." *Annals of the New York Academy of Sciences* 1036 (1): 141–151.

Polsky, H. 1962. *Cottage Six: The Social System of Delinquent Boys in Residential Treatment.* New York: Russell Sage Foundation.

Puzzanchera, C., and B. Adams. 2011. *National Disproportionate Minority Contact Databook.* Washington, DC: US Department of Justice, Office of Justice Programs, Office of Juvenile Justice and Delinquency Prevention. www.ojjdp.gov/ojstatbb/dmcdb/.

Puzzanchera, C., B. Adams, and M. Sickmund. 2011. *Juvenile Court Statistics 2008.* Washington, DC: US Department of Justice, Office of Justice Programs, Office of Juvenile Justice and Delinquency Prevention, National Center for Juvenile Justice. www.ojjdp.gov/ojstatbb/njcda/pdf/jcs2008.pdf.

Rabb, L. 2011. *Kids Claim Abuse and Violence at Juvenile Lockup Thompson Academy.* www.miaminewtimes.com/2011–04–07/news/kids-claim-abuse-and-violence-at-thompson-academy-a-for-profit-juvenile-lockup-in-pembroke-pines/.

Reamer, F., and D. Siegel. 2008. *Teens in Crisis: How the Industry Serving Struggling Teens Helps and Hurts Our Kids.* New York: Columbia University Press.

Redding, R. E. 2003. "The Effects of Adjudicating and Sentencing Juveniles as Adults: Research and Policy Implications." *Youth Violence and Juvenile Justice* 1 (2): 128–155.

Reich, A. D. 2010. *Hidden Truth: Young Men Navigating Lives in and out of Juvenile Prison.* Berkeley, CA: University of California Press.

Ron & Don Show, The. n.d. "School Bus Attack: Is Suspension Enough?" www.mynorthwest.com/index.php?nid=108&sid=212968.

Roper v. Simmons. 2005. 543 U.S. 551.

Rosen, J. 2007. "The Brain on the Stand." *New York Times Magazine*, March 11, 49.

Ryan, L., and J. Ziedenberg. eds. 2007. *The Consequences Aren't Minor: The Impact of Trying Youth as Adults and Strategies for Reform.* Washington, DC: Campaign for Youth Justice.

Ruddell, R., and M. O. Thomas. 2009. *Juvenile Corrections.* Richmond, KY: Newgate Press.

Sabo, D., T. Kupers, and W. London, eds. 2001. *Prison Masculinities.* Philadelphia: Temple University Press.

Schlossman, S. J. 1977. *Love and the American Delinquent. The Theory and Practice of "Progressive" Juvenile Justice, 1825–1920.* Chicago: University of Chicago Press.

Schlossman, S. J., and S. Wallach. 1978. "The Crime of Precocious Sexuality: Female Juvenile Delinquency in the Progressive Era." *Harvard Educational Review* 48 (1): 65–94.

Schneider, E. C. 1992. *In the Web of Class: Delinquents and Reformers in Boston, 1810s–1930s.* New York: New York University Press.

Scott, E. S., and L. Steinberg. 2008a. "Adolescent Development and the Regulation of Youth Crime." *The Future of Children* 18 (2): 15–33.

———. 2008b. *Rethinking Juvenile Justice.* Cambridge, MA: Harvard University Press.

Sercombe, H. 2010. "The Gift and the Trap: Working 'the Teen Brain' into Our Concept of Youth." *Journal of Adolescent Research* 25 (1): 31–47.

Shoemaker, D. J. 2009. *Juvenile Delinquency.* Lanham, MD: Rowan and Littlefield.

Sickmund, M. 2003. *Juveniles in Court: National Report Series Bulletin.* Washington, DC: US Department of Justice, Office of Justice Programs, Office of Juvenile Justice and Delinquency Prevention. www.ncjrs.gov/html/ojjdp/195420/contents.html.

————. 2010. *Juveniles in Residential Placement, 1997–2008*. Washington, DC: US Department of Justice, Office of Justice Programs, Office of Juvenile Justice and Delinquency Prevention. www.ncjrs.gov/pdffiles1/ojjdp/229379.pdf.

Sickmund, M., A. Sladky, and W. Kang. 2010. *Easy Access to Juvenile Court Statistics: 1985–2007*. Washington, DC: US Department of Justice, Office of Justice Programs, Office of Juvenile Justice and Delinquency Prevention. http://ojjdp .gov/ojstatbb/ezajcs/.

Sickmund, M., T. J. Sladky, W. Kang, and C. Puzzanchera. 2011. *Easy Access to the Census of Juveniles in Residential Placement*. Washington, DC: US Department of Justice, Office of Justice Programs, Office of Juvenile Justice and Delinquency Prevention. http://ojjdp.gov/ojstatbb/ezacjrp/.

Sowell, E. R., P. M. Thompson, K. D. Tessner, and A. W. Toga. 2001. "Mapping Continued Brain Growth and Gray Matter Density Reduction in Dorsal Frontal Cortex: Inverse Relationships during Postadolescent Brain Maturation." *Journal of Neuroscience* 21 (22): 8819–8829.

Snyder, H. N., and M. Sickmund. 2006. *Juvenile Offenders and Victims: 2006 National Report*. Washington, DC: US Department of Justice, Office of Justice Programs, Office of Juvenile Justice and Delinquency Prevention. http://ojjdp.gov/ ojstatbb/ezacjrp/.

Snyder, H. N., M. Sickmund, and E. Poe-Yamagata. 1996. *Juvenile Offenders and Victims: 1996 Update on Violence*. Washington, DC: US Department of Justice, Office of Justice Programs, Office of Juvenile Justice and Delinquency Prevention. http://ojjdp.gov/ojstatbb/ezacjrp/.

Stanfield, R. n. d. *The JDAI Story: Building a Better Juvenile Detention System*. Baltimore: The Annie E. Casey Foundation. www.aecf.org/upload/publicationfiles/ jdai%20story.pdf.

Steinberg, L. 2009. "Should the Science of Adolescent Brain Development Inform Public Policy?" *American Psychologist* 64: 739–750.

Steinhart, D. 1988. *Public Attitudes on Youth Crime*. Washington, DC: National Council on Crime and Delinquency.

Stimson, C., and A. Grossman. 2009. *Adult Time for Adult Crimes: Life without Parole for Juvenile Killers and Violent Teens*. Washington, DC: Heritage Foundation.

Szalavitz, M. 2009. "Why Juvenile Detention Makes Teens Worse." *Time*, August 7. www.time.com/time/health/article/0,8599,1914837,00.html.

Thompson, E. H., Jr., and J. H. Pleck. 1995. "Masculine Ideologies: A Review of Research Instrumentation on Men and Masculinities." In R. F. Levant and W. S. Pollack, eds. *A New Psychology of Men*, 129–163. New York: Basic Books.

Thornberry, T. P., D. Huzinga, and R. Loeber. 1995. "Implications from the Program of Research on the Causes and Correlates of Delinquency." In J. C. Howell, J. B. Krisberg, D. Hawkins, and J. J. Wilson, eds. A *Sourcebook: Serious, Violent, and Chronic Juvenile Offenders*, 213–237. Thousand Oaks, CA: Sage.

Trulson, C. R., J. W. Marquart, J. L. Mullings, and T. J. Caeti. 2005. "In Between Adolescence and Adulthood: Recidivism Outcomes of a Cohort of State Delinquents." *Youth Violence and Juvenile Justice* 3 (4): 355–387.

Ungar, M., and E. Teram. 2000. "Drifting Towards Mental Health: High-Risk Adolescents and the Process of Empowerment." *Youth & Society* 32 (2): 225–252.

United States Census. 2010. www.census.gov/prod/cen2010/briefs/c2010br-02.pdf.

VanderVen, K. 1995. "'Point and Level Systems': Another Way to Fail Children and Youth. *Child & Youth Care Forum* 24 (6): 345–367.

————. 2000. "Cultural Aspects of Point and Level Systems." *Reclaiming Children and Youth* 9 (1): 53–59.

Vera Institute of Justice. 2009. *Charting a New Course: A Blueprint for Transforming Juvenile Justice in New York State.* New York: Vera Institute of Justice. http://ocfs.ny.gov/main/rehab/http___www%20vera%20org_download_file2944_Charting-a-new-course-A-blueprint-for-transforming-juvenile-justice-in-New-York-State.pdf.

Vorrath, H. H. and L. K. Brendtro. 1976. *Positive Peer Culture.* Chicago: Aldine.

Walker, J. 1925. "Factors Contributing to the Delinquency of Defective Girls." *University of California Publications in Psychology.* 3 (4): 148–213. Berkeley: University of California Press.

Way, N. 1998. *Everyday Courage: The Lives and Stories of Urban Teenagers.* New York: New York University Press.

Way, N., and J. Chu. eds. 2004. *Adolescent Boys: Exploring Diverse Cultures of Boyhood.* New York: New York University Press.

Weis, L., and M. Fine. eds. 2000. *Construction Sites: Excavating Race, Class and Gender among Urban Youth.* New York: Teachers College Press.

West, C., and D. Zimmerman. 1987. "Doing Gender." *Gender & Society* 1 (2): 125–151.

Wilkinson, D. L. 2003. *Guns, Violence, and Identity among African American and Latino Youth.* New York: LFB Scholarly Publishing.

Williams, A. 2009. "Mass Incarceration as Social Control." *Policy Innovations,* May 22. www.policyinnovations.org/ideas/briefings/data/000112.

Wooden, K. 1976/2000. *Weeping in the Playtime of Others: America's Incarcerated Children.* New York: McGraw-Hill.

Young, M. C., and J. Gainsborough. 2000. *Prosecuting Juveniles in Adult Court: An Assessment of Trends and Consequences.* Washington, DC: The Sentencing Project.

YouthFacts. 2010. *Crime Tables: Violent Crime (Murder, Rape, Robbery, Aggravated Assault.* www.youthfacts.org/crimetables.html.

Zahn, M. A., S. Brumbaugh, D. Steffensmeier, B. C. Feld, M. Morash, M. Chesney-Lind, J. Miller, A. A. Payne, D. C. Gottfredson, and C. Kruttschnitt. 2008. *Girls Study Group: Understanding and Responding to Girls' Delinquency.* Washington, DC: US Department of Justice, Office of Justice Programs, Office of Juvenile Justice and Delinquency Prevention. www.ncjrs.gov/pdffiles1/ojjdp/218905.pdf.

Ziedenberg, J., and V. Schiraldi. 1997. *Risks Juveniles Face When They Are Incarcerated with Adults.* San Francisco: The Justice Policy Institute.

INDEX

Abbott, Edith, 9

Abbott, Grace, 9

academic performance, 92; of Brad, 42; of Eric, 63; of Josh, 45; of Kei, 45; of Nino, 46; of Thomas, 47; of Trevor, 47. *See also* education

acceptance of identity changing, 103–106; of Humphrey, 124, 127; of Kei, 103–104, 106, 124, 127; of Trevor, 103, 104–106, 124–127, 127–128. *See also* patterns of change

Addams, Jane, 9

Adolescence (Hall), 9

adolescence as construction, 9, 19

adult correctional facilities, 129–130; youth in, 21–22, 138

adult court, youth sentenced in, 14, 21, 23, 129, 131, 138

advocacy view of juvenile corrections reform, 15, 18–25, 28–29, 129–130, 131

African Americans, 14; mass incarceration and, 30; ratio of in juvenile corrections, 17; on staff at Wildwood House, 41

aftercare status, 113–114, 115, 119; Trevor and, 124. *See also* community reentry

aggression, 72, 89–90

aggression replacement training (ART), 23

aging out of system, 16, 111–112

all-boys facilities, 4

ambivalent pattern of identity change, 100–103, 109, 119–124; of Elijah, 100–101, 102, 119, 121–123, 128,

131; of Jason, 44, 100, 102, 119–121, 122, 128; of Josh, 102, 124; of Mario, 124; of Nino, 102–103, 123–124. *See also* patterns of change

American Association of Child and Adolescent Psychiatry, 19

American Medical Association, 19

American Psychiatric Society, 19

Annie E. Casey Foundation, 24

Ayers, William, 4

behavioral management system at Wildwood House, 37–39, 51, 124, 132, 133; Mr. Lund and, 100, 101. *See also* treatment/punishment tension

Berkeley Media Studies Group, 27

blended systems of care at Wildwood House, 31, 33, 36–40. *See also* treatment/punishment tension

border crossings, 91–92, 99, 112

boredom, 53, 54

Bortner, M. A., 4

boys, 4, 134–135; child savers' beliefs about, 10; emotional expression and, 74; juvenile placements of, 16. *See also* gender; girls; men

Brad (Unit C resident), 41–42, 73–74, 75; community reentry, 114–116, 119, 127, 128; criminal history, 42, 108, 130; family of, 42, 108–109, 115, 130; self-preservation of identity of, 108, 114–116, 119, 127, 128; treatment program views of, 93, 108–109, 115–116, 128, 130, 132, 144

About the Author

Laura. S. Abrams, associate professor of social welfare at the UCLA Luskin School of Public Affairs, has dedicated her research to understanding identity formation and transitions among incarcerated youth. She has authored over forty scholarly articles and book chapters and regularly consults with youth-serving organizations on program design and research.

Ben Anderson-Nathe, associate professor and program director of child and family studies at Portland State University, is the author of *Youth Workers, Stuckness, and the Myth of Supercompetence* and coeditor of *Child & Youth Services*. His practice and teaching emphasizes relational engagement with youth in multiple service systems.

CPSIA information can be obtained at www.ICGtesting.com
Printed in the USA
BVOW040005211212

308770BV00001B/3/P